THOMSON
━━★━━
COURSE TECHNOLOGY™

Professional ■ Trade ■ Reference

GAME ART
FOR TEE

LES PARDEW

Premier
p
Press

INCLUDES CD-ROM

D1307532

ISBN: 1-59200-307-9

Library of Congress Catalog Card Number: 2003115724

Printed in the United States of America

04 05 06 07 08 BA 10 9 8 7 6 5 4 3 2 1

THOMSON

COURSE TECHNOLOGY

Professional ■ Trade ■ Reference

Course PTR, a division of Course Technology
25 Thomson Place
Boston, MA 02210
http://www.courseptr.com

SVP, Course Professional, Trade, Reference Group:
Andy Shafran

Publisher:
Stacy L. Hiquet

Senior Marketing Manager:
Sarah O'Donnell

Marketing Manager:
Heather Hurley

Manager of Editorial Services:
Heather Talbot

Acquisitions Editor:
Mitzi Foster Koontz

Associate Marketing Manager:
Kristin Eisenzopf

Project Editor/Copy Editor:
Cathleen D. Snyder

Technical Reviewer:
Daniel Whittington

Teen Reviewer:
Jacob Nobbe

Retail Market Coordinator:
Sarah Dubois

Interior Layout Tech:
William Hartman

Cover Designer:
Mike Tanamachi

CD-ROM Producer:
Brandon Penticuff

Indexer:
Kelly Talbot

Proofreader:
Kim V. Benbow

This book is dedicated to all the young artists.
Keep the dream alive.
Without art, much of beauty would be lost.
You are needed.

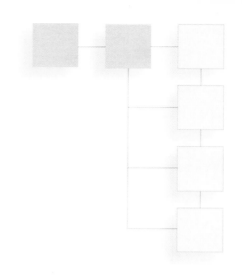

ACKNOWLEDGMENTS

This book is the culmination of the work of many individuals. Some, such as Mitzi Koontz, Cathleen Snyder, Dan Whittington, and Jacob Nobbe, have worked on the book directly. Others, such as Carl Lundgren, Dave Wolverton, and Don Seegmiller, have helped by teaching me their craft. My biggest thanks go to my wife and family, who have put up with my countless hours away from them to write this book, and to my parents, who have always believed in me. To all who had a role in helping me to write this book, I express my deepest appreciation and gratitude.

ABOUT THE AUTHOR

In 1987, **Les Pardew** started his career by creating the animation for *Magic Johnson Fast Break Basketball* on the Commodore 64. He soon found that he loved working on games and has been in the industry ever since. His work encompasses more than 100 video game titles, including some major titles such as *Super Star Wars*, *NCAA Basketball*, *Starcraft: Brood War*, *James Bond 007*, *Robin Hood: Prince of Thieves*, and *CyberTiger*.

He currently serves as President of Alpine Studios, which he founded with Ross Wolfley in the fall of 2000. Alpine Studios is a game development company focusing on family-friendly games. Alpine Studios' products include *Kublox, Combat Medic, Motocross Mania 2*, and *Ford Truck Mania*.

CONTENTS AT A GLANCE

CONTENTS

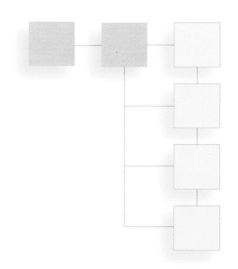

Introduction

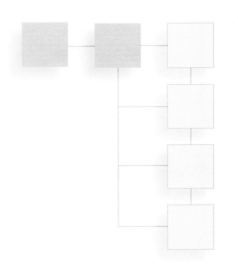

I remember growing up in a small town in southern Idaho. Our high school didn't have an art teacher. The only place that I could gain any instruction in art was from books. I loved reading about artists and I loved the step-by-step instruction books. Now, after years of success in commercial art, I felt it was time to help the young students who are looking for guidance with their dream of becoming game artists.

This book is designed to give real-world instruction with solid examples of game art creation. The chapters are full of step-by-step projects that show you in detail how game art is created. The examples are taken from projects that could be right out of any game.

To best understand and learn from this book, you should complete each project as shown in the step-by-step instructions. From there, you should practice the concepts on your own to broaden your knowledge of the tools and master the techniques.

The CD contains tools and links to all the resources you will need to complete the projects. The tools are trial versions or learning versions of professional software.

I hope you enjoy reading this book and doing the projects. I wish you success and fulfillment as an artist in this dynamic and exciting field. If you need help or just want to talk, you can e-mail me at les@alpine-studios.com.

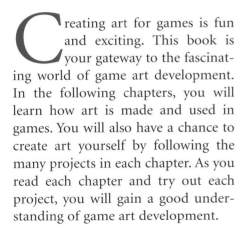

CHAPTER 1

GETTING STARTED IN GAME ART

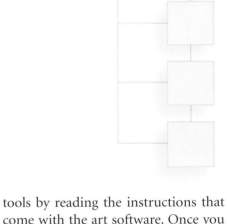

Creating art for games is fun and exciting. This book is your gateway to the fascinating world of game art development. In the following chapters, you will learn how art is made and used in games. You will also have a chance to create art yourself by following the many projects in each chapter. As you read each chapter and try out each project, you will gain a good understanding of game art development.

In this book I only want to deal with game art. Completing each project will require some level of artistic talent. Because you are interested in reading this book, I will assume that you have some skill in art. I will not go into the basics of drawing and painting. There are many great books about those subjects, but in this book I only want to deal with the exciting field of creating art for games.

The book contains step-by-step instructions on a number of topics. I have worked hard to be as detailed as possible so you can follow along with me; however, no book can provide every single step to every process in something as complex as game art development. The best way to use this book is to become familiar with the tools by reading the instructions that come with the art software. Once you are comfortable with the basic features of the art software, following the step-by-step instructions will be easier.

How Art Is Displayed

The best way to begin any discussion on game art is to clarify how art is displayed in a game. Most people play games on a computer, handheld device, or console game system. The pictures we see in games on these systems are made up of small, colored square dots of light called *pixels*. More precisely, a *pixel* could be defined as the smallest controllable segment of a display. Back when computer games first came out, the resolution of video-game pixels were very low and appeared as big blocks of color. As technology has advanced, the size of pixels has shrunk to the point that in some game systems it is difficult to see a single pixel.

Figure 1.1 shows a character typical of those used in early PC games. The character is 32 pixels high. Notice that the pixels are very easy to see.

Figure 1.2 shows a scene from a PlayStation 2 game. Notice that the pixels are so small that they are very difficult to distinguish as small blocks of light. As new game platforms continue to become more powerful,

screen resolutions will increase and individual pixels will be harder to detect.

Pixels are small dots of colored light that make up pictures on a computer screen. This is very important. In traditional art, artists work mostly with the reflected light of a painted surface. For games, artists work with pure light as it is displayed on a screen instead of painting on a canvas. This fundamental difference takes a little getting use to, particularly in the area of color.

A game artist uses colored light to create images. Most other forms of art use reflected light. For example, when a person looks at an oil painting, he sees colors that are reflected from

light in the room. On the other hand, when a person looks at the same painting displayed on a color monitor or TV he is looking at direct light, not reflected light (see Figure 1.3).

Reflected light is not as bright and vibrant as direct light; however, we live in a world of reflected light. When you are creating game art, it is important to remember that the art will look unrealistic or cartoon-like if you don't take care to reduce the intensity of the color to match how things look in real life.

Working with Pixels

Artists use a variety of computer programs to work with pixels on the screen. These programs fit into two

Figure 1.1 This game character for an old PC game is 32 pixels high. The pixels are blocky and easy to see.

Figure 1.2 This scene is from a PlayStation 2 game system.

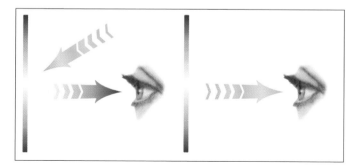

Figure 1.3 Reflected light and direct light

basic categories—two-dimensional (or 2D) programs and three-dimensional (or 3D) programs. 2D programs are the easiest to understand because computer screens and video game screens are basically flat. A 2D art program directly manipulates pixels on screen. Many of these programs are very sophisticated, and some even simulate natural media such as airbrush, oil paint, or even watercolor. 3D programs create virtual 3D objects used in the creation of 3D characters and worlds in games.

Included on the CD for this book are links to trial versions of several 2D programs and one 3D program:

- Corel Painter
- CorelDRAW suite
- Alias SketchBook Pro
- Alias Maya Personal Learning Edition

Hint

Take some time to explore and become familiar with the art programs available through the accompanying CD-ROM. Each program is a professional tool. The better you understand these programs, the more you will gain from the projects in this book.

In later chapters I will get into several specific exercises that deal directly with these programs. They are all programs that I use regularly in my own work, and each one is a true professional program. In this chapter, I will give you a brief overview of these programs.

Using Painting Programs

Game artists use painting programs to create 2D art for games. 2D art is often created by the artist from scratch instead of through manipulation of other art or photographs. Both Corel Painter and Alias SketchBook Pro are great programs for creating art. They both have very powerful features that allow you to use tools that simulate natural drawing and painting tools.

To use a painting program properly, you need to have a *digitizing tablet*—a flat tablet with a special pressure-sensitive stylus used to input direction to the computer, similar to a mouse (see Figure 1.4). The advantage of the digitizing tablet is that you can use the stylus like a pen, pencil, or paintbrush. The stylus is built like a pen and can

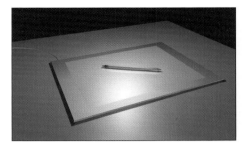

Figure 1.4 A typical digitizing tablet

be held like a pen over the tablet. When you move the pen over the tablet, the cursor on the computer screen moves. Like clicking with a mouse button, you can select or execute commands on the screen by touching the tip of the stylus to the tablet. Unlike the mouse, however, the stylus has a pressure-sensitive tip, which paint programs use to simulate the pressure the artist uses in drawing.

If you are serious about doing art for games, I highly recommend getting a digitizing tablet because it helps make the drawing and painting process on the computer more natural. Don't worry if you don't have one, though. You can still complete the projects in the book because all of the art programs used in the projects work fine with a mouse.

Hint

The purpose of this initial chapter is not to train you in all aspects of the tools that will be used in this book; rather, I want to give you a quick example of how the programs will be used. Greater detail on each art program will be provided later in the book.

Using Brushes

Painting programs simulate natural drawing and painting with a set of tools called *brushes*. Imagine a fully equipped artist studio with all the latest tools and media. In the studio you might see things like watercolor brushes, oil paint brushes, pastel chalks, airbrushes, and any number of other artist tools. Now imagine all those tools and media in a painting program. That is exactly what a painting program is meant to simulate.

In a painting program, the brush defines not only the type of instrument the painting program is trying to simulate, but also the media. Painting programs allow for a wide range of flexibility in the brushes. For example, an artist might start a picture by sketching in a rough outline with a pencil brush.

The following example uses Corel Painter. Painter is a great program with a very powerful set of drawing and painting tools.

Figure 1.5 shows a sketch of a young boy for a sports game. Notice the sketchy outlines. In this example, the boy is first drawn lightly with minimal pressure put on the stylus. Once the general shape is defined by these loose outlines, the darker lines are added to the drawing.

Some artists prefer to draw their initial sketches on paper and then scan them into the computer; other artists work directly on the computer. I like to sketch by working directly on the computer because it saves me several steps in production.

When the drawing is complete, the next step is to clean up all the excess lines. Painter has an Eraser tool, which works much the same as a brush except instead of adding lines or color, it removes the lines and returns the image to its original color.

Figure 1.6 shows a finished line drawing of the character. Now you need to add color to complete the drawing. Save the line sketch to a file for later use.

Painter also has a Magic Wand selection tool, which will select all

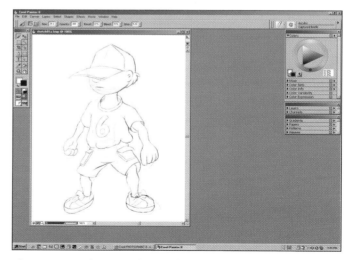

Figure 1.5 Character sketch of a young boy

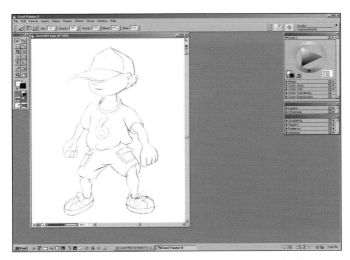

Figure 1.6 The cleaned drawing

instances of a color in a picture. You can use the tool to mask out an area of the drawing, making only that area available to paint. This makes coloring the character very easy.

In Figure 1.7, the character's arm has been selected and painted using the Airbrush tool.

By selecting each area, you can add color to the character. Notice, however, that the coloring process has obscured most of the original lines of the drawing (see Figure 1.8).

Usually at this stage it makes sense to switch to a different program. Save the colored image to a file for use later.

Hint

Often when I am working on a project, I will have a paint program, a photo paint program, and a 3D program all running on my computer at the same time. I often switch between programs.

Figure 1.7 The selected area is painted using the Airbrush tool.

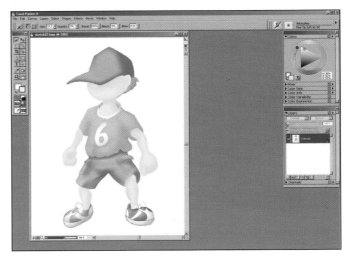

Figure 1.8 The color has obscured the lines of the drawing.

Photo Paint Programs

A photo paint program is designed for photo manipulation and retouching. Some artists use them for creating art, but I find painting programs work better for the former purposes. The CD for this book includes a link to the CorelDRAW suite; one of the programs in the suite is Corel Photo Paint. This is an excellent program for working with photographs or drawings.

Finishing the Character Sketch

Because Photo Paint has some very powerful tools for color adjustments, it is an excellent choice to finish the character sketch you started in the painting program. Load the two images of the character into the program.

Figure 1.9 shows the two images I created earlier. The one on the left is the original line drawing; the one on the right is the colored drawing. By putting the two together or by layering one on top of the other, you can create a finished colored character sketch. The first step will be to copy and paste the colored sketch over the line drawing.

Next you use the Transparency tool to make the desired color appear transparent so the line drawing shows through it (see Figure 1.10). As you might have guessed, the Transparency tool is used to make an image transparent.

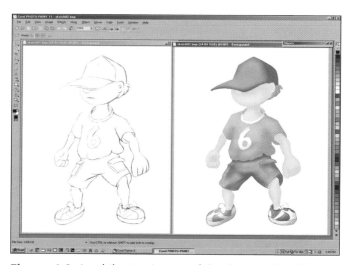

Figure 1.9 Load the two images of the character into Photo Paint.

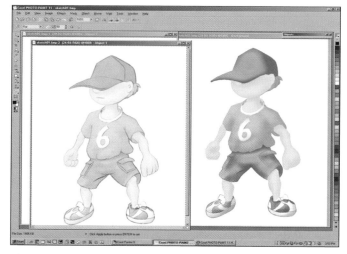

Figure 1.10 The line drawing shows through the transparent color.

Now adjust color and brightness to bring the sketch to a finished state (see Figure 1.11).

Creating a Door Texture

This section will provide an example of how you might use a photo paint program to create a door texture for a game. First you load the digital photograph into the program. Figure 1.12 shows a nice picture of a door I took a few years ago.

The first step to converting the photo of the door into a usable texture is to isolate the door from the rest of the picture. Drag a mask around the door to select it (see Figure 1.13). A *mask* is a selected area of a picture. You cannot manipulate areas outside the selected area; you *can* manipulate areas inside the mask.

Figure 1.12 A picture of a door loaded into Photo Paint

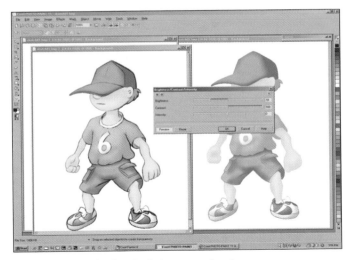

Figure 1.11 The finished character sketch

Figure 1.13 Select the door from the picture.

Notice that the door is not square with the camera. A photo is seldom perfectly flat with the viewer. Textures need to be flat, so you should copy the selection and then paste it over the original picture (see Figure 1.14). You can then distort and rotate the pasted image to fit a flat rectangular shape.

Once the door is fit into a flat rectangle, you can copy and paste it into a new image without the rock wall that surrounds the door in the original picture (see Figure 1.15). At that point you could use the door for a texture, but it really needs more work to be a good texture. Notice that the lighting of the door is dark and uneven. There are also some hints of stone on the bottom and some black areas near the lower-left side of the door.

You need to fix the lighting of the door. The first step is to adjust the brightness and contrast of the door, as shown in Figure 1.16.

Figure 1.15 Paste the door into a new image without the doorframe.

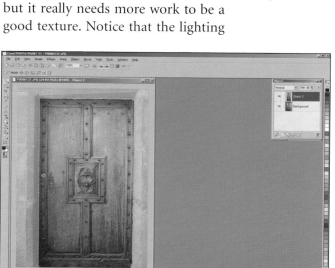

Figure 1.14 Distort the door to fit a flat rectangle.

Figure 1.16 Adjust brightness and contrast to lighten the door.

The door looks better now that it is brighter, but the lighting is still uneven. The top of the door is lighter than the bottom. In fact, the bottom of the door is obscured in shadows. You can even out the lighting of the door by making a new image that is lighter and merging the two images.

You make the new image by copying the door and pasting it over the old image. Now there are two images of the door—one directly over the other. You then brighten the top image so the shadowy lower door is as light as the rest of the door in the original picture (see Figure 1.17). Notice that when the lower door is brightened, the lighter parts of the door toward the top become too bright, and you lose much of the door's detail.

The next step is to give the new, brighter top image a linear transparency. In a *linear transparency*, an image is completely transparent on one side and completely opaque on the other. The transparency is graded evenly from the transparent side to the opaque side. In this example, the top of the new picture is washed out because I brightened it to make the bottom of the door less dark. I want the bottom of the door but not the top. I also don't want to simply copy the bottom of the door into the old image because it will cause a noticeable line between the old and new art.

Using the Linear Transparency tool in Photo Paint, you can make the top of the new door transparent and the bottom opaque. The transition from the opaque to the transparent is gradual, so when you place the new image over the old image it appears to be one image. The lighting of the bottom of the door is now even with the top (see Figure 1.18).

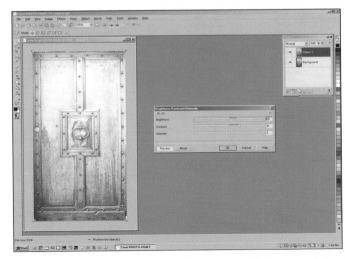

Figure 1.17 Brighten the new image to match the rest of the door.

Figure 1.18 You can merge the two images to even the lighting.

Now that the door is more uniform in its lighting, you simply need to touch up the problem areas on the bottom of the door. Photo Paint has a very effective tool for touching up a photograph, called a *Clone tool*. The Clone tool basically takes a selected part of a picture and allows you to transfer that part of the picture by painting it into another part of the picture. You do this by selecting the Clone tool and clicking on the area *from* which you want to transfer, and then selecting the area *to* which you want to transfer. The Clone tool takes part of an image

and transfers it to another part of the image. In Figure 1.19, I selected a part of the lower door and painted it over the stone that was in the lower corner.

You can use the Clone tool in the same way to clean up the black areas on the lower-left area of the door. Figure 1.20 shows the Clone tool working on the left side of the door.

The end result of using the Clone tool is a cleaner door on which the detail is visible (see Figure 1.21).

Now the door texture is finished and usable in a game (see Figure 1.22).

Working with Vector-Drawing Programs

Vector-drawing programs are art tools in which you create images using vector graphics. Unlike painting on pixels, every line or shape in a vector program is defined by a line or curve between two points. Vector-drawing programs are primarily used in print production, but occasionally they come in handy for creating art for games. The CD for this book includes a link to the CorelDRAW suite. CorelDRAW 11 is one of the programs in the CorelDRAW Suite. It is

Figure 1.19 Use the Clone tool to clean up the lower-right area of the door.

Figure 1.20 Use the Clone tool to clean up the lower-left portion of the door.

Figure 1.21 A close-up of the door area after the Clone tool is used

Figure 1.22 The finished door texture

arguably the most powerful vector-drawing program on the market.

Vector-drawing programs are great for anything that deals with typography, such as signs or interface art for menus. This section shows you a simple example of how you could use a vector-drawing program to create a graphic for a game.

Figure 1.23 shows a rendered image of a banner imported into Corel-DRAW. This banner will be part of an interface screen with type running across it.

You input the type into the banner using the Type tool (see Figure 1.24). For this banner, I selected Garamond Bold Condensed.

Now you need to size the title to fit the banner (see Figure 1.25). Because you are using a vector-drawing program, each character in the title is an

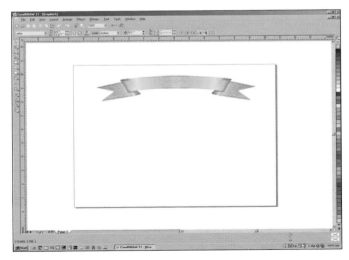

Figure 1.23 The rendered banner

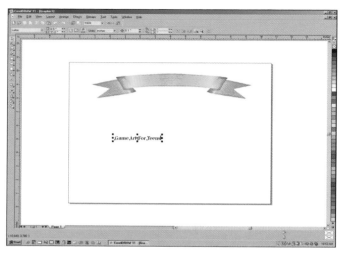

Figure 1.24 Type in the banner title.

Figure 1.25 Move the type to the banner and size it to fit.

individual object. This makes it possible to move and size the title as if it were a picture object.

The title is now sized correctly for the banner, but it doesn't fit because it is the wrong shape. One of the nice things about a vector-drawing program is you can fit type to a path. Drawing an ellipse that follows the lower curve of the banner creates the path for the title (see Figure 1.26).

Now you need to attach the title to the path. This is a simple process in a vector-drawing program. First you select the title, and then you select Fit Text to Path from the Text menu (see Figure 1.27).

The program will bring up an arrow so you can select the path the title is to fit. Click on the ellipse to attach the type to the path of the ellipse (see Figure 1.28).

Now the only thing left to do is get rid of the ellipse. You can make objects in

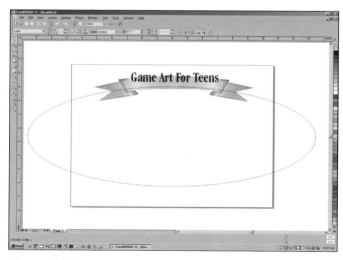

Figure 1.26 Drawing an ellipse creates the path.

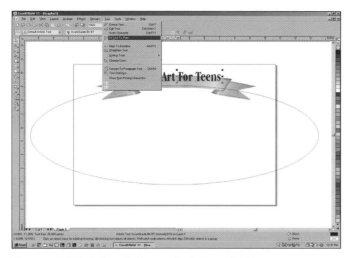

Figure 1.27 Select Fit Text to Path from the Text menu.

CorelDRAW transparent by selecting Transparent from the palette. If you look at the palette on the right side of the screen, you will see that the top palette slot has an X through it. Click on that palette slot to make the ellipse transparent. The ellipse is still there, but because it is now transparent

you don't see it anymore. The banner is now finished and ready to put into the game (see Figure 1.29).

Working with 3D Modeling Programs

3D modeling programs have become the standard of the game industry. Almost all games on the market today use 3D models for creating the worlds, characters, and objects. A *3D model* is a virtual three-dimensional object in a virtual three-dimensional space. The computer calculates

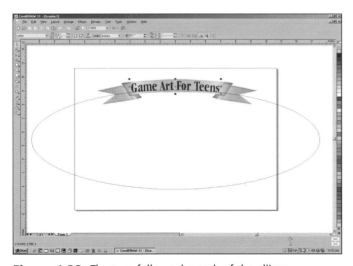

Figure 1.28 The type follows the path of the ellipse.

Figure 1.29 Make the ellipse transparent.

position, rotation, and movement of the objects in the virtual space, giving 3D models a realistic look you can't achieve using two-dimensional art programs.

At first, building game objects in a 3D program might seem a little intimidating. However, once you get used to the program, it will become an invaluable tool. 3D programs have opened a whole new world of possibilities in film, art, and gaming. Good 3D artists are in high demand in the game industry, so taking the time to learn how to create art in 3D programs is worthwhile for the beginning artist.

The CD that comes with this book contains a copy of the Personal Learning Edition of Maya. The program is a full-featured version of the professional software, but because it is designed for educational purposes, it contains an embedded watermark so you can't use the images or commercial projects. Maya is considered by many in the game industry to be the best 3D modeling and animation program on the market.

A marble column will be the example for how 3D models are created in

games. The first step is to create a primitive. A *primitive* is a simple three-dimensional geometric shape. In this case, make a polygonal cylinder. A *polygon* is a flat plane of either a triangle or a rectangle bounded by points that are called *vertices*. Vertices is the plural for *vertex*, which refers to a single point on a polygon. Between each vertex runs a vector or line called a *segment*. In Maya, select Polygonal Primitives from the Create menu. This will bring up a submenu with a cylinder on it. Select the small square at the end of the menu to bring up the Polygon Cylinder Options dialog box (see Figure 1.30).

Cylinders have many attributes. The Polygon Cylinder Options dialog box gives you the ability to control the size of the cylinder and the density of the polygonal mesh that will be created for it. *Polygonal mesh* is another term for the number and placement of polygons on a 3D object.

For this column, I created a cylinder that is 8 units high and has a radius of 0.5 units. The number of subdivisions on the height is also 8. After you enter your specifications, click Apply to create the cylinder.

You can change the camera view of the 3D model to make it easier to

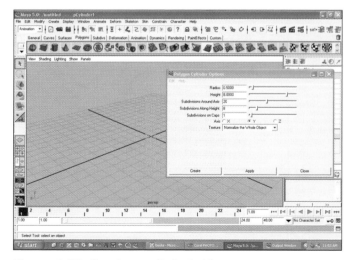

Figure 1.30 Creating a cylinder in Maya

adjust some of the polygons. The current camera view is a Perspective view, which simulates how an object looks in real life. For the next step, change the view by selecting Orthographic, Front from the Panels drop-down menu, as shown in Figure 1.31.

From the Front view it is easy to see the polygonal bands around the cylinder. A cylinder makes a boring column. To add more realism to the column, you need a base and a crown for the bottom and top, respectively. Right-click on the cylinder to bring up a floating marking menu. Hold down the right mouse button and

drag the cursor toward the word "vertex," then release the button. Now the cylinder is in what is called *Component mode*. In this mode, rather than selecting the entire object on the screen, you can select parts of the object, such as vertices, segments, or faces. By dragging a bounding box around a row of vertices, you can select all vertices within the box, as shown in Figure 1.32.

On the left side of the program window there are several manipulator tools, which you can use to modify polygonal objects or components. The third one from the top (with the

picture of a cone and an arrow) is the Move tool. The Move tool allows you to move objects or components in 3D space. Select the green arrow to move the previously selected vertices up and down in the y-axis. Move the rows of vertices until they appear as in Figure 1.33.

These vertices will make up the base of the column. You can use the Scale tool to form the base by scaling the rows of vertices. Like the Move tool, the Scale tool is a model manipulator tool. The Scale tool is the fifth tool down from the top. (It has two arrows and a cube on it.) When you select it,

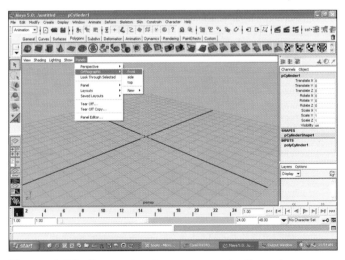

Figure 1.31 Change the view screen to the Front view.

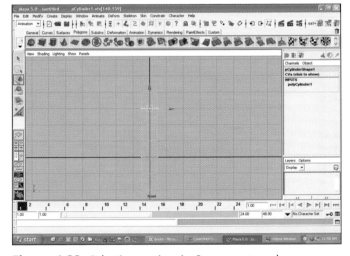

Figure 1.32 Selecting vertices in Component mode

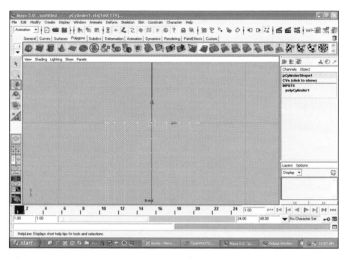

Figure 1.33 Move the vertices of the column.

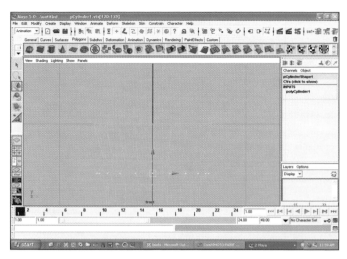

Figure 1.34 Creating the base of the column

a new manipulator appears. By clicking on the center (or yellow) block on the tool and moving the mouse to the right or left, you can scale the selected vertices larger or smaller in all three dimensions. Scale each row of vertices as shown in Figure 1.34.

Repeat the same process for the bottom of the column to create an upper and lower base on the column. Now the shape of the column is finished and ready to have a surface texture applied to it (see Figure 1.35).

Most 3D objects in games use either a color or a texture to give them a

realistic look. In this case, I will use textures. *Textures* are 2D images that are applied to 3D objects. In Maya, the Hypershade tool is used to organize and apply textures to 3D objects. You access the Hypershade tool through the Window menu, as shown in Figure 1.36.

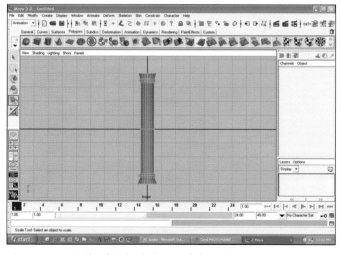

Figure 1.35 The finished shape of the column

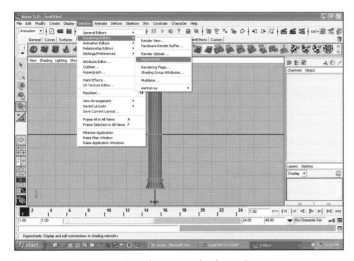

Figure 1.36 Accessing the Hypershade tool

Maya creates *materials* for each texture. You use materials to adjust a texture's attributes after it is loaded in Maya. To create a material, go to the Create menu in Hypershade and choose Materials, Blinn, as shown in Figure 1.37. (Blinn is a type of material.)

A new material will appear in Hypershade. Press Ctrl+A to bring up the attribute editor, which is used for manipulating a material (see Figure 1.38). In this case, I will use the attribute editor to load a texture.

In the attribute editor, click on the little checkerboard icon to the right of Color to bring up the Create Render Node dialog box, as shown in Figure 1.39.

The Create Render Node dialog box contains several options for creating

Figure 1.37 Creating a new material in Hypershade

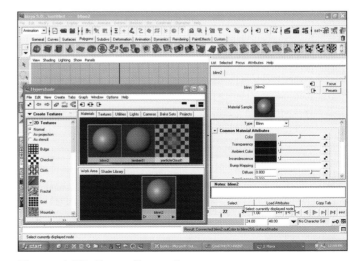

Figure 1.38 The attribute editor

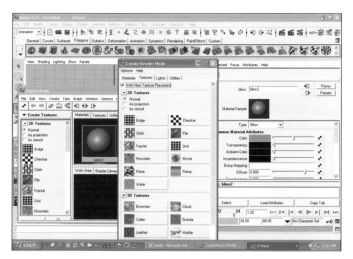

Figure 1.39 Calling up the Create Render Node dialog box

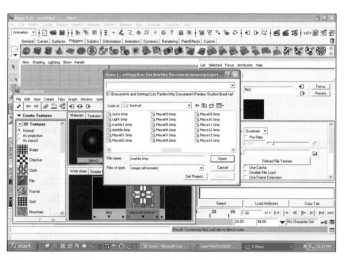

Figure 1.40 The texture-loading dialog box

textures or patterns for materials. For this column, I will use the File icon to load a texture that was previously created in a 2D photo-paint program. Click on File to bring up a new menu on the attribute editor. Notice that there is a file folder icon to the right of the image name. Clicking on this icon will bring up a new dialog box in which you can select the marble texture and load it into Maya (see Figure 1.40).

The texture is now loaded into Maya (see Figure 1.41).

Now minimize Hypershade and the attribute editor, and then change the main view window to Perspective view. The object is still in Component mode. There are several icons below the main menu bar at the top of the program window, two of which are mode select icons (see Figure 1.42).

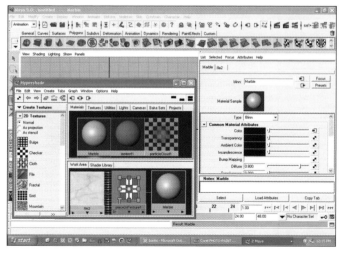

Figure 1.41 The texture loaded into Hypershade

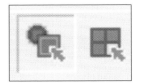

Figure 1.42 Mode select icons

These two mode select icons control the viewing mode of the main window. The icon on the right is for Component mode, and the icon on the left is for Object mode. Return the view window to Object mode by first clicking on the Component mode icon to clear the object, and then clicking on the Object mode icon.

Now you can apply the texture to the object. If the column is selected, it will show the polygons in bright green. If the column is not highlighted in bright green, select it by clicking on it. Now bring up the Hypershade tool and right-click on the new material to bring up the marking menu. From the menu, select Assign Material to Selection. The texture will be applied to the column. Press 6 on the keyboard to see the texture applied to the column in what is known as *hardware texturing*.

You need to adjust the texture so it looks correct on the column. Maya has several texture manipulators called *projectors*. Projectors take their name from slide projectors because they project an image onto the surface of the object. The Cylindrical Mapping projector would be the best choice for this project. You access it through the Edit Polygons menu, as shown in Figure 1.43.

The Cylindrical Mapping projector is used to map an object onto a cylinder. Click the Apply button to bring up the onscreen manipulators (see Figure 1.44). Now the object is mapped correctly.

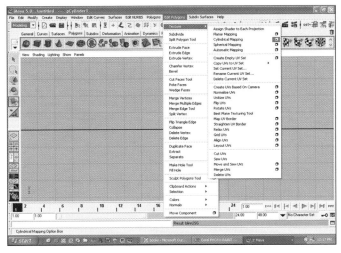

Figure 1.43 Accessing the Cylindrical Mapping projector

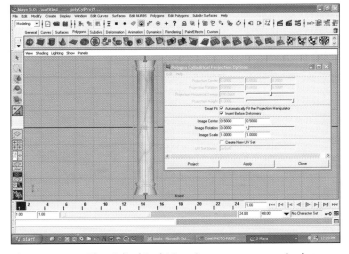

Figure 1.44 The Cylindrical Mapping onscreen manipulators

The column could be finished now, but with only one texture it is a little boring. It would be a lot more interesting to look at if it had a second texture for the base and crown. To add a second texture, go back to Hypershade and load the second texture the same way you did the first (see Figure 1.45). This time the texture will be marble1.

The darker marble1 texture only needs to be applied to the top and bottom of the column. To select and apply a texture to only a part of an object, the object needs to be in Component mode. Press 4 on the keyboard to go back to Wire-Frame view, and then right-click on the object and select Faces by holding down the right mouse button and moving the cursor down toward Faces on the marker menu. *Face* is the component name for a polygon. Now you can draw a bounding box around the faces that make up the bases of the column by holding the left mouse button down and dragging, as shown in Figure 1.46.

Apply the texture to the faces with Hypershade the same way you applied it to the object earlier. Now you have a completed column, as shown in Figure 1.47.

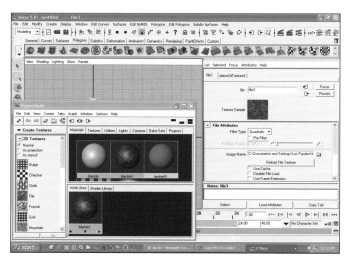

Figure 1.45 Loading the second marble texture into Hypershade

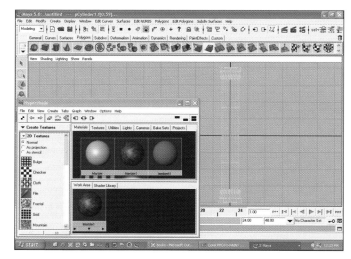

Figure 1.46 Selecting the column's bases

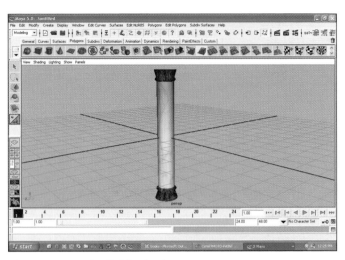

Figure 1.47 The finished column

Summary

This chapter has been an overview of the tools used in the creation of art. This chapter also provided brief examples of how you might use these programs in a production setting.

CHAPTER 2

2D ARTWORK IN GAMES

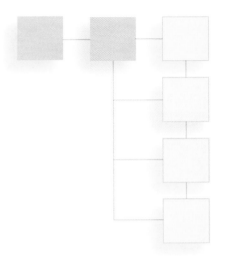

Before 3D games hit the market, games were created using 2D artwork. Even now there are many facets of game creation that require good two-dimensional artwork. The main areas for which 2D artwork is required for games include

- Textures for 3D models
- Titles, menus, legal screens, and other interface art
- Concept art

In this chapter I will provide an overview of each type of 2D art used in games and give you some examples of how the art is created.

Learning about Textures

Textures are 2D images that are applied to a three-dimensional model to give the model surface detail. In real life every surface has a texture. Sometimes the textures are only a color, while other times they might be very complex, such as the bark of a tree. Take a quick look around and study some of the many textures you see in everyday life. You will notice on close examination that every surface has some qualities that you can fit into a few specific categories.

- Color
- Roughness
- Translucency
- Reflectivity
- Luminance

Each one of these qualities or attributes is part of what gives the surface the look and feel it has. To make a 3D model look believable in a game, the artist needs to capture the inherent qualities of the surfaces he is trying to depict by creating textures that match the surface as closely as possible. The metallic sheen of a kitchen appliance has a very different look than a weathered fencepost. The hard gray of a sidewalk is very different than the spiky look of the lawn right next to it.

To better understand how you can create surface attributes in 2D artwork, take a look at each one individually.

Color in Textures

One of the most noticeable characteristics of any surface is its color. We often refer to an object by its color. We say "the red car" or "the blue sweater." Some colors are tied to emotional states. We call a person who is on a lucky streak "red-hot" or a person who is depressed "blue." We even assign temperatures to colors. Red, yellow, and orange are considered warm colors, while purple, blue, and green are thought of as cool colors.

How Light Affects Colors

To better understand color, you first need to look at light. When pure light strikes an object, some of the light energy is absorbed and some is reflected. The light you see is the light that is reflected. For example, when you see a red object, you are really seeing an object that reflects red light. The object is absorbing all the non-red light and reflecting the red.

The light that your eyes process so you can see the world around you is called the *visible band* of light. The visible band of light is made up of a spectrum of colors. If you have ever seen a rainbow, you have seen the spectrum of visible light (see Figure 2.1). Rainbows are made from light bouncing off water particles in the air. Because each color has its own unique characteristics, some colors are bounced in one direction and some are bounced in another, forming bands of pure color. These bands of color are always in the same order, with red at one end and violet or purple at the other end. All the rest of the colors are between those two colors.

© Corel Corporation
Figure 2.1 A rainbow in nature

Pure light is often called *white light*. White light contains the full spectrum of colors. When you see a white color, you are really seeing an object that reflects a full spectrum of color toward you. On the other hand, when you see a black object, you are really seeing an object that is not reflecting any band of light back to you. The black object is absorbing the full spectrum of light, while the white object is reflecting the full spectrum of light. That is why black objects tend to heat when placed in light, while white objects tend not to heat as much.

Hint

Light is a very important topic for artists. I encourage every person that I teach to learn as much as he or she can about the physics of light. The better an artist understands the nature of light, the better he or she will understand how to create realistic and believable art.

Understanding light is very important to understanding how color works. Unless you are in a completely dark room, every object sends light to your eyes (see Figure 2.2). This light not only affects the object itself, but also

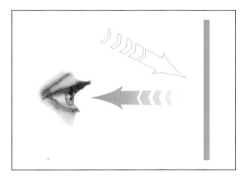

Figure 2.2 When white light strikes a red object, only red light is reflected.

other objects around it. Try an experiment. Place a white card next to a bright red object. You can see the red light from the object bouncing off the white of the card. The effect is similar to shining a red light on the card, just not as pronounced.

Any light you see that is not pure is missing part of the full spectrum of color. In some ways you can call colored light *deficient light*. Because colored light is deficient in one or more bands of color, it affects the objects it lights. Because red light does not contain blue light, objects that are blue in normal light will look very different in red light. The same thing is true for all other colored light.

Using the Color Wheel

Earlier I gave the example of the rainbow. A common tool for artists is a color wheel (see Figure 2.3). A *color wheel* is an ordered placement of colors in a circle based on their relative positions in the full spectrum of light. Remember that one end of the bands of color on a rainbow is red and the other is purple or violet. On a color wheel, these two colors are next to each other, and the other colors are arranged around the circle in order.

Some art programs actually use the color wheel as part of the color palette. Corel Painter provides a good example of the color wheel in a program. Load Painter and look at the

Figure 2.3 The color wheel in Corel Painter

color palette. Notice the color ring around the color triangle. The colors in the ring represent the different bands of color in the full spectrum of color. The inside triangle shows the current color of the spectrum from the color wheel. Look for the small ring on the color wheel. Move the ring around the wheel and notice how the color of the inside triangle changes to match the color on the wheel.

Understanding Color Saturation

Color saturation is the intensity and purity of a color. When a color is fully saturated it contains a pure band of color from the color wheel. The color is not grayed or tinted; it is the pure color at its full strength. You almost never see fully saturated colors in real life. However, every color that you see has some level of saturation.

The color palette in Corel Painter shows the fully saturated color at one corner of the inside triangle. Move the small circle inside the triangle. The right side of the triangle is the purest color. As you move the small circle away from the right, the color is less pure and more muted.

Understanding Value in Color

Color value does not refer to how expensive a color is; rather, it refers to how light or dark it is. The full *value scale* is from pure black to pure white. The value scale is represented in Corel Painter on the left side of the triangle color palette (see Figure 2.4). The lower corner of the triangle is black, and the upper corner is white. Between the two left-hand corners is grayscale without any color saturation.

Figure 2.4 The left side of the triangle is for the light-to-dark value.

All colors have values. Colors such as red and blue tend to have dark values, while a color such as yellow tends to have a lighter value. When you look at a black-and-white photograph, you are really looking at a picture of value.

As an artist, I often will convert a color picture to grayscale so I can see the values of each color. If your pictures look drastically different in color than they do in grayscale, you are probably dealing with a value problem.

Roughness in Textures

Every surface you see in real life has some degree of roughness. Some surfaces, such as glass or polished metal, have such a low degree of roughness that it can only be seen using a microscope. Other surfaces, such as a rock wall or gravel, have noticeable roughness. The rougher a surface is, the more it refracts light. *Refraction* is the scattering of light when it hits an uneven surface. When light hits a surface, it bounces off the surface at a direct angle from the light source (see Figure 2.5).

Roughness is usually simulated in textures rather than built with geometry in the 3D model. Moving polygons around in a virtual world requires many mathematical calculations. The fewer polygons an artist can use to create 3D models, the faster the game will be able to run.

Figure 2.6 shows a rough rock wall. You could create this wall using nothing more than color and geometry, but that would be an extreme waste of computer processor time that you could devote instead to more critical game needs. It would also be an extreme waste of your time. A better method would be to create the

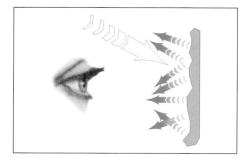

Figure 2.5 Light refracting from a rough surface

Figure 2.6 The rough surface of a rock wall

appearance of the rough rock wall in a 2D picture and paste that picture on a relatively simple object.

Translucency in Textures

In nature, not all surfaces are opaque; some surfaces are *translucent*. A translucent surface allows some amount of light to pass through it, making it possible to see through the surface. Figure 2.7 shows a good example of a translucent surface. Notice how the glass of the pyramid changes the color and detail of the building seen through it.

Figure 2.7 The glass of the pyramid is translucent, which allows light to pass through it.

Some of the more advanced game engines will allow you to use translucent textures. Sometimes you will need to create a translucent texture in a 2D paint program, but most of the time the translucency is added in the 3D art program.

Reflectivity in Textures

Reflectivity is related to roughness in textures. The more even and polished a surface is, the more it will tend to reflect light directly back to the viewer. A *reflective* surface acts like a mirror, reflecting its surroundings back to the viewer. True reflections can only be generated in the game environment; however, sometimes reflections can be simulated, as in Figure 2.8.

Figure 2.8 Simulated reflections on the surface of a door texture

Even though the reflection on the door is static, it still gives the impression of a reflection. For many objects in 3D games, building true reflections is impractical. In those instances, a static reflection will get the job done. The problem with a static reflection is that it does not move with the viewer.

Surface Luminance in Textures

Luminance is the brightness of a color. For the purposes of this book, I will discuss luminance when dealing with a light source as seen in a game. For example, a light bulb will have a high degree of luminance when the light is turned on and no luminance when it is turned off. Like reflections, real-time luminance is a property of the game engine. Many times, though, luminance needs to be part of a 2D image. In Figure 2.9, the texture is a wall that is lit by a wall-mounted light. The wall-mounted light will be added in the 3D modeling program, but the pattern or the luminance of the light was added to the texture itself.

Figure 2.9 A lighting effect was added to the texture.

Creating Textures

To create textures for games, artists use one of two different methods. The first method is to create a texture from scratch by painting it. This method is great for artists who have a high degree of artistic ability because it allows for endless variety in the types of textures that can be produced. The only limitations are the imagination and ability of the artist. The other method of creating textures is to use photographs. Many times a photograph of a surface is the best choice because the artist is trying to simulate a real object.

Hint

One thing I learned about working as an artist for games is that artists use whatever method they can to create the art as quickly and accurately as possible. There is no rule that states every piece of art has to be drawn by hand. If a photograph will work better, use the photograph. You will need permission to use a photograph if it isn't your property. Using a photograph without the owner's permission is illegal.

Painting Textures

For this example I will create a weathered stucco texture using Corel Painter, which has some nice features for creating textures.

1. First open Corel Painter. Select New from the File menu to bring up the New dialog box, as shown in Figure 2.10. Set the size at 256×256 pixels.

Figure 2.10 The texture size is set for 256×256 pixels.

Hint

It is a good idea to get in the habit of making your texture's dimensions a power of two. This is of particular importance on console systems such as the PS2 because of the limited bandwidth of the bus. It is a good rule to make the dimensions one of the following numbers: 8, 16, 32, 64, 128, 256, 512, or 1024. Texture sizes should be as small as possible but still look good in the game.

2. The next step is to select the color of the texture. I used the color wheel on the right side of the screen to select a color partway between blue and green, and then I used the triangle palette to give me a cool gray color (see Figure 2.11). The Fill tool on the left side of the screen is used to apply the color to the texture.

3. Next select the Show Papers window from the Window menu, as shown in Figure 2.12.

4. The Show Papers window has a number of preset surface textures. The small icon in the upper-right corner of the window is used for selecting surfaces. I clicked on the little triangle to bring up the Paper Surface drop-down menu, and then I selected Simulated Woodgrain for the texture (see Figure 2.13).

5. Now the texture in the window shows the simulated wood grain. Adjust the three slider bars at the bottom of the window to the numbers shown in Figure 2.14 (67%, 85%, and 65%).

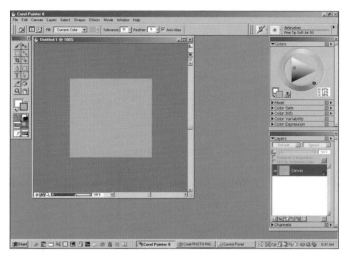

Figure 2.11 I selected a cool gray color for the texture.

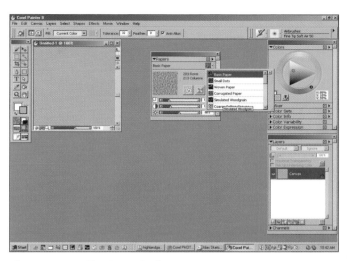

Figure 2.13 The Paper Surface menu

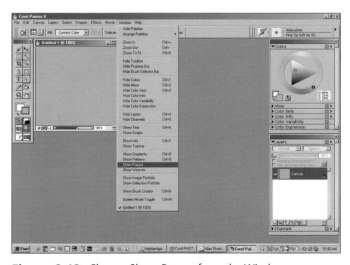

Figure 2.12 Choose Show Papers from the Window menu.

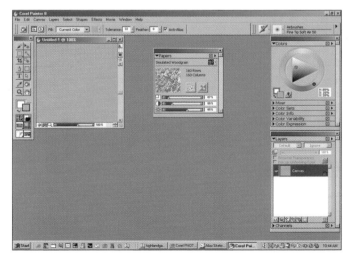

Figure 2.14 Adjust the texture using the three slider bars.

6. Now you have the surface texture you want. The next step is to apply the surface texture to the image. In the Effects menu, choose Surface Control, Apply Surface Texture, as shown in Figure 2.15. This will bring up the Apply Surface Texture dialog box.

7. The first thing you should change in the Apply Surface Texture dialog box is the lighting. I chose to offset the cool gray color with a warm orange light (see Figure 2.16). The

mixture of a warm light source with a cool color will gray the image further, but it also adds a second color, which will become very important later.

8. I made several adjustments to the slider bars to get just the right look (see Figure 2.17). Feel free to do the same or make adjustments as you like. A little experimentation with these slider bars will result in a number of dramatic changes to the surface texture. For this texture, I reduced the shine and

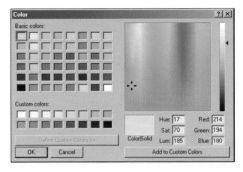

Figure 2.16 Select the lighting color.

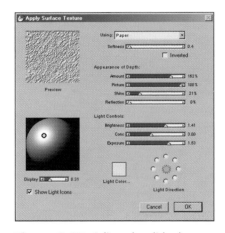

Figure 2.17 Adjust the slider bars.

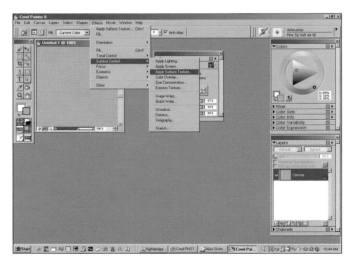

Figure 2.15 The Apply Surface Texture dialog box can be accessed from the Surface Control submenu in the Effects menu.

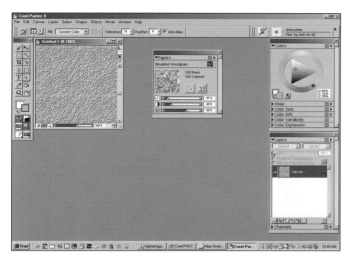

Figure 2.18 The texture is a good start but it needs more work.

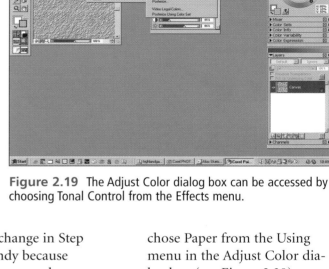

Figure 2.19 The Adjust Color dialog box can be accessed by choosing Tonal Control from the Effects menu.

increased the amount. I also adjusted the three light controls.

9. Now you should have a nice-looking stucco texture (see Figure 2.18). You could finish here, but I want to add some more interest to my stucco. Right now it is too much like freshly painted stucco, and I am looking for a more weathered look with maybe a hint of moss growing on the wall.

10. Now the lighting change in Step 8 will come in handy because you have both a warm and a cool color in the texture. You can modify these colors to get the weathered look by accessing the Adjust Color dialog box, which is found under Tonal Control in the Effects menu (see Figure 2.19).

11. I didn't want to make a uniform change to the colors, so I

chose Paper from the Using menu in the Adjust Color dialog box (see Figure 2.20).

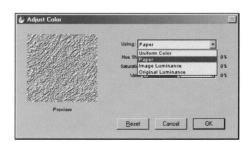

Figure 2.20 Select Paper from the Using menu in the Adjust Color dialog box.

12. I shifted the Hue Shift, Saturation, and Value slider bars to get the weathered stucco look (see Figure 2.21). Notice how some colors are shifted to more of a reddish tint, while others are shifted to more of a greenish tint.

Now the texture is finished and ready to use in a game (see Figure 2.22).

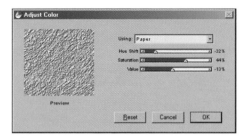

Figure 2.21 Adjust the slider bars to get the final look for the texture.

Using Photographs for Textures

This section is an example of taking a part of a picture and using it to create a repeatable texture for trim on a building. After searching through a number of photographs from a previous excursion to the city, I found just what I wanted (see Figure 2.23). For this example I will use Corel Photo Paint. As I stated earlier, photo-painting software is geared specifically toward photo manipulation.

1. The first step is to crop the picture down to the area with which you want to work. You can use the Crop tool to drag a box around the area on the picture, as shown in Figure 2.24.

2. Figure 2.25 shows the cropped image. Notice that the image is

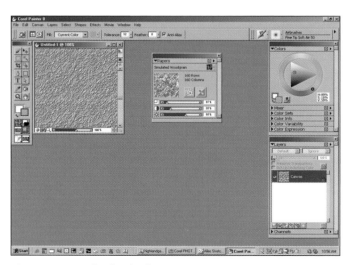

Figure 2.22 The finished stucco texture

Figure 2.23 The base photo used to start the process of creating a texture

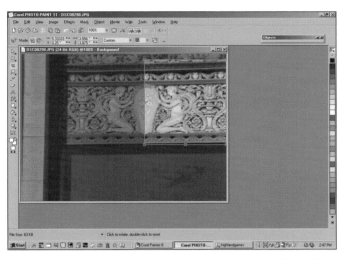

Figure 2.24 Crop to the area where the texture will be taken from the picture.

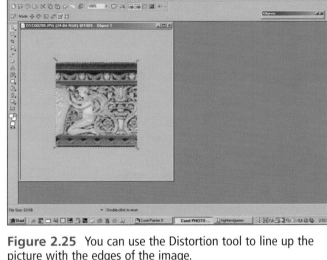

Figure 2.25 You can use the Distortion tool to line up the picture with the edges of the image.

warped. The edges of the building decoration do not line up perfectly with the edges of the image. I want this texture to repeat, so it needs to be completely square with the edges of the image.

3. The easiest way to get a picture to line up with the edges of an image is to use the Distort tool. First you copy the image, and then you paste it over itself. Now you have two images, one exactly on top of the other.

4. Corel Photo Paint provides you with four different ways to manipulate the pasted image. To change the manipulation tool, all you have to do is click on the image. Try clicking on the image a few times. Notice that the handles around the image change. These handles are used for manipulating the image. The default tool is the Scale tool, which is depicted by a set of black squares around the edge. After you click once inside the image, the manipula-

tor will change to arrows that curve around the corners. This tool is the Rotate tool. The third click will bring up the Distortion tool, which is used to adjust the shape of the image by allowing you to move individual corners. The Distortion tool is represented by small arrows painted away from the picture. You can grab and move these arrows. I used these arrows to line up the picture with the edges of the image, as shown in Figure 2.25.

5. Once the image is adjusted so it is even with the edges, you can combine the two images using the Combine All Images with Background option, as shown in Figure 2.26.

6. Now that the image is flat, you can crop it again to only the area you want for the repeatable texture (see Figure 2.27).

7. The image is now cropped and parallel with the edges so it will repeat accurately. Notice that I cut off the image in the middle of the decorative pattern on both ends (see Figure 2.28). Later I will show you how to get a full pattern by flipping the image.

8. Now the texture needs to be resized so that it will work better in the game. I could make this texture square by resizing it to 256×256 pixels. However, in this example it would be better to make the texture a rectangle instead of a square because a square will distort the image too much (see Figure 2.29). You can use the Resize tool, as I did in the first example, to make this texture 128 pixels wide and 256 pixels high. Notice that the width and height are still a power of two even though they are not the same.

9. Now the texture is ready to be put in the game. However, before you do that, you should make sure it repeats correctly. You can do this in a paint program; you don't have to go to a

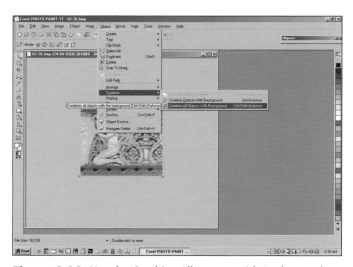

Figure 2.26 Use the Combine All Images with Background option.

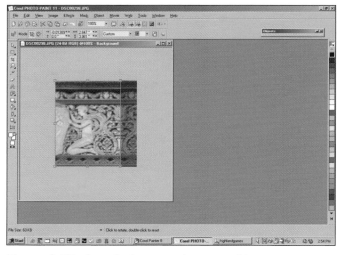

Figure 2.27 Crop the image to the repeatable area.

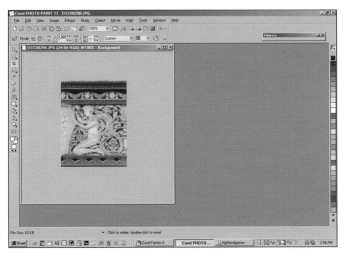

Figure 2.28 The texture after cropping

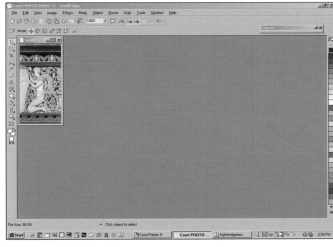

Figure 2.29 The image resized to a power of two

3D program. Simply bring up a new image and set it for 256 pixels high and 512 pixels wide (see Figure 2.30).

10. You now have two images—one of the texture and a white image that is as high as the texture but four times as wide. Click on the texture image to make it active, and then press Ctrl+C to copy the texture.

11. Now that the image is copied into the computer, you can paste it into the new image. Click on the new image to make it active, and then press Ctrl+V to paste the texture into the new image. You now have a copy of the texture in the new image.

Hint

In this example I am using hot keys, which are keystroke combinations. Hot keys are shortcuts that can save you time, but you can also use the menus to accomplish the same tasks. In this case, the Copy and Paste menu items are in the Edit menu.

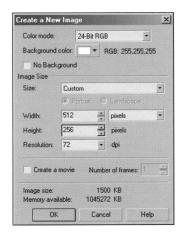

Figure 2.30 The new image is 256×512.

12. You can move the copy of the texture in the new image because it floats above the background. You should check how your image repeats, so you want to move the copy of the texture to the far left of the new image. It is easy to move the texture; you simply use the Move tool that is represented by an arrow icon on the Toolbox on the left side of the screen. The Move tool allows you to select and move floating images above the background. So for this example, click on the texture and drag it to the far left of the new image.

13. Now that you have placed the first copy of the texture, repeat Step 11 to paste another copy of the texture into the new image. Then move that copy to the left so it is lined up next to the first image (see Figure 2.31).

14. You need the second floating copy of the texture to be facing in the opposite direction of the first copy of the texture. To accomplish this, select Flip, Horizontally from the Object menu (see Figure 2.32).

Hint

When you move floating objects in an image, it is sometimes useful to lock one of the directions. If you hold down the Ctrl key while you are moving an image, you can move the image either up and down or left and right, but not in the other direction. Try it. Hold down the Ctrl key and click on one of the floating images. Now move the image either up and down or left and right. Notice how the image is locked in one direction.

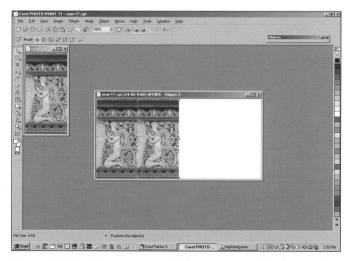

Figure 2.31 The two copies of the texture are lined up to the left of the new image.

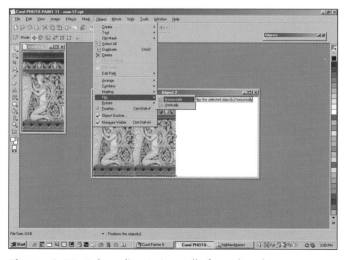

Figure 2.32 Select Flip, Horizontally from the Object menu.

Figure 2.33 The flipped copy of the texture lines up with the first copy of the texture.

15. The first and second textures are lined up now (see Figure 2.33). Notice how the symmetrical shape of the vase works in the two textures.

16. Repeat the process of adding new copies of the texture and flipping them when necessary for the rest of the new image. Figure 2.34 shows how the texture will look when you place it on a 3D model of a building. This method works best if the lighting on the original picture is perpendicular to the direction of the repeating texture. The lighting in this instance was directly overhead, so the repeating texture didn't have any shading conflicts.

Figure 2.34 The texture is repeated and flipped across the new image.

Tiling Textures

Large textures take up memory in a game system, and some console game systems have very limited texture memory. To make better use of texture memory, game artists have developed a system of tiling textures. *Tiling* a texture is the process of taking a small texture and repeating it numerous times over the surface of a 3D object. For example, think about a brick wall. Most of the bricks look very similar, so there is no need to make one large texture image for the entire wall. It is much more efficient to create a small image of a few bricks and repeat it over the surface of the wall multiple times. The texture in the last example is a form of tiling a texture in one direction, but textures can also be tiled in two directions.

In addition to repeating textures such as bricks, you can tile more organic images. In the following example, I will show you how a photo of a bush is adapted to a texture that tiles in two directions. If you have a similar image, you can follow along with these steps.

1. Figure 2.35 shows a photo of a bush. Notice all the organic shapes of the leaves.

Figure 2.35 A close-up source image of a bush

2. Select the upper-right corner of the picture (see Figure 2.36). When you are tiling, always pick an area of a photograph with the least amount of unique differences in it.

3. The next step is to resize the image to a good texture size. In this case, resize the picture to 256×256 pixels (see Figure 2.37). Bring up the Resample dialog box by selecting Resample from the Image menu.

4. Tiling textures line up on all sides so there is no noticeable seam between pictures. If I tried to use the current picture as a tiling texture, the seams between each picture would be very noticeable (see Figure 2.38).

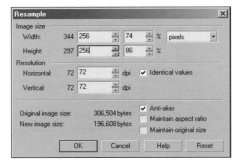

Figure 2.37 Resize the image to 256×256 pixels.

Figure 2.36 Select the upper-right corner for the texture.

Figure 2.38 The current picture will not tile properly because of the seams between each picture.

5. The easiest way to remove seams is to use the Offset function to move the seams to the middle of the picture. Select Distort, Offset from the Effects menu (see Figure 2.39).

6. You want to move the seams to the center of the picture. Make sure the Wrap Around feature is selected and the Shift Value as % of Dimensions box is checked in the Offset dialog box. Then adjust the slider bars to 50 so the seams cross in the

middle of the image (see Figure 2.40).

7. One of the best tools for removing seams is the Clone tool, which you will find in the

Figure 2.40 Offset the texture image by 50 percent.

Toolbox on the left side of the screen (see Figure 2.41).

8. Use the Clone tool to transfer parts of the picture over the seams to remove them. First click on an area of the picture from which you want to transfer, and then click on the area to which you want to transfer. Then simply paint with the brush (see Figure 2.42). Do this several times—try to keep the image as natural-looking as possible.

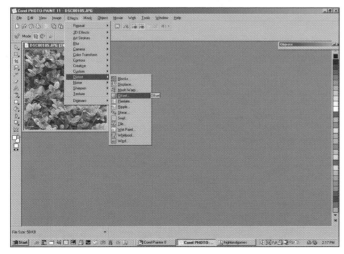

Figure 2.39 Select Distort, Offset from the Effects menu.

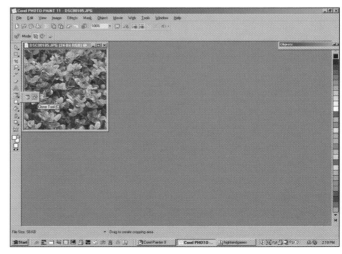

Figure 2.41 Select the Clone tool from the toolbar.

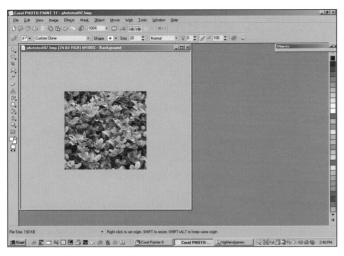

Figure 2.42 Use the Clone tool to remove all the seams in the texture.

Figure 2.44 Remove the darker areas using the Clone tool.

9. Now that you have removed all the seams, the texture is a tiling texture. However, just because it doesn't have seams does not mean that it is a good tiling texture. Sometimes textures will create repetitive patterns when tiled over a large area. These patterns are very noticeable in organic textures. An easy way to check whether a texture creates an annoying pattern is to use the Tile tool. Select Distort, Tile from the Effects menu. In the Tile dialog box, set Overlap to 0 and adjust the Horizontal Tiles and Vertical Tiles slider bars to 5, as shown in Figure 2.43.

10. Notice in Figure 2.42 that there is an obvious pattern. The

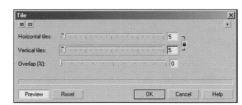

Figure 2.43 Check for patterns in the tiling of the texture.

problem is that there are distinct light and dark areas in the texture; these areas form the pattern. To remove the pattern, you can again use the Clone tool and remove as much of the darker areas as possible (see Figure 2.44).

11. Figure 2.45 shows the final texture repeated four times. As you can see, the pattern is much less noticeable. This texture is now ready to use on rows of bushes in a game.

Figure 2.45 The texture is repeated four times with minimal pattern and no seams.

Creating Game Interfaces

Significant 2D art is used in the opening and closing of most games. This art includes title screens, legal screens, navigation menus, heads-up displays, credit screens, and so on. These screens are all part of the work that an artist must create to complete a game. Collectively they are called *interface art* because they make up the art that is used for controlling and navigating a game.

A cool-looking interface can go a long way toward making a game look and feel like a professional product. Some game companies spend thousands of dollars for artists to design and create great interfaces for their games. Take a look at some of your favorite games and study how the interface was created. You will soon see that there is a lot of art created for the interface in many of these games.

Interface art can be divided into two major categories—information art and navigation art. Information art is used to inform the player of important information in a game, such as how to play the game, who owns the game, and most importantly, who created the game. Navigation art is used to help a player move through or play a game; this might include selection menus, life meters, or load/save features.

In the following example, I will create a menu screen for loading saved games. To start with, I will set up the screen using CorelDRAW.

1. The first step is to define the size of the Save menu. Use the Rectangle tool on the Toolbox on the left side of the screen and drag a rectangle around the area in which you want the menu to appear (see Figure 2.46).

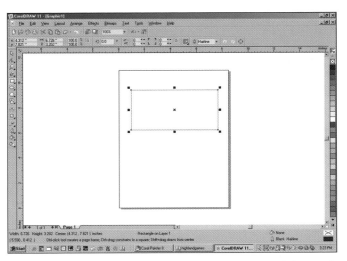

Figure 2.46 The Rectangle tool defines the size and shape of the menu.

2. You will want to have a pattern for the base of the menu. Select Pattern Fill from the flyout menu for the Fill tool (see Figure 2.47). The Pattern Fill dialog box will appear.

3. Select the Bitmap radio button to get a full-color pattern, and then click on the small triangle next to the pattern image. A menu will appear, from which you can select a pattern for the background (see Figure 2.48). I selected the center pattern on the third row.

4. The new pattern will appear in the pattern image area. Set the image size in the Size area. I set my image size to 2 inches by 2 inches (see Figure 2.49).

5. The menu now has a pattern-filled background, as you can see in Figure 2.50.

6. You want a readable, heavy typeface for the menu. Select the Type tool from the Toolbox to access a Formatting toolbar across the top of the page. Select a font from the control

bar (see Figure 2.51). I selected Arial Black as the typeface.

7. Now set the size of the font. I changed the size to 100, as shown in Figure 2.52.

8. Type **SAVE** in all capitals below the menu area, and make sure you can see your type clearly (see Figure 2.53).

9. Flat typefaces are boring. Don't you want to add a little flare to this typeface? For this example, I selected Fountain Fill from the Fill flyout menu, as shown in Figure 2.54.

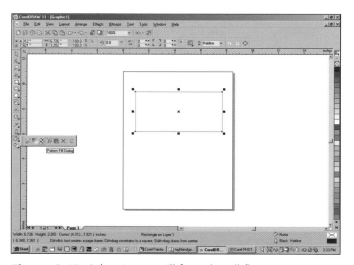

Figure 2.47 Select Pattern Fill from the Fill flyout menu.

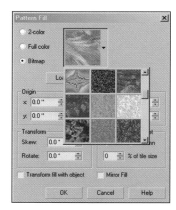

Figure 2.48 Select a pattern from the menu.

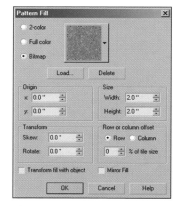

Figure 2.49 The image size is set to 2 inches by 2 inches.

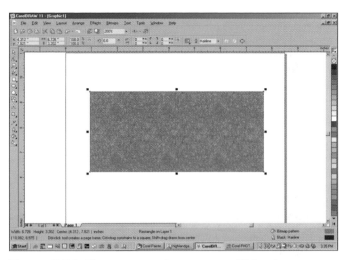

Figure 2.50 The menu now has a pattern fill for the background.

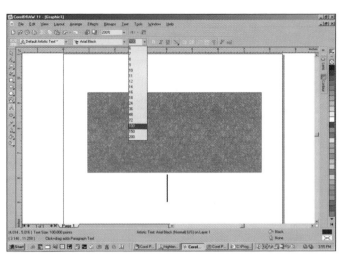

Figure 2.52 I chose 100 for the size of the typeface.

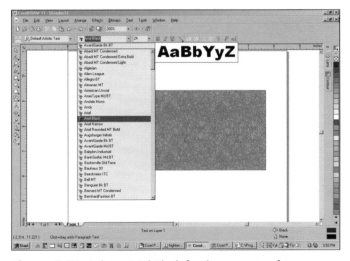

Figure 2.51 I chose Arial Black for the menu typeface.

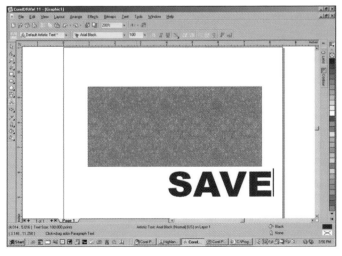

Figure 2.53 I typed SAVE below the menu area.

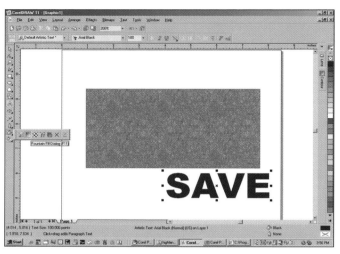

Figure 2.54 I chose Fountain Fill from the Fill flyout menu.

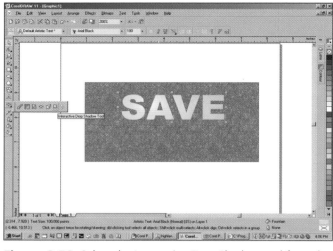

Figure 2.56 Select the Interactive Drop Shadow tool from the flyout menu.

10. The Fountain Fill dialog box has several preset fills from which you can choose. I selected Circular - Orange 01 from the Presets drop-down menu, as shown in Figure 2.55.

11. Now that you have a nice fill, move the type to the menu area. The type seems a little flat. Suppose you want to add a drop shadow to add a little depth to the image. Select the Interactive Drop Shadow tool from the Toolbox, as shown in Figure 2.56.

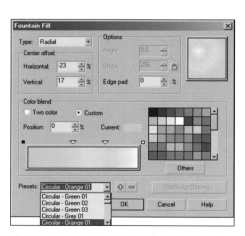

Figure 2.55 I chose Circular - Orange 01 from the Presets menu.

12. The Interactive Drop Shadow tool works with two click-and-drag movements. The first click and drag determines the size of the shadow. The second click and drag moves the shadow. Make a moderately large shadow and then position it so that the shadow is down and to the right of the type, as shown in Figure 2.57.

13. In addition to Save, you also need two more buttons on the menu. Type **Back** and **Quit** below the menu. You might also

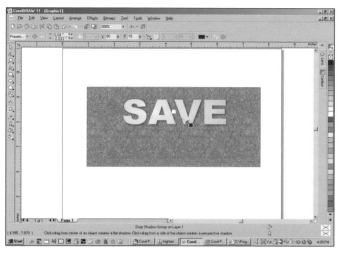

Figure 2.57 A drop shadow is added to the type.

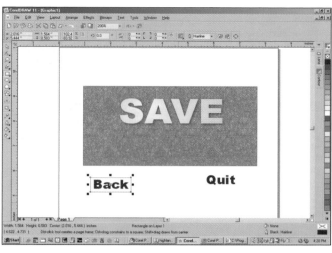

Figure 2.58 Draw a rectangle around one of the two words.

want to add a border around one of the menu words. Draw a rectangle around Back using the Rectangle tool, as shown in Figure 2.58.

14. Right-click on orange in the palette on the right side of the screen to change the rectangle line color to orange. On each corner of the rectangle there will be a small open square. Click on the square and round the corners of the rectangle to give it more of a button look.

15. The rectangle line needs to be a little thicker, don't you think? Click on the Line tool, which looks like a pen nib. It is the third icon from the bottom in the left Toolbox. When you click on the Line tool, a flyout menu will appear with several line widths (see Figure 2.59). Select the 2 Point Outline line width.

16. Now you can add color. Give the word Back the same fountain fill you gave the word SAVE earlier.

Hint

Shapes in CorelDRAW have both an outline and a fill. When they are first drawn, the fill color is transparent. Choosing an outline and fill color is very easy. A click of the left mouse button on any palette color on the right side of the screen will fill the shape with the selected color. A right-click will change the outline color to the selected color from the palette.

17. Move the newly colored button up to the menu area and add a drop shadow, as you did for the word SAVE earlier (see Figure 2.60).

18. Now repeat the process to make the Quit button, and then add it to the menu area. At the top of the work area there is a ruler. Click on the ruler and drag downward to create a dashed guideline. You can do this three times and use the guidelines to line up the two buttons (see Figure 2.61).

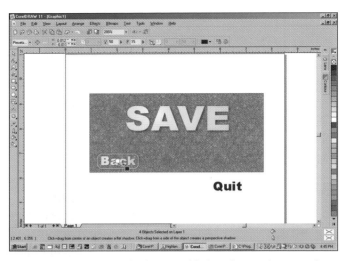

Figure 2.60 A drop shadow is added to the newly created button.

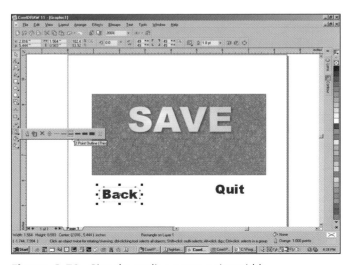

Figure 2.59 Give the outline a two-point width.

Figure 2.61 Add guidelines to help line up the words.

Creating Concept Art for Games

Concept art is not art that is actually used in a video game; rather, it is the design art that is created to visualize the game. Concept art is in the form of character designs, world designs, and storyboards.

Character designs are drawings of characters and creatures that will appear in a game. They are often in color with multiple views of the character. Designing great characters for a video game is not an easy process. It often takes artists several iterations before a final character sketch is approved to go into the game. When we were creating the new characters to go into *StarCraft: Brood War*, the artists designing the characters spent weeks working on some of them, with multiple changes and revisions.

World designs are drawings of the game environments. They might include pictures of scenes and maps of levels. Some game worlds are simple, but others are very sophisticated and complex. The game world for a fighting game might be nothing more than a simple room, but the game world for an adventure game might have an entire city with surrounding countryside that needs to be designed. As game systems advance in power, game worlds are becoming more and more complex.

Storyboards are drawings of the progression in a game. They usually are series of pictures depicting how a game is played to give the development team a good idea of how the game will be played once it is finished. They are also used to help convey how a game should look when it is finished.

Storyboards are a great help in solving complex game play issues. While working on a platform game, I remember doing a detailed storyboard of a very complex level. The main character was a robot that could roll around the level and make small jumps. I had to design the level so it was interesting to look at but functional from the standpoint of the robot's limitations. By creating a series of storyboards, I was able to work out both the look of the level and the game play challenges within the level.

When I first started in the industry, almost all concept art was created by hand on paper. With the advancement of art programs such as Alias SketchBook Pro and Corel Painter, more and more artists are turning to the computer to create their concept drawings. In the following example, I will use Alias SketchBook Pro to create a character for a game.

1. Alias SketchBook Pro is designed a little differently than other art programs. All the tools are located on the lower-left of the screen. There are four icons that will bring up marking menus. For this example you want to draw a character so select the second icon, which is the Brush tool, and, while holding the stylus down, slide it toward the Pencil icon. With this brush, draw very lightly the basic shape of the character (see Figure 2.62).

2. The Toolbox contains a Zoom and Move tool. It is represented by the top icon on the marking menu, with a picture of a hand and a magnifying glass. The Zoom and Move tool looks like a doughnut. Clicking on the

outside ring allows you to move the image around on the screen. Clicking on the doughnut hole allows you to magnify or reduce the image. Play with the tool a little to get used to how it works. When you are ready, zoom into the image.

3. With the image enlarged, you can add detail to the drawing. In this example, I start by adding detail around the head and shoulders of the character, as shown in Figure 2.63.

4. Continue to add detail to the rest of the drawing. Take a look at Figure 2.64 to see the detail I've added for this example.

5. Once you have the drawing defined, clean off the unwanted construction lines using the Eraser. First bring up the Brush Selector palette as a floating window from the Brush tool icon (see Figure 2.65). Notice that there is set of Eraser icons at the bottom of the palette. These icons represent various

sizes of erasers. I used several of them to clean up the drawing for this example.

6. After you clean up the drawing, save the file so you can bring it back later.

7. The next step is to color the drawing. Use the Airbrush tool to block in the basic colors and values of the picture. In this example I worked on the face and hands. I used the Airbrush tool from the Brush Selector palette. I also brought up the

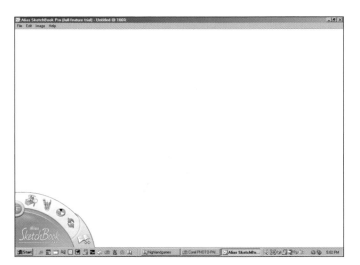

Figure 2.62 Draw light beginning strokes to start defining the character.

Figure 2.63 Add detail to the drawing.

Figure 2.64 Add detail to the rest of the drawing.

Figure 2.65 Use the Eraser tool to clean up unwanted lines in the drawing.

Color Selector tool from the Color Selector icon. Like in CorelDRAW, the Color Selector has a color wheel and a value/saturation triangle (see Figure 2.66).

8. Continue to add color to the drawing, and don't worry too much about the lines (see Figure 2.67).

9. Again, use the Eraser tool to clean up the drawing (see Figure 2.68). One of the nice things about drawing on a computer screen is that you don't have to worry about the drawing surface. You can use the Eraser to clean off anything—something you can't always do with real paper.

10. Now you are ready to add the line drawing you saved earlier to the colored version. Save the colored version under a different name and close Alias SketchBook Pro.

11. You can merge your two drawings in Corel Photo Paint. Bring up that program and load the two images, as shown in Figure 2.69.

12. Copy the line drawing and paste it over the color drawing (see Figure 2.70). That way you have two drawings—one on top of the other.

13. Now make the top line drawing transparent so the color drawing shows through it. Select the Transparent tool, as shown in Figure 2.71, and then select Flat from the Toolbox.

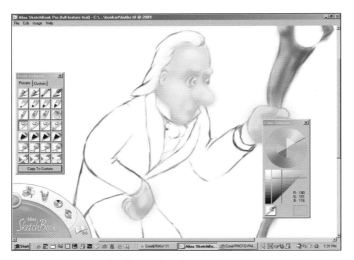

Figure 2.66 Add color to the picture.

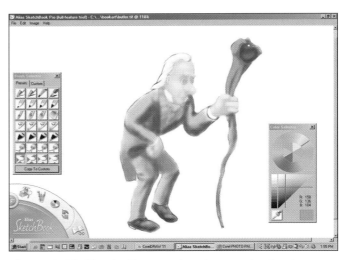

Figure 2.68 Use the Eraser tool to clean up the drawing.

Figure 2.67 Use the Color Selector and the Airbrush tool to add color to the drawing.

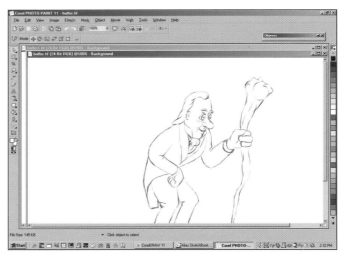

Figure 2.69 Bring up the two images in Corel Photo Paint.

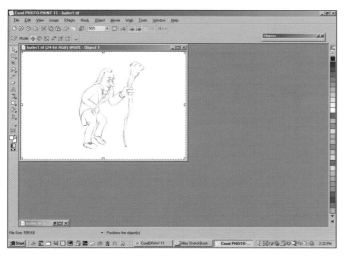

Figure 2.70 Paste the line drawing over the top of the color drawing.

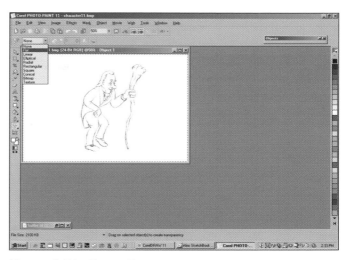

Figure 2.71 Choose Flat transparency.

14. Now adjust the transparency to 70 so the top image is 70 percent transparent (see Figure 2.72). The color drawing will be clearly visible under the line drawing, yet the lines will be clear as well.

15. Next combine the two images by selecting Combine, Combine All Layers with Background from the Object menu, as shown in Figure 2.73.

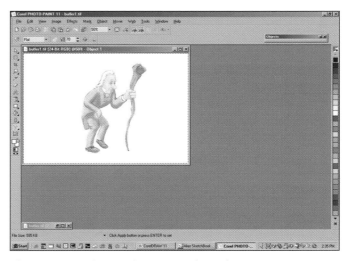

Figure 2.72 The top drawing is adjusted to 70 percent transparency.

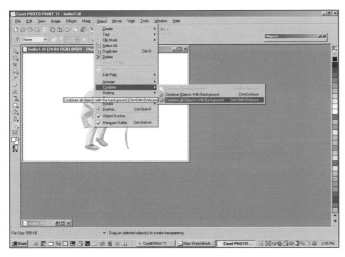

Figure 2.73 The two drawings are combined.

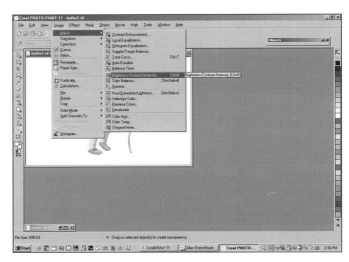

Figure 2.74 The Brightness/Contrast/Intensity tools are in the Adjust submenu of the Image menu.

16. Now you have the colored version and the line version of the drawing combined, but the drawing is dull. You need to brighten the colors. Select Adjust, Brightness/Contrast/Intensity from the Image menu, as shown in Figure 2.74.

17. Decrease the brightness and increase the contrast to bring out the colors and lines on the drawing, as shown in Figure 2.75.

Figure 2.75 Increase the contrast and decrease the brightness.

18. Now the drawing is finished as far as you probably want to take it for a concept sketch. Some sketches will require more finishing than others. This drawing is detailed enough to give you a good idea of the character (see Figure 2.76).

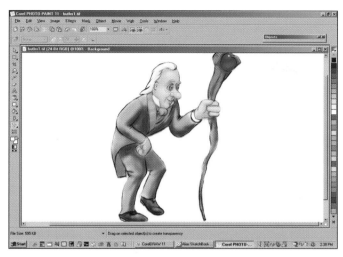

Figure 2.76 The finished concept sketch

Summary

Even though three-dimensional art is used in almost all current games on the market, two-dimensional art still plays a major role in the creation of a game. Even the most advanced 3D games use significant amounts of textures for 3D models within the game. 2D art is also used in the creation of interface art and concept sketches.

Understanding light and color is very important in developing textures for games. Textures also simulate shininess, roughness, transparency, and luminance.

Corel Painter is a good tool for creating textures when you use its paper texture features. Corel Photo Paint has several powerful tools for preparing photographs for textures and for creating tiling textures. CorelDRAW is a good choice for creating menus. And Alias SketchBook Pro is a good program for drawing characters.

CHAPTER 3

2D Animation

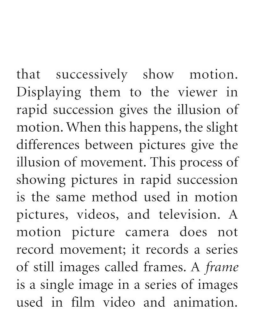

W hen I first started creating games, all animation was done in 2D or what is sometimes referred to as cell animation. The term *cell animation* comes from the motion picture industry. It refers to how animation was once created on clear plastic pages called *cells*. These cells were laid over background art and photographed one at a time.

How Does Animation Work?

Animation is the process of taking a series of drawn or rendered pictures that successively show motion. Displaying them to the viewer in rapid succession gives the illusion of motion. When this happens, the slight differences between pictures give the illusion of movement. This process of showing pictures in rapid succession is the same method used in motion pictures, videos, and television. A motion picture camera does not record movement; it records a series of still images called frames. A *frame* is a single image in a series of images used in film video and animation. If a motion picture camera is recording a scene from an action car-chase movie, each picture of the cars will be slightly different. The first frame of the car chase might be of the cars in the distance coming toward the camera. Each successive frame will have the cars a little closer to the camera. When all the frames are played back in order, the cars will actually appear to move toward the camera.

In motion pictures and television, the frames are presented so quickly that the normal human eye does not register that they are individual frames. In motion pictures, the normal rate of pictures projected on the screen is 24 frames per second, although some will go as high as 70 frames per second.

TV and video run at 30 frames per second. Frame rates in games are not set because often the speed of the computer and the complexity of the program determine the frame rate. However, most game developers target 60 frames per second. Games that drop below 30 frames per second are harder to play because the controls often seem sluggish.

Hint

The number of frames per second is very important to the animator. The most common mistake of beginning animators is that they make the difference in movement between frames even. They do not take into account that faster movements have greater differences between frames, while slower movements have lesser differences between frames. However, movement between frames should not be sporadic, causing the animation to have a jerky appearance. Differences in movement rates should be smooth.

Artists use animation to make things move in video games. In 2D animation each movement is drawn by hand. This is a very time-consuming process that requires several artists working on a single project.

Creating a Simple 2D Animation

For this example I will use Corel Painter to create a simple animation.

1. Animations in Corel Painter are set up the same way as new pictures. Choose New from the File menu (see Figure 3.1).

2. In the New dialog box, select the Movie radio button (see Figure 3.2). Change the frame count to 16 and the image size to 512×512. Click on OK.

3. Corel Painter automatically saves animations, so the Enter Movie Name dialog box will appear, as shown in Figure 3.3. Name the animation Ball and click on Save.

4. The New Frame Stack dialog box allows you to set up Painter's Onion Skin feature. Onion skin is a simulation of the velum used by traditional animators to see multiple drawings. Set the levels to 4 and the color depth to 24, as shown in Figure 3.4. Click on OK to continue.

5. Now the Animation window will appear. In addition to the Animation window, there is also a Frame Stacks window. *Frame stack* is the term used in Corel Painter for the series of frames in an animation. The Frame Stacks window has controls for advancing frames forward and backward. The current frame is on the right with the red arrow above it.

6. Now you need an image to animate in the frame. Corel Painter has some preset images you can use. To call up the Image Portfolio, select Show Image Portfolio from the Window menu, as shown in Figure 3.5.

7. Drag the marble image from the Image Portfolio to the Animation window (see Figure 3.6).

8. Now position the marble as high in the upper-left corner as possible (see Figure 3.7). You will be animating the marble to drop from the left side of the screen and bounce to the right. This is the simplest form of

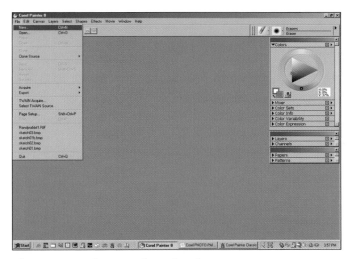

Figure 3.1 Select New from the File menu to set up a new animation.

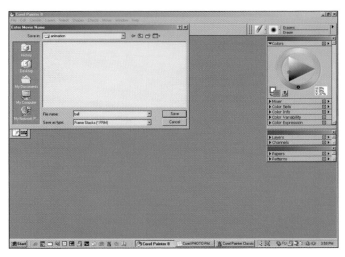

Figure 3.3 The Enter Movie Name dialog box

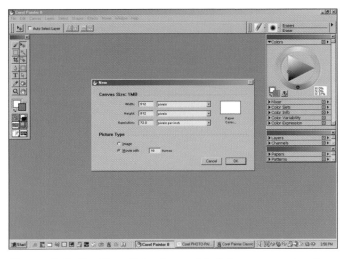

Figure 3.2 The New dialog box, set to bring up an animation

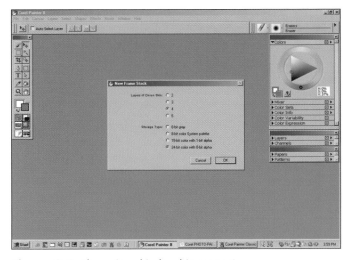

Figure 3.4 The onion skin level is set to 4.

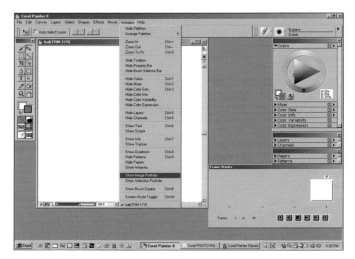

Figure 3.5 Select Show Image Portfolio from the Window menu.

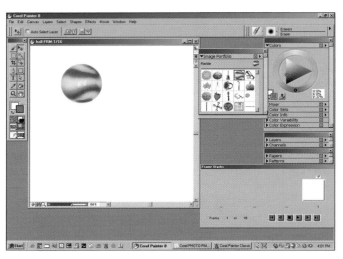

Figure 3.6 Move the marble image to the Animation window.

animation because all you are doing is moving the marble. Later, you will work on moving a character.

Hint

Artists seldom move objects on the screen in game animation. Typically, movement of objects and characters is done in the game and is part of the game computer code.

9. To bring up the Onion Skin effect and see the four levels of animation you selected at the beginning, you need to select Tracing Paper from the Canvas menu, as shown in Figure 3.8.

10. Next click the Advance One Frame button in the Frame Stacks window. (It's the second button from the right.) Notice that the marble remains in the same position. If you look at the Frame Stacks window, you will see frames 1 and 2 both have the marble in the upper-left corner.

11. Drag the marble down and to the right, as shown in Figure 3.9. The marble is an object that floats above the animation background. When a frame is advanced, all floating objects are combined with the background of the previous frame. The floating object is then transferred to the current frame.

12. Now drag the marble down to a position near the bottom of the Animation window, as shown in Figure 3.10.

Figure 3.7 Position the marble in the top-left corner of the screen.

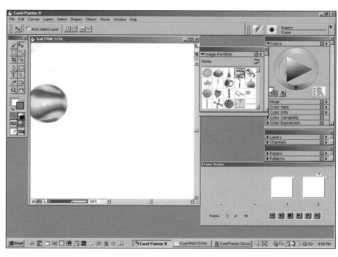

Figure 3.9 The marble is moved to a new position in frame 2.

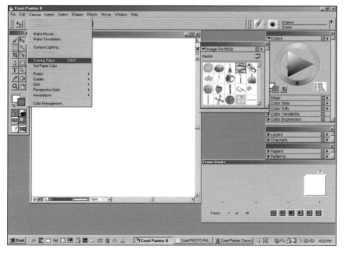

Figure 3.8 Select Tracing Paper to turn on the Onion Skin effect.

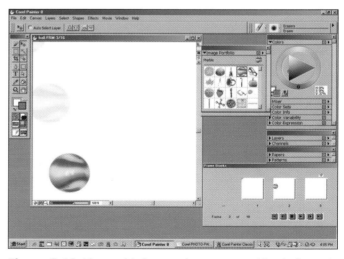

Figure 3.10 The marble is moved to a new position in frame 3.

13. Animation is about timing. As the marble drops, it accelerates toward the ground. As it hits the ground, some of the energy from the falling marble is transferred to the ground and the rest is redirected in the bounce of the marble. This slows the marble. In frames 5 and 6, the marble isn't moved as far because it is moving slower (see Figure 3.11).

14. Continue moving the marble through its first bounce and into its second by positioning the marble and advancing the frame (see Figure 3.12).

15. Once the marble is through the second bounce and is moved off the window, delete the floating marble object so it will not be part of the last few frames of the animation. To delete a float-ing object, select Delete Layer from the Layers menu (see Figure 3.13).

16. Now click on the Play button in the Frame Stacks window. The animation should play, showing the marble bouncing from left to right across the Animation window (see Figure 3.14).

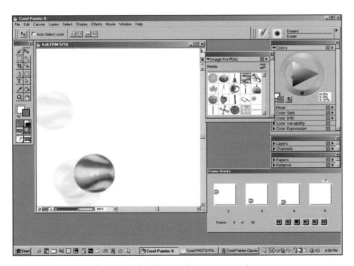

Figure 3.11 The marble slows down on its bounce.

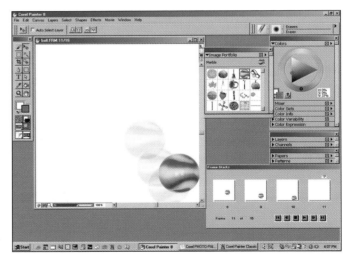

Figure 3.12 The marble's position in frame 11

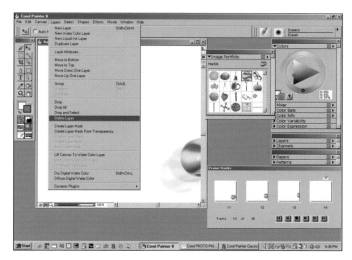

Figure 3.13 Delete the floating marble object.

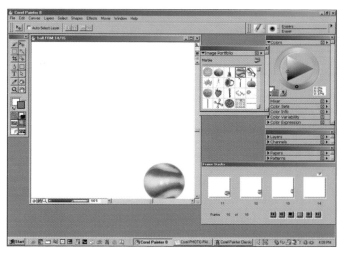

Figure 3.14 Play the animation.

Creating Character Animation

Animating a character is a complex task. There are many things to consider when an animator simulates the movement of a person or creature. The length of this book does not allow me to go over every aspect of good character animation; instead, I will focus on the basics. I highly recommend that you experiment with the concepts in this book. You should also study great animated videos or DVDs to see how animators create the illusion of movement. If you can go through a video or DVD frame by frame, you will learn a lot about animation.

As I stated earlier, the artist generally will not deal with movement of a character or object on the screen. The game programmer usually does that work. What the artist is more likely to deal with is the character or object's internal animation. *Internal animation* is the movement *within* a character or object, rather than the movement across a screen. For example, if a character is walking, the movement of the legs is an internal

animation while the progress the character makes across the screen is not. When an artist animates a character walking for a game, he will animate the character walking in place. This is very important because if the artist moves the character, it will be much more difficult for the programmer to move the character in the game.

Many animations in computer games are looping cycles. A *looping cycled animation* is an animation that ends where it starts. For example, most walking and running animation in a game is one full step repeated several times. In the industry it is referred to as a *walk* or *run cycle*. In the following example, you will create a walk cycle for a character.

1. To start this animation you need to bring up an Animation window in Corel Painter, as you did in the previous example (see Figure 3.15).

2. Set the dimensions to 256×256 and the frames to 12. Select the Movie radio button and click on OK. Save the movie as Walk in the Enter Movie Name dialog box (see Figure 3.16).

3. Set the layers to 4 and the color depth to 24-bit in the New Frame Stack dialog box (see Figure 3.17).

4. For this animation you will start with a character. You can load Randy Rabbit from the sample art on the CD that came with this book. Randy is already in the process of taking a step, as shown in Figure 3.18.

5. Now select Randy using the Box Selection tool on the left side of the screen (see Figure 3.19).

6. Once the character is selected, it is easy to click on the character and drag him over to the Animation window (see Figure 3.20). He is now a floating object similar to the marble in the first example.

7. It is easier to draw an animation if it is larger on the screen. At the bottom of the Animation window there is a blue slider bar. This is the magnification control. Slide the bar to the right until it is set to 200%.

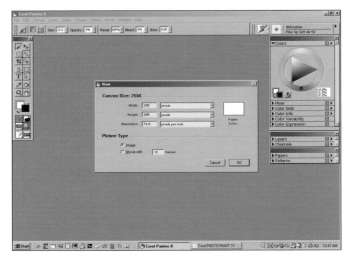

Figure 3.15 Bring up the Animation window.

Figure 3.16 Save the movie as Walk.

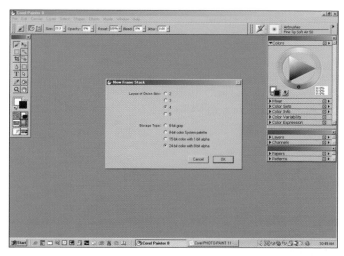

Figure 3.17 The New Frame Stack dialog box

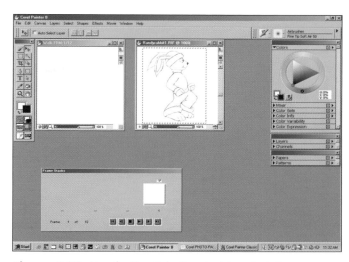

Figure 3.19 Use the Box Selection tool to select the character.

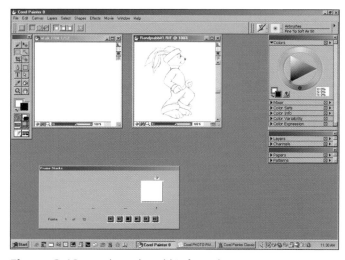

Figure 3.18 Load Randy Rabbit from the CD.

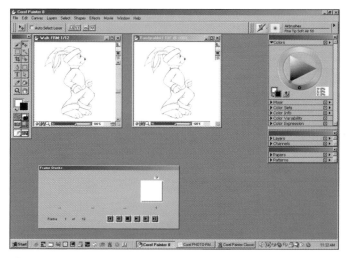

Figure 3.20 The selected character is moved to the Animation window.

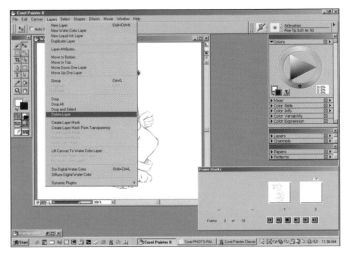

Figure 3.21 Delete the floating layer from frame 2.

Figure 3.23 Frame 2 of the animation is drawn.

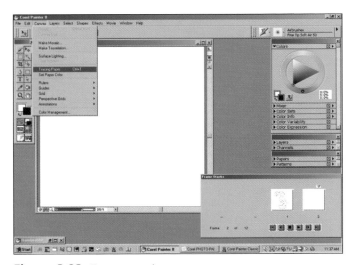

Figure 3.22 Turn on tracing paper.

Figure 3.24 Frames 1 through 4 of the animation sequence

8. Now grab the lower-right corner of the window and enlarge it to hold the animation.

9. Use the animation controls to move the animation forward one frame. The drawing of Randy is now flattened onto the first frame. You will want to change Randy for the second frame, so you need to delete the floating drawing. Select Delete Layer from the Layers menu, as shown in Figure 3.21.

10. Next turn on the tracing paper feature, as shown in Figure 3.22.

11. Now you can see the first drawing through the second frame so you can use it as a guide for drawing the second frame of the animation. You draw the second frame with Randy's feet and hands moved to a new position (see Figure 3.23). Notice that you also are raising the character slightly in this frame.

12. Continue to draw new frames of the animation of Randy's walk using the previous drawings as a guide (see Figure 3.24).

Hint

One of the biggest challenges of animation is timing. In a walk cycle the rate of movement is fairly constant, meaning that the act of walking generally does not have uneven movement. In most cases the animator can divide the distance of movement between each frame evenly. In a 12-frame animation, frames 1 and 7 will look much the same, with the only exception being that the left and right sides of the character are reversed (see Figure 3.25).

The same thing will be true for frames 2 and 8, frames 3 and 9, frames 4 and 10, frames 5 and 11, and finally frames 6 and 12 (see Figure 3.26). If the artist does a good job with the first half of the walk cycle, the second half becomes easier because the first half can be used as a template.

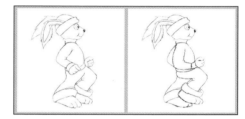

Figure 3.25 Frames 1 and 7

Figure 3.26 Similarity between frames of animation

13. Continue drawing each frame. Once you have reached the last frame and you have compared each frame (as in Figure 3.25), review the motion by moving through animation frames 1 to 12 (see Figure 3.27). Be careful to only go to 12. Corel Painter will automatically add unwanted frames if you go beyond 12.

14. Reduce the animation back to 100% size and click the Play button (see Figure 3.28). The animation will run fast, but you will be able to see your work.

Summary

In this chapter you looked at 2D animation. You should have a good understanding of creating 2D animation with Corel Painter. I went over setting up an animation, importing objects, moving between frames, and enabling onion skinning. I also covered basic animation for games, including timing and cycles.

Figure 3.27 Frame 12 of the animation sequence

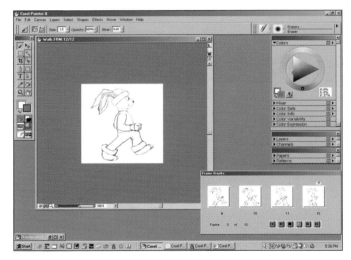

Figure 3.28 Playing the animation

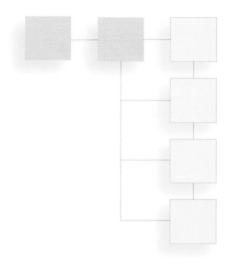

CHAPTER 4

INTRODUCTION TO 3D

Most of the art you create as a game artist will probably be in a 3D art program. These programs are very complex because creating believable 3D models is not a simple process. In the next several chapters I will attempt to simplify model creation so it will be easy to follow. Each exercise in this book will build on the previous exercises so that when you finish, you should have a good foundation to continue learning about 3D art and how it is used in games.

The 3D Art Program

Although the programs and processes are complex, they are not necessarily hard. The biggest challenge with most of the professional 3D programs is getting to know the many features. Of the many 3D art programs available, I have chosen Maya for use in this book. I chose Maya not because it is the simplest—far from it!—but because it is considered to be the standard in the industry. By learning Maya, I am hoping you will have a head start on gaining the skills necessary for becoming a real game artist.

Building 3D Worlds

One of the basic elements in game art is the game world. A *game world* is the environment in which the game takes place. The game world could be tracks in a racing game or a stadium in a sports game. Sometimes they are extensive, like in adventure games, while other times they might be very small, like in a puzzle game.

Game worlds can have a huge impact on a game. Their main purpose is to set the stage for the action, but they are becoming more interactive themselves. In many games, characters can pick up objects and use them just as they would in real life.

Building a 3D Castle

You will start by building a castle with four turrets, one in each corner. This will be a simple castle because it is your first project, but it will form the base of what could be a very unique building, depending on how far you want to take the design.

1. The first part of the castle you will build will be the turret or tower. Start by opening Maya. When Maya first comes up, it will display a window that offers several tutorials to help you learn how the program works (see Figure 4.1). You can click out of the tutorial window for now. I suggest you take a look at the tutorials later. They have some very valuable information on the program that will be helpful as you progress in your 3D studies.

2. You will start by using a primitive object. In this case, you are building a turret so you should use a cylinder. To bring up the Polygon Cylinder Options dialog box, select Polygon Primitives, Cylinder from the Create menu, as shown in Figure 4.2.

3. You want the base of the turret to be about 8 units high and about 4 units in diameter. Set the radius to 2 and the height to 8 in the Polygon Cylinder Options dialog box (see Figure 4.3). Then set the subdivisions

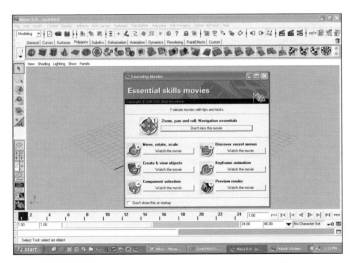

Figure 4.1 The opening window in Maya Personal Learning Edition

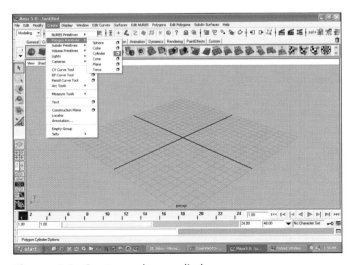

Figure 4.2 Create a polygon cylinder.

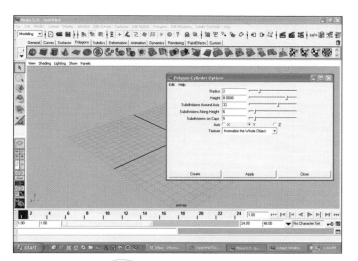

Figure 4.3 The Polygon Cylinder Options dialog box

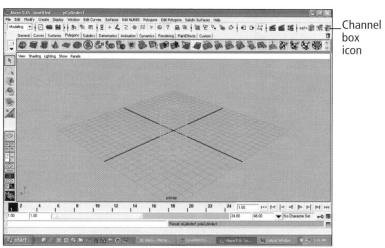

Channel box icon

Figure 4.4 The channel box in Maya is on the right side of the screen.

around the axis to 32, the subdivisions on height to 6, and the subdivisions on the cap to 5. Click on either Create or Apply to create the cylinder. The Create button will create the cylinder and close the dialog box. The Apply button will create the cylinder and leave the dialog box open.

4. You now have a cylinder to work with, but it is in the wrong position. By default Maya will always create an object centered on the exact center of the grid. You can easily adjust the object with the channel box. The channel box is activated by clicking on the Channel Box icon on the far right side of the screen (see Figure 4.4). The channel box is used to alter or modify an object after it is created.

5. Your cylinder is 8 units high. You want to bring it up level with the grid, so you need to move it up 4 units in the y-direction. In the channel box, type 4 in the Translate Y box and then hit Enter (see Figure 4.5). The cylinder will now be positioned where you want it.

6. Some artists like to work with multiple views of an object on the screen at the same time. Maya supports almost every screen configuration common in 3D development. Personally, I prefer to work in only one view at a time and change it

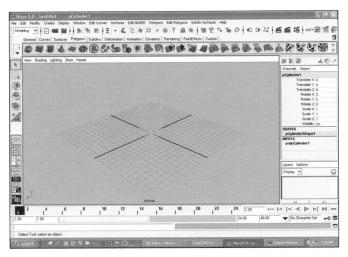

Figure 4.5 Type 4 in the Translate Y box.

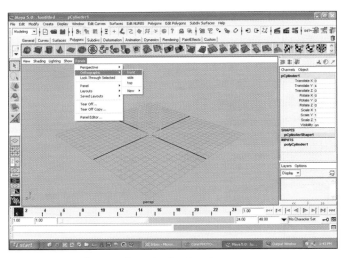

Figure 4.6 Change views in the Panels menu.

when I need to see the object from another view. In some cases it is easer to work with an object in Orthographic view than in Perspective view. In Orthographic view, everything is square with the camera and there is no perspective. It is similar to a drawing created in a drafting program. Select the Front view from the Orthographic option under the Panels menu, as shown in Figure 4.6.

7. Now that the view is from the front, it is easy to see the bands of polygons that make up the sides of the cylinder. Use the marking menu to change the cylinder from Object view to Vertex view by right-clicking on the object and selecting Vertex.

8. The next step is to shape the tower. Start by selecting the row of vertices three down from the top, as shown in Figure 4.7. Draw a bounding box around the vertices to select the row.

9. Once the vertices are selected, you can manipulate them using the tools on the left side of the screen. Select the Scale tool (the one that looks like a box with two arrows around it). A manipulator will appear on the screen. You want to size the tower in all three dimensions. The middle yellow block on the Scale tool sizes in all three dimensions, so pick that one. Press and hold the mouse button on the yellow block and slide the mouse to the left until your screen matches Figure 4. 8.

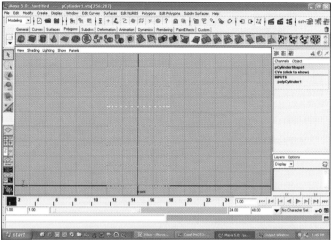

Figure 4.7 Select the row of vertices three down from the top.

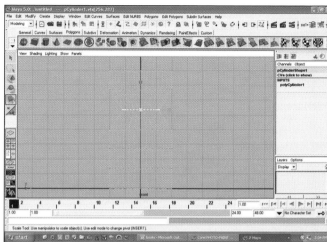

Figure 4.8 Scale the third row of vertices.

10. Now continue to scale each row of vertices until they match Figure 4.9. The cylinder should now look a lot like a rook from a chess set.

11. The tower is starting to take shape. Next you need to build the top. Select the top row of vertices and change the view to the Perspective view.

12. Sometimes it is easier to work on a model if you only have to deal with the area on which you want to work. You are finished with the lower part of the tower, so you really don't need it hanging around and getting in your way. Select Isolate Select, View Selected from the Show menu, as shown in Figure 4.10.

13. You now want to raise blocks to make the tower look like a real turret. In the Perspective view, change the object to Face using the marking menu. Right-click on a vertex and drag the mouse toward Face in the marking menu.

14. Now select every other face on the outer ring of the tower top, as shown in Figure 4.11.

15. You want to keep the faces together, so before you go any farther, you need to set the software to Keep Faces Together. The menu item is found in the Tool Options submenu in the Polygons menu, as shown in Figure 4.12.

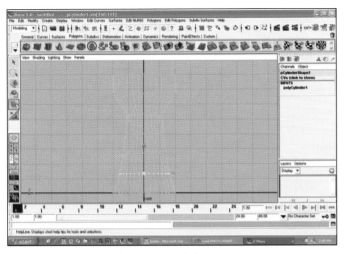

Figure 4.9 Size the lower part of the tower.

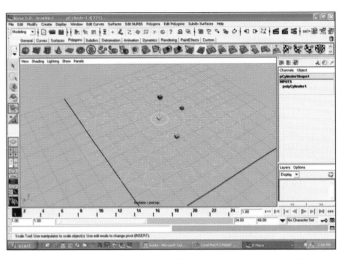

Figure 4.11 Select every other face on the outside of the tower top.

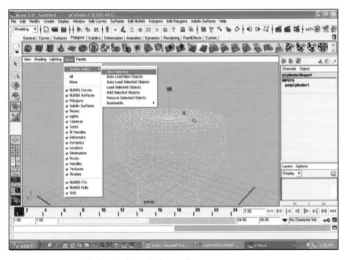

Figure 4.10 Select View Selected.

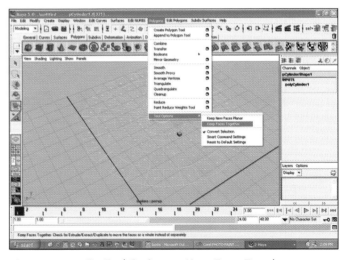

Figure 4.12 Set Tool Options to Keep Faces Together.

16. Next select Extrude Face from the Edit Polygons menu, as shown in Figure 4.13.

17. When you use the Extrude Face tool, it will automatically bring up a special manipulator tool. You will use that tool on another project, but for this one you only want to move up the faces. Click on the Move tool from the manipulator tools on the left side of the screen. Now click on the green up arrow, hold down the mouse button, and pull up the faces until they match Figure 4.14.

18. Now select all the faces on the second ring from the outside, as shown in Figure 4.15.

19. Change the view to Smooth Shading by pressing the 5 key at the top of the keyboard so you can better see the next step.

20. Now extrude the ring of faces downward, as shown in Figure 4.16.

21. You don't want your characters to get wet while they are guarding the castle, so you need to build a roof over the top of the tower. Change the view to the Top view and select the rest of the rings of faces, as shown in Figure 4.17. Be careful not to select any faces except for the three remaining rings.

22. Now switch to the Front view again and pull the faces upward, as shown in Figure 4.18.

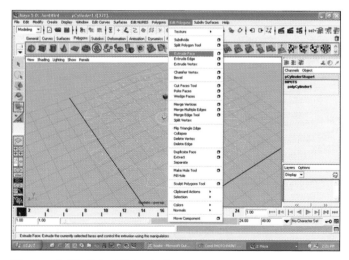

Figure 4.13 Select Extrude Face.

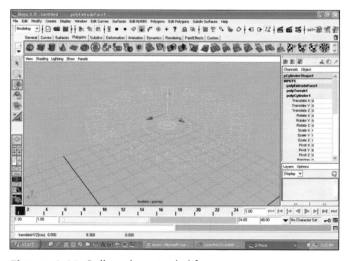

Figure 4.14 Pull up the extruded faces.

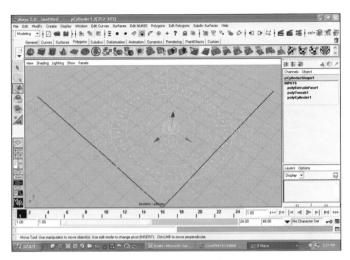

Figure 4.15 Select the second ring of faces.

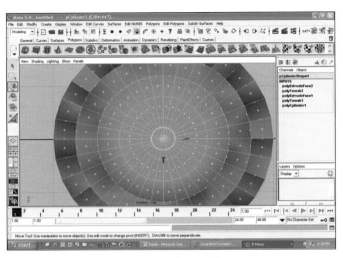

Figure 4.17 Change views in the Panels menu.

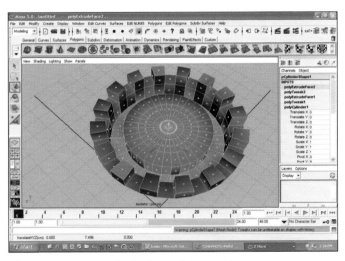

Figure 4.16 Extrude the faces downward.

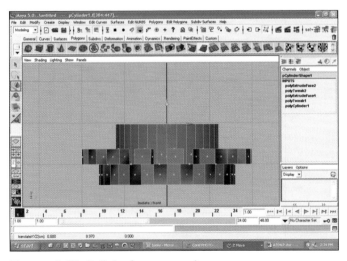

Figure 4.18 Pull the faces upward.

23. Next go back to the Top view and select the two inside rings of faces (see Figure 4.19).

24. Use the Scale tool to expand the two rings of faces until they are slightly larger than the diameter of the tower top, as shown in Figure 4.20.

25. The next step is to create the peaked roof. Select the inside ring of faces, as shown in Figure 4.21.

26. From the Front view, pull the faces upward to start the peaked roof (see Figure 4.22).

27. Now you need to go back to the vertices to get the peak. Return to the Top view and change the view mode to Vertex in the marking menu.

28. Select the centermost vertex, as shown in Figure 4.23.

29. Go back to the Front view and pull the center vertex upward, as shown in Figure 4.24. Now you have a peaked roof. Your characters won't have to get wet from the rain—unless of course the wind is blowing.

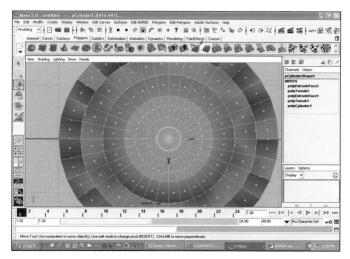

Figure 4.19 Select the two inside rings of faces.

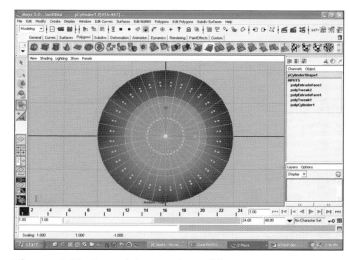

Figure 4.20 Expand the two rings of faces.

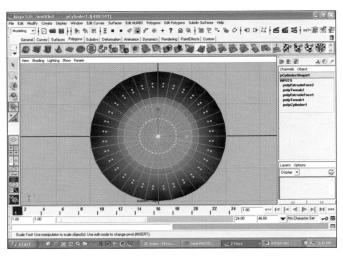

Figure 4.21 Select the inside ring of faces.

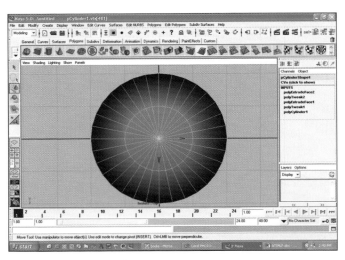

Figure 4.23 Select the center vertex.

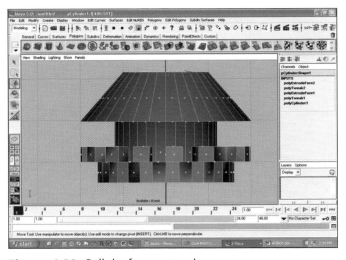

Figure 4.22 Pull the faces upward.

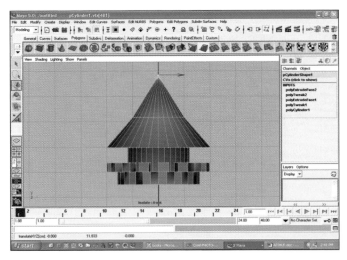

Figure 4.24 Pull the center vertex upward.

30. You could stop here, but notice that the bottom roofline looks unnatural, like it has no depth. Select the faces in the roof and extrude them upward to form an edge around the bottom of the roof (see Figure 4.25).

31. Next go back to the Front view. You want to see how your tower is looking with the lower part that you hid earlier. Go back to the Show menu and select View Selected again. Notice that the option has a checkmark by it. When it is active, it has a checkmark; when it is not, it does not have a checkmark by it.

32. The roof does not look peaked enough. Change the object back to Vertex mode and shape the roof until it looks like Figure 4.26.

33. Now you have a completed tower. While pressing the Alt key and the left and middle mouse buttons, slide the mouse to the left to pull back in the Front view to see the entire tower, as shown in Figure 4.27.

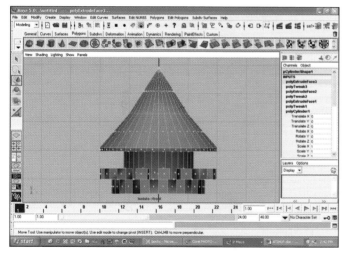

Figure 4.25 Extrude the faces in the roof upward.

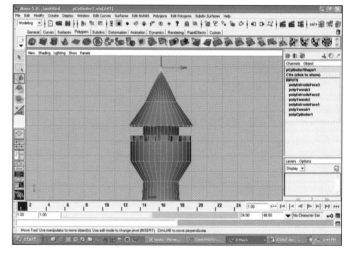

Figure 4.26 Shape the roof.

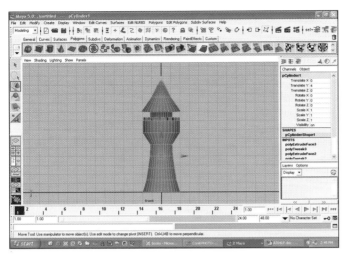

Figure 4.27 View of the tower

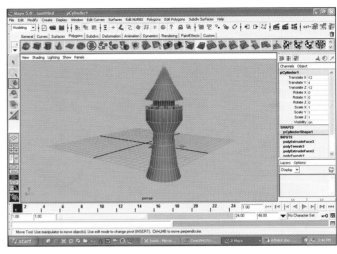

Figure 4.28 Move the tower to the corner of the castle.

Building the Walls

You now have the geometry for a nice medieval-looking tower. But one tower does not a castle make. You need to build some walls for your castle. It won't be much of a castle if there are no walls.

1. Before you can build the walls, you need to place the tower at the corner of the castle. In the channel box, enter 12 in both the Translate X and Translate Z fields (see Figure 4.28).

2. You now have one tower in one corner of the castle. You still have three other corners that need towers as well. It would sure be nifty if you didn't have to rebuild each tower. Well, guess what? You don't. Maya has this neat little feature called Duplicate Object. With the object selected, press Ctrl+D on the keyboard and voilà—you have a new tower.

3. Type a minus sign in front of the 12 in the Translate X box. Now the duplicated tower will be in position on the other end of the castle (see Figure 4.29).

4. Repeat the process twice more to duplicate two more towers, and position them on the other corners of the castle (see Figure 4.30). The coordinates for tower three are X -12, Y 4, and Z -12. The coordinates for tower four are X 12, Y 4, and Z -12.

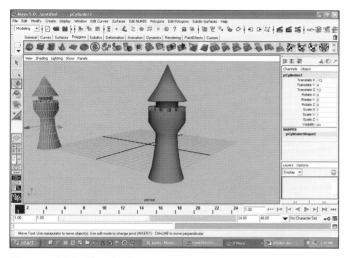

Figure 4.29 The duplicate tower

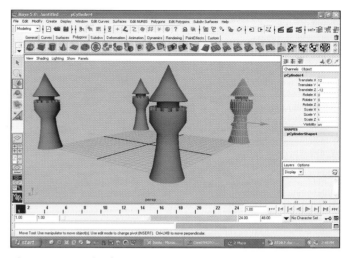

Figure 4.30 The four towers are positioned at each corner of the castle.

5. Now that the towers are in position, you can hide them so they won't be in the way while you build the walls. Select all four towers and then press Ctrl+H to hide the towers.

6. Now select Polygon Primitives, Cube from the Create menu (see Figure 4.31).

7. Set the preferences to match the ones shown in Figure 4.32.

8. Now you have the polygon cube you will use to make a wall.

Move it up four in Translate Y and over 12 in Translate X so it fits between the two towers on that end of the castle (see Figure 4.33).

9. Now go to the Side view and shape the wall similar to how you did the tower, except instead of sizing in all three dimensions, only size in the x-direction (see Figure 4.34). Select the box on the left of the Scale tool and slide it toward the center box.

10. Go to the next row of vertices and continue shaping the tower to match Figure 4.35.

11. Select the inside top four vertices and size them in the x-direction to match Figure 4.36.

12. Now go back to the Perspective view and change the view mode to Face by right-clicking on the object and sliding the cursor toward Face.

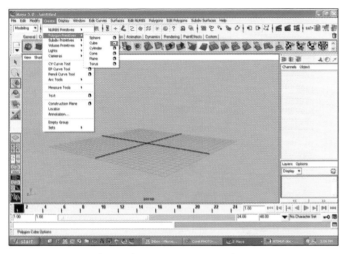

Figure 4.31 Select Polygon Primitives, Cube.

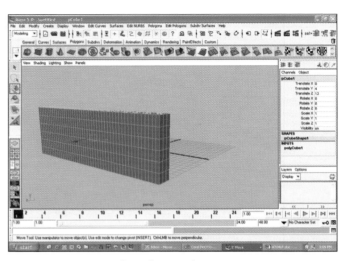

Figure 4.33 Move the polygon cube to X 12.

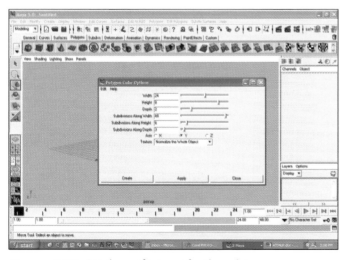

Figure 4.32 Set the preferences for the cube.

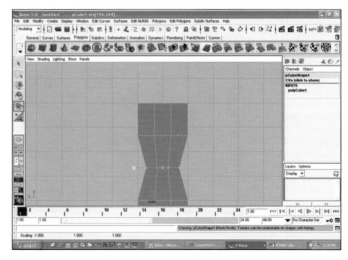

Figure 4.34 Size the wall in the x-direction.

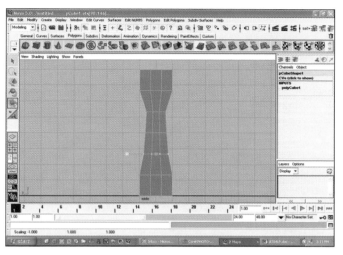

Figure 4.35 Shape the wall.

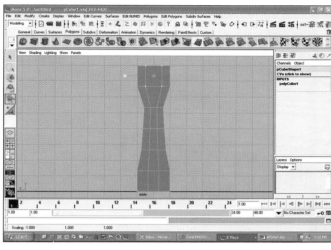

Figure 4.36 Size the inside top four vertices.

13. On the outside of the wall, select every other face and extrude it upward (see Figure 4.37).

14. Next select the center row of faces and extrude them downward (see Figure 4.38).

15. Now the general shape of the wall is finished. Take a look to see how the entire castle will look. You need to duplicate the wall for all four sides of the castle. Select the wall and press Ctrl+G. This will center the pivot of the wall to the x–0,

z–0, and y–0 position (see Figure 4.39).

16. Now duplicate the wall and rotate it 90 degrees.

17. Next duplicate the wall and rotate it 180 degrees.

18. Finally duplicate the wall and rotate it 270 degrees (see Figure 4.40).

19. Now you need to bring back all the towers to see how the walls and towers fit together (see Figure 4.41). Go to Show, Show All in the Display menu.

20. Now you are beginning to see the completed castle. There is still some work to do, but it is starting to take shape. Notice that the walls run into the towers. This is fine for the lower areas, but it looks out of place at the top. You need to fix that area. Select one tower and one section of the wall and then hide the rest of the castle by going to the View Selected option, as you did earlier when you built the tower (see Figure 4.42).

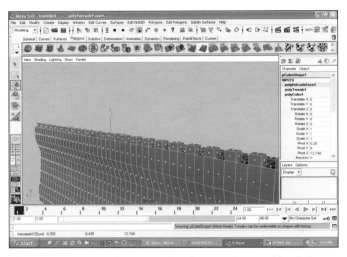

Figure 4.37 Extrude every other face on the outside of the wall top.

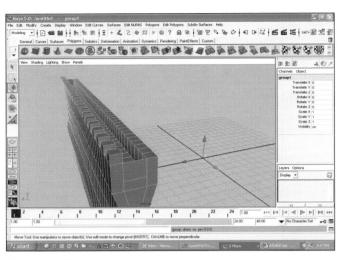

Figure 4.39 Center the pivot.

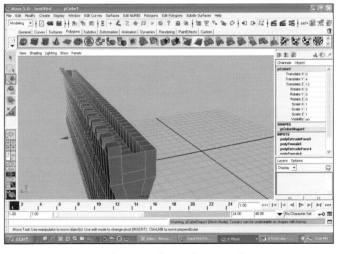

Figure 4.38 Extrude center faces downward.

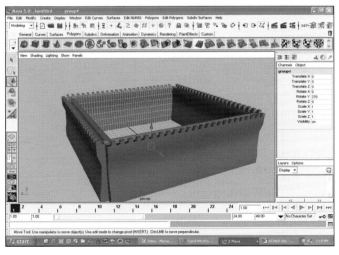

Figure 4.40 All four sides of the castle walls

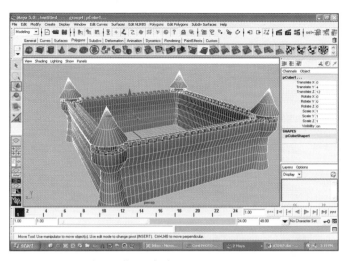

Figure 4.41 The walls with the towers

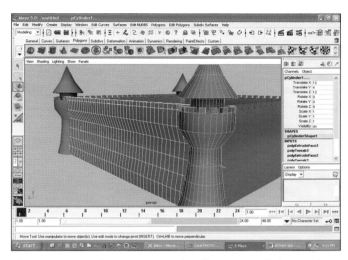

Figure 4.42 Select a tower and wall section and choose the View Selected option.

21. Now change the view mode back to Wire-Frame by pressing the 4 key at the top of the keyboard. This will help you see the inside of the intersection of the tower and the wall.

22. Notice that the wall extends into the tower. Select the wall section and change the view mode to Face.

23. Now select the top faces that extend into the tower, as shown in Figure 4.43.

24. Next press the Delete key to remove those faces (see Figure 4.44).

25. While in the Wire-Frame view, you also need to line up the tower with the wall. From the Side view, select the tower and change it to Vertex mode.

26. Using the wall as a guide, line up the tower elements with the wall (see Figure 4.45).

27. This next part will be a little tricky because you have to create the connection of the

walkways from the walls to the towers. You will need to come in very close to that area, so pull the camera in close (looking at the tower and the wall from the side), as shown in Figure 4.46.

28. The wire mesh is a little complicated here, so you need to simplify it and only work with the area where the two objects meet. Bring back the hidden elements by unchecking the View Selected menu item. Then change the view to Component

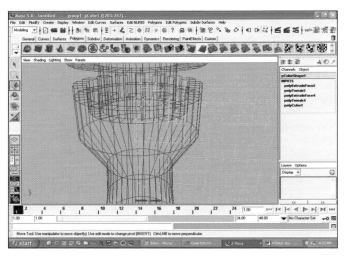

Figure 4.43 Select the top faces.

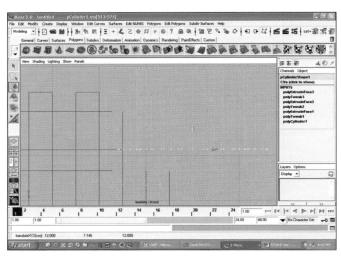

Figure 4.45 Line up the tower with the wall.

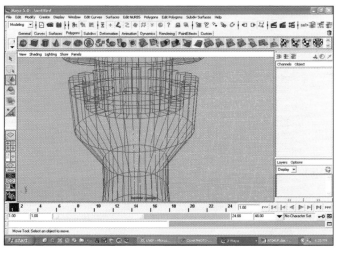

Figure 4.44 Delete unwanted faces.

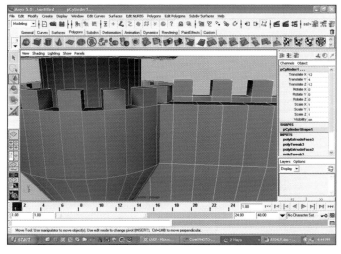

Figure 4.46 Closeup of the connection of the wall and tower

mode by clicking on the Select by Component Type icon (see Figure 4.47). The icon is located in the upper row of icons, just below the pull-down menu bar toward the left side of the screen. Look for the icon that shows a blue square with a small red arrow on the lower-right side. In Component mode you can select faces from more than one object.

29. Select all the faces surrounding the area where the two objects

meet, as shown in Figure 4.48.

30. With the faces selected, turn on the View Selected function as you have done in the past (see Figure 4.49).

31. Now you can get a better look at the area where the two objects meet. You will be working on the tower so deselect the wall, as shown in Figure 4.50.

32. It will be easier to see all the faces you need to remove by

going back to Wire-Frame mode. Press the 4 key.

33. Now carefully select the faces, as shown in Figure 4.51.

34. With these faces removed, your characters will be able to walk from the wall to the tower. However, there is a problem: You now have holes in your geometry. You will need to clean those up. Change the selection type to Vertex, as shown in Figure 4.52.

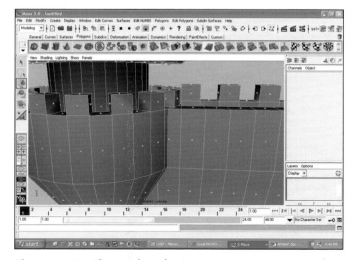

Figure 4.47 Change the selection type to Component mode.

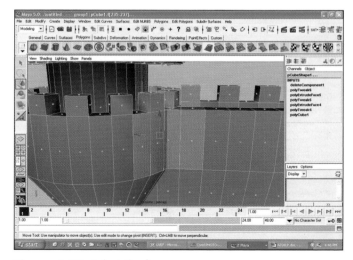

Figure 4.48 Select the faces.

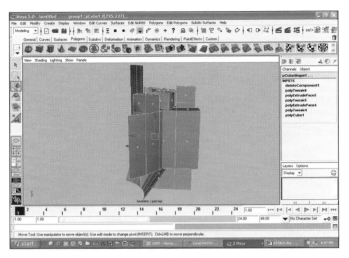

Figure 4.49 Turn on View Selected.

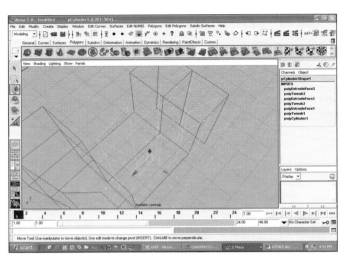

Figure 4.51 Select the faces you don't need.

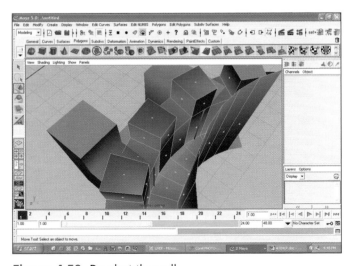

Figure 4.50 Deselect the wall.

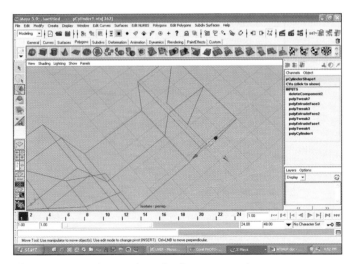

Figure 4.52 Change the selection type on the tower to Vertex.

35. Using the Move tool, press and hold the V key and move the vertex shown in Figure 4.53 toward the corner of the wall (as shown). The V key activates the Snap to Vertex feature. Notice that the vertex will move to match the intended vertex.

36. It will be easier to see the holes in Shaded view, so change to that mode by pressing the 5 key. Continue to snap vertices until all the holes are gone (see Figure 4.54).

37. You will need to do the same thing for each place where a wall joins with a tower. Go to the other wall that connects with the tower that you are working on and repeat the process for that wall/tower connection (see Figure 4.55).

38. You could go through each tower and fix the connections, but that would be a long and unnecessary process. It is easier to simply delete the other wall sections and then duplicate the one you fixed (see Figure 4.56). It will also make it easier for you to apply the textures if you only have to do it to one tower and one wall.

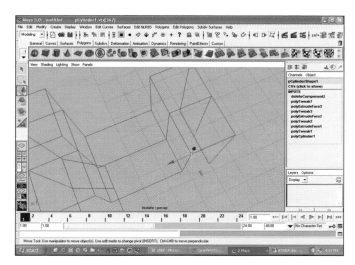

Figure 4.53 Snap to vertex to close the hole in the geometry.

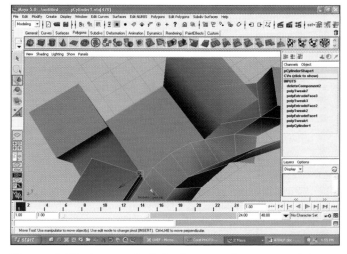

Figure 4.54 Remove the holes between the tower and the wall.

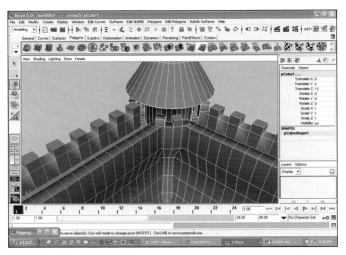

Figure 4.55 Connect the other wall to the tower.

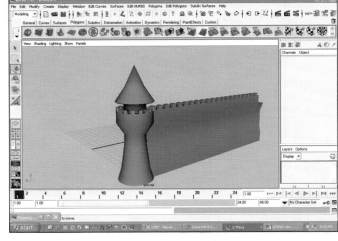

Figure 4.56 Delete all other walls and towers.

Texturing the Castle

Now the geometry is finished, and you are ready to add the surface textures. Your tower and wall look pretty good, but they are flat-shaded so they aren't very interesting. By adding a surface texture to the models, you can give them an almost lifelike look.

For this example, I will be using two textures for the wall and the tower. You could use many more, but for this lesson two textures will be enough to give you the look you want. The two textures are on the CD that came with this book; their names are wall.bmp and roof.bmp.

1. You will need to work in the Hypershade editor to bring your textures into Maya. Bring up Hypershade by selecting it from the Rendering Editors submenu in the Window menu, as shown in Figure 4.57.

2. Create a new material in Hypershade by selecting Materials, Blinn from the Create menu, as shown in Figure 4.58.

Hint

You will notice that Maya supports a number of material types. Each type has its own purposes. The many different game engines do not always support all material types found in Maya. Make certain that the game engine supports the material type you want to use. Most game engines support blinn materials, so I will use those in this book. Blinns are used primarily for metallic surfaces, but they have a wider range of editing capabilities than lamberts and phongs, so they are often used as good all-around materials for games.

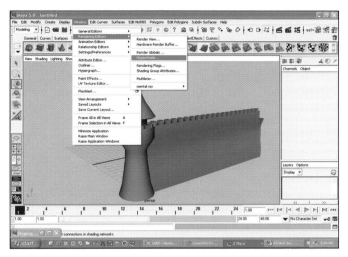

Figure 4.57 Select the Hypershade editor.

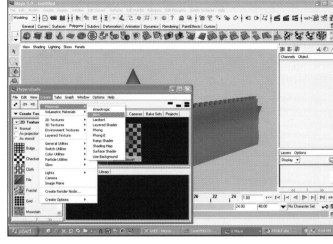

Figure 4.58 Select the Blinn option.

3. You will be using a texture from the CD, so select the new material in Hypershade and then press Ctrl+A. This will bring up the attribute editor.

4. Click on the checkerboard icon to the right of Color to bring up the Create Render Node dialog box (see Figure 4.59).

5. In the Create Render Node dialog box, select File. The dialog box will disappear, and the file will appear in the attribute editor. Now all you need to do is load the texture file into the material.

6. Look for the small file folder icon next to the Image Name box. Notice that the Image Name box is empty. Click on the file folder to bring up the Open dialog box (see Figure 4.60).

7. You will need to browse the CD and look for one of the two texture files. They are in the Chapter 4 directory in the Resources directory. Choose the wall.bmp file and click on Open.

8. Now that the texture is loaded, go back to Hypershade and rename it *wall* by right-clicking on the material and selecting Rename from the menu that appears (see Figure 4.61).

9. Now repeat the same process for loading the roof texture (see Figure 4.62).

10. You will need the Hypershade editor to apply the textures to the model, but the window is so large it is hard to see your model. It will be much easer to work with if you don't have the

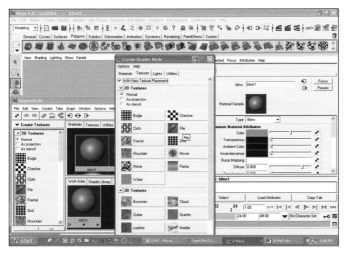

Figure 4.59 Bring up the Create Render Node dialog box.

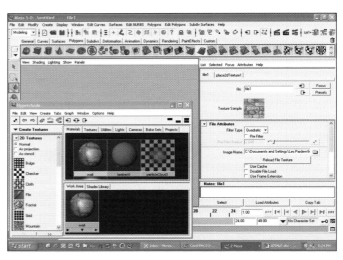

Figure 4.61 Rename the material *wall*.

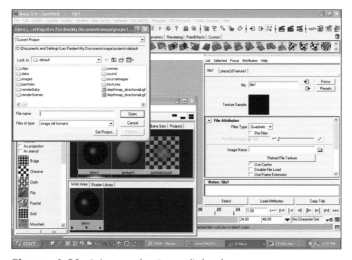

Figure 4.60 Bring up the Open dialog box.

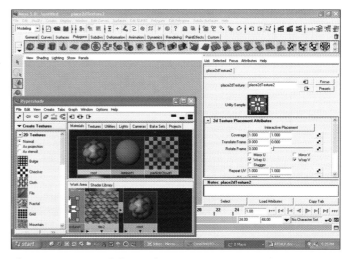

Figure 4.62 Load the roof texture.

editor covering up the model. Exit out of the editor by clicking on the red X in the upper-right corner.

11. Now click on the Two-Panel view. It is the third view icon from the top just under the manipulator icons on the left side of the screen.

12. You can now change the first panel to Hypershade by selecting it from the Panels menu, as shown in Figure 4.63.

13. That's much better. You can see both Hypershade and the

model. Select the wall and apply the wall material to it by right-clicking on it in Hypershade and selecting Apply to Selected from the menu (see Figure 4.64). Press the 6 key to change the view of the model to Textured view so you can see the material on the model.

14. The wall material is a tile material, so you will want it to repeat several times. The easiest way to tile a texture is to have it repeat once for every polygon. In Maya that process is called

unitizing. With the wall selected, select Texture, Unitize UVs from the Edit Polygons menu, as shown in Figure 4.65.

15. Now go to the Side view and do the same thing with the lower part of the tower, as shown in Figure 4.66.

16. Next apply the roof texture to the upper part of the tower. You could unitize the roof textures as well, but that would make the shingles get smaller at the peak of the roof. Unitizing works best when the polygons

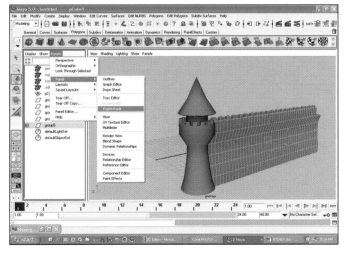

Figure 4.63 Call up the Hypershade editor in the first panel.

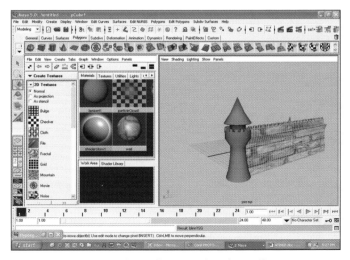

Figure 4.64 Apply the wall material to the wall.

Figure 4.65 Unitize the material on the model.

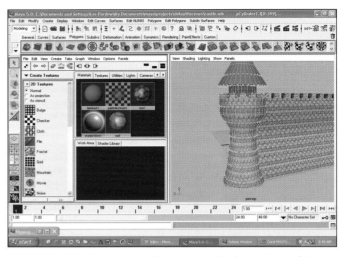

Figure 4.66 Apply the wall texture to the lower part of the tower.

are all similar sizes. In this case you need to use something different.

17. In Chapter 1 you learned about cylindrical projections. Bring up the Polygon Cylindrical Projection Options dialog box by clicking on the small box next to Cylindrical Mapping on the Texture submenu under the Edit Polygons menu.

18. In this case you will be using the Cylindrical Mapping tool to tile the roof texture. Select Texture, Cylindrical Mapping from the Edit Polygons menu. Change the image scale from 1 to 4 in both boxes (see Figure 4.67).

19. Now the shingles look more natural (see Figure 4.68). There is some shrinking of the shingles as they go up to the peak, but not nearly as bad is it would have been if you had unitized them.

Finishing the Castle

Now the wall and the tower are mapped (see Figure 4.69). All you have to do to finish the castle is duplicate the towers and walls.

1. Select both the wall and the tower and press Ctrl+G to center the pivot to the 0 position, as shown in Figure 4.70.

2. Now duplicate the group three times and rotate each duplicate 90, 180, and 270 degrees, respectively, to form the four sides of the castle (see Figure 4.71).

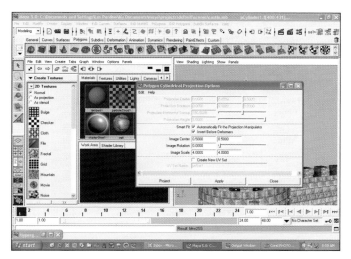

Figure 4.67 Change the image scale to 4.

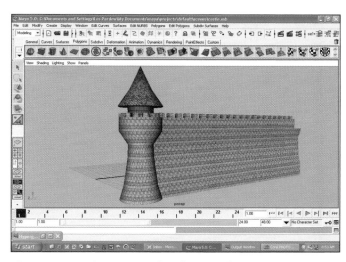

Figure 4.69 The tower and wall mapped

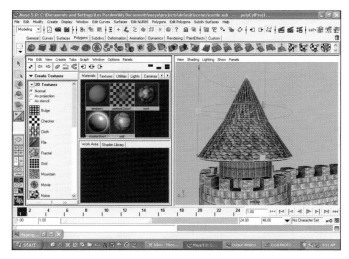

Figure 4.68 The roof cylindrically mapped

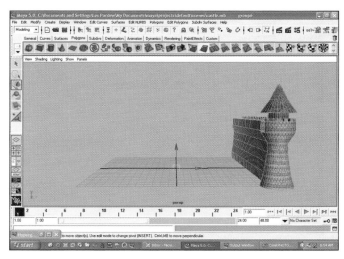

Figure 4.70 Group the tower and the wall.

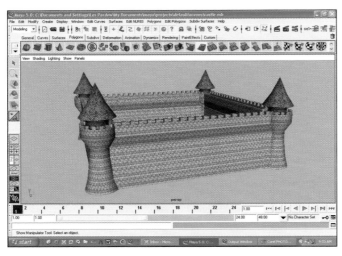

Figure 4.71 The castle with all four walls and towers

The castle is not complete because you don't have any doors or entryways. There needs to be a gatehouse with a drawbridge and some buildings on the inside of the walls. Using the knowledge you have gained in this chapter, you should be able to complete these details with no problem.

Summary

This chapter covered how to build exterior objects in Maya. You had a chance to gain some experience with the 3D program by building simple objects with polygons. You also learned how to texture and duplicate the objects. Practice what you have learned to build a variety of outdoor buildings. Try building a small village around your castle—this could be the set for your first video game.

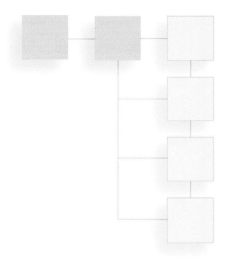

CHAPTER 5

BUILDING GAME INTERIORS

In the last chapter you built a castle. A castle from the outside is a grand and inspiring site that will inspire a game player to try to get inside it. Therefore, you should spend some time learning about building game interiors.

A *game interior* is any enclosed play area in a game. The main difference between building a model of an interior and a model of an exterior is that unless they are huge caverns or halls, interiors can get a little cramped and difficult to see. When you build an exterior object you can view it from almost any angle because you are on the outside looking in. When you build an interior, it is meant to be viewed from the inside looking out.

Interiors are typically viewed much closer to the camera than exteriors are. Closer viewing generally means you need to give your models more detailed textures because the camera will often come right up to a wall or an object. If the textures are too small they will appear blocky when the camera gets close to them. In addition to larger, more detailed textures, an interior will generally need more detail in the geometry.

Building the Interior

In this chapter you will build a two-story domed room with columns and a balcony. This model will be more complex than the model in the previous chapter. It will also require more textures. I have included the textures on the CD under the Chapter 5 directory, so put the CD in your drive if you haven't already done so. As with all the exercises in this book, you will be using Maya, so bring up the program and let's get started.

1. Bring up the Polygon Cylinder Options dialog box and set the options to those shown in Figure 5.1.

2. Translate the cylinder up 8 units and change the view to the Side view so it looks like Figure 5.2.

3. You will create a round room, and the cylinder will form the basic shape. Now you need to adjust the cylinder to give it the desired features of your two-story room. Change the selection mode to Face and select the row of faces shown in Figure 5.3.

4. Scale the row of faces inward just a bit, as in Figure 5.4.

5. Now make some wainscoting on the wall. Change the selection mode to Vertex. Using the Move tool, pull together the vertices above and below the faces you scaled in the last step until they look like Figure 5.5.

6. Next you need to build the balcony. Change the selection mode back to Face and select the faces in the fifth row from the top. You will be using them to create the balcony. Make the faces smaller by scaling them in

the y-direction and then move them to the position shown in Figure 5.6.

7. Use the Extrude tool to create the balcony. Select Extrude Face from the Edit Polygon menu and then scale the balcony inward, as shown in Figure 5.7. In an earlier chapter you turned on the Keep Faces Together option. If you haven't changed that option, it should still be on. If it's not, turn it on by selecting Tool Options from the Polygons menu.

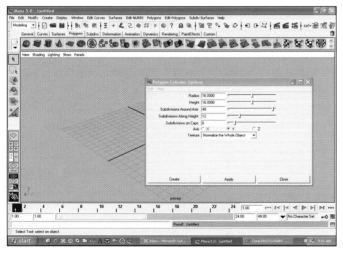

Figure 5.1 The Options screen for creating a polygon cylinder

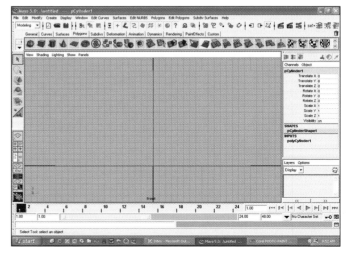

Figure 5.2 Side view of the newly created cylinder

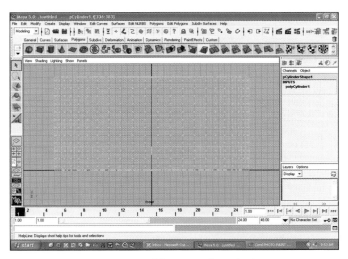

Figure 5.3 Select a row of faces on the cylinder.

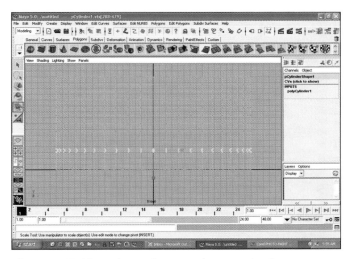

Figure 5.5 Move the vertices together to make the wainscoting.

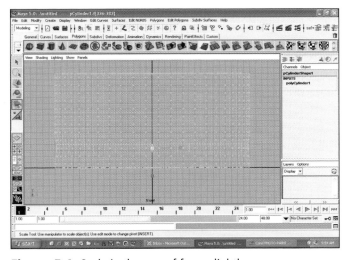

Figure 5.4 Scale in the row of faces slightly.

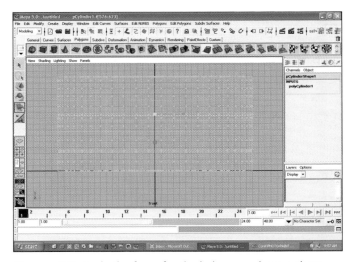

Figure 5.6 Scale the faces for the balcony and move them into position.

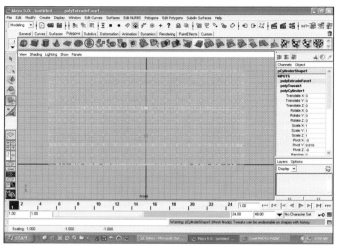

Figure 5.7 Extrude the faces to form the balcony.

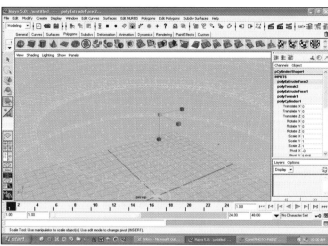

Figure 5.8 Extrude the faces in slightly.

8. Pull the faces up using the Move tool so the top of the balcony is parallel with the ground.

9. You are going to need some railing around the balcony so your characters don't just walk off it. Use the Extrude Face tool again and scale it in just a bit, as shown in Figure 5.8.

10. You will come back later to finish the balcony. For now you can continue building the rest of the room. In the Side view,

select the faces at the top of the cylinder, as shown in Figure 5.9.

11. Choose View Selected from the Show menu.

12. Now select the third ring of vertices from the outside and move them down to form a lip around the edge of the dome, as shown in Figure 5.10.

13. Expand the ring until it is just below the second ring of vertices, as shown in Figure 5.11.

14. Now you need to build a dome roof for the room. Select all the

vertices on the inside of the third ring of vertices. Your room should now look like Figure 5.12.

15. Pull the selected vertices upward until they match what is shown in Figure 5.13.

16. Next deselect the outer ring of selected vertices. Pull the remaining vertices upward. Continue working your way inward, pulling vertices upward until they match the dome shown in Figure 5.14.

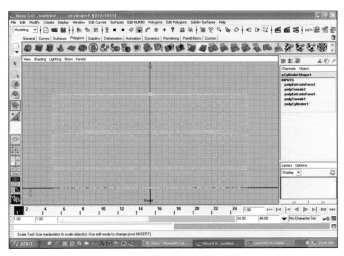

Figure 5.9 Select the faces at the top of the cylinder.

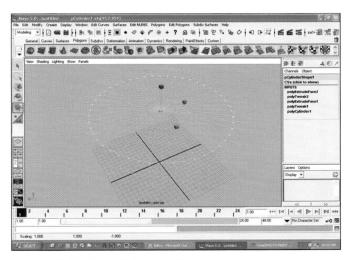

Figure 5.11 Expand the ring of vertices.

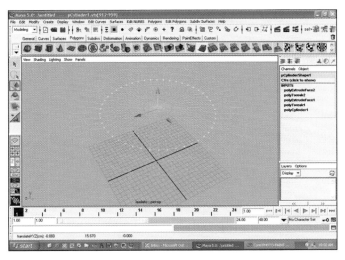

Figure 5.10 Pull down the third ring of vertices.

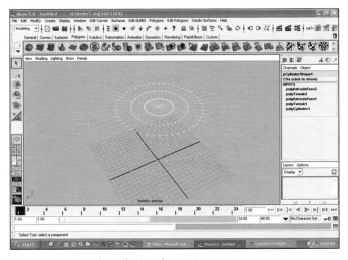

Figure 5.12 Select the inside vertices.

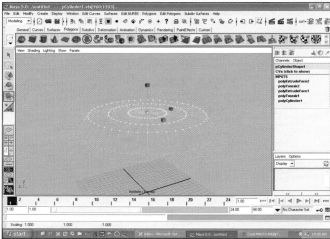

Figure 5.13 Pull the vertices upward.

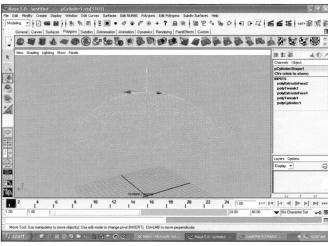

Figure 5.14 The upper dome of the room

17. Bring the rest of the room back by going to Isolate Selected, View Selected in the Show menu on your view area.

18. Now select the bottom of the room similar to the way you selected the top earlier, as shown in Figure 5.15.

19. Remove the other faces from the view by selecting View Selected, as you did earlier. You are going to place a large chalice-shaped pool at the bottom of the room. You can use the floor geometry to create the pool. Select the center vertex and the inner ring of vertices.

20. Pull the selected vertices upward, as shown in Figure 5.16.

21. Select the next ring of vertices outward from the ones you just moved.

22. Move these vertices upward until they match Figure 5.17.

23. Scale the ring of vertices inward until it is directly above the inner ring of vertices, as shown in Figure 5.18.

24. Now select the next ring of vertices outward from the last ring selected.

25. Move the ring up until it is level with the last ring.

26. Scale the ring in until it is just outside of the last ring, as shown in Figure 5.19.

27. You now have the basin and the upper lips of the chalice-like pool. Select the next ring of vertices outward from the last set.

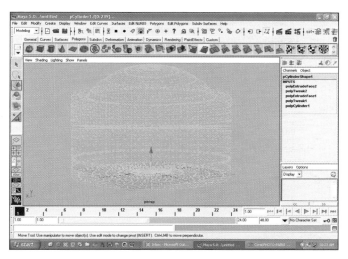

Figure 5.15 Select the faces at the bottom of the cylinder.

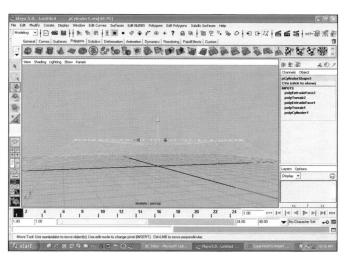

Figure 5.17 Move the next ring of vertices upward.

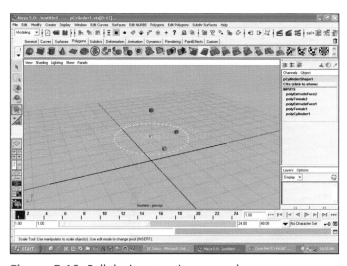

Figure 5.16 Pull the inner vertices upward.

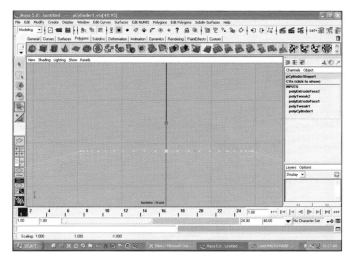

Figure 5.18 Scale the ring of vertices.

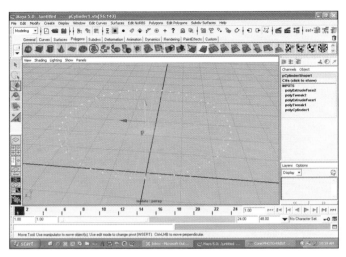

Figure 5.19 Scale the next ring inward.

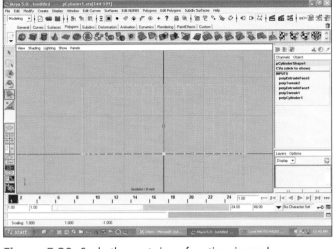

Figure 5.20 Scale the next ring of vertices inward.

28. Scale this ring of vertices until they are directly below the outer ring of the lip of the pool. Use Figure 5.20 as a guide.

29. Select the next ring of vertices from the last ring selected and scale it about halfway between the outer ring and the pool, as shown in Figure 5.21.

30. To finish building the pool and the platform it sits on, you will need more vertices. You can create them by extruding them out of your current geometry.

Change the view mode to Face and select all the faces except the outer ring. Check your work to make sure it matches Figure 5.22.

31. Select Extrude Face from the Edit Polygons menu and move the faces upward to form the platform.

32. Next select the faces of the pool, as shown in Figure 5.23.

33. Now extrude the faces and move them upward three times. (Refer to Figure 5.24.)

34. You now need to shape the base of your chalice pool. Change the view mode back to Vertex view and scale the new rings of vertices until they match those in Figure 5.25.

35. Bring back the rest of the geometry and check the scale of the pool with the room. It should look like Figure 5.26. You might have to adjust a few things to get the pool to fit in the room correctly.

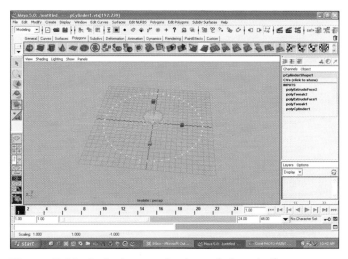

Figure 5.21 Scale the next ring inward about halfway between the other rings.

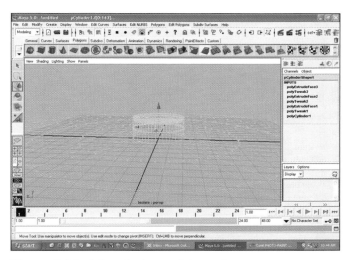

Figure 5.23 Select the faces of the pool.

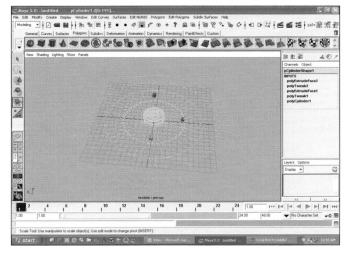

Figure 5.22 Select the inner faces.

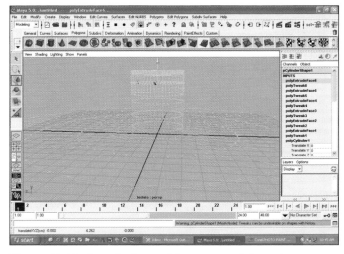

Figure 5.24 Extrude the pool faces upward three times.

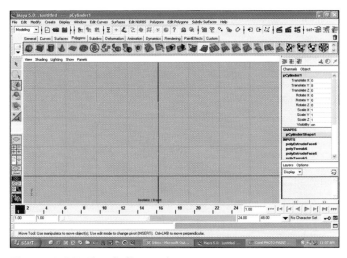

Figure 5.25 The chalice pool

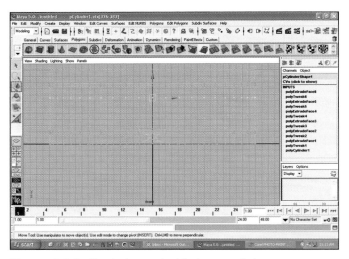

Figure 5.26 Check the pool with the rest of the room.

You could have built the chalice pool out of a separate piece of geometry, but whenever possible I prefer to use the geometry of the room. If an object is built out of the room's geometry, it will remove any possibility of there being a seam between the two pieces of geometry. Not all objects can be built out of the room geometry, as you will see when you build the columns to support the balcony. In those cases, you need to pay special attention to make sure the two objects intersect past each other.

Building the Columns

So far, so good. You now have the beginnings of a room built from your original cylinder. If you haven't already, this would be a good time to save your work. It is always a good idea to save your work often. You never know when something might happen and all your hard work will be lost.

Now you can continue building your room. You will need some supports for your balcony, so you will build some columns to hold it up.

1. Bring up the Polygon Cylinder Options dialog box, as you did for the room. Change the settings to match those shown in Figure 5.27.

2. Hide the room so you can work on the column by itself.

3. Adjust the vertices in the column to match those in Figure 5.28.

4. You will only build one column right now. After you texture it, you will duplicate the column and move the duplicates to form several supports. Unhide

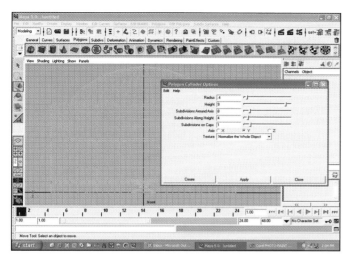

Figure 5.27 The Polygon Cylinder Options dialog box

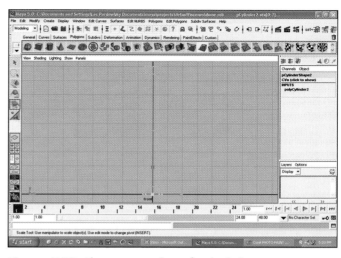

Figure 5.28 The support column for the balcony

the room so you can continue to work on it.

5. You need to have a way into and out of the room. Create doors for the room on four sides at the base and two on the balcony. Using the grid as a guide, select the faces of the room's wall, as shown in Figure 5.29.

6. Extrude the faces and pull them outward from the room.

7. The room's walls are rounded, but you don't want to have a rounded door. With the faces still selected, use the Scale tool to flatten the door. Go to a Side view of the room and pull the perpendicular box toward the center box. Be careful not to pull it past the center box or you will flip the face, which will cause problems later (see Figure 5.30).

8. Repeat the process for creating the door for the other three sides of the room at the base.

9. Now create two doors on opposite sides of the balcony. You want these doors to be smaller than the ones on the ground floor. Refer to Figure 5.31 to see how the finished doors should look.

10. Now go back to the balcony and create the railings so your characters will not fall into the pool. Select the faces at the edge of the balcony, as shown in Figure 5.32.

11. Extrude the faces upward, as shown in Figure 5.33.

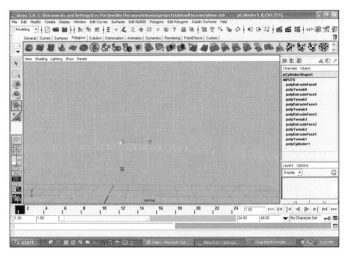

Figure 5.29 Select the group of faces to form a door.

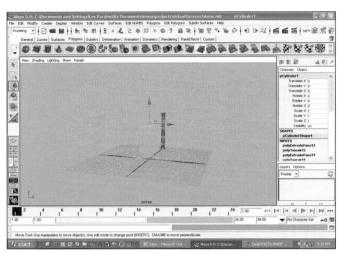

Figure 5.31 The room with doors

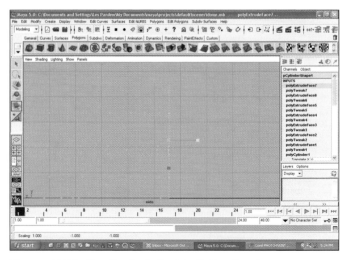

Figure 5.30 Use the Scale tool to flatten the door.

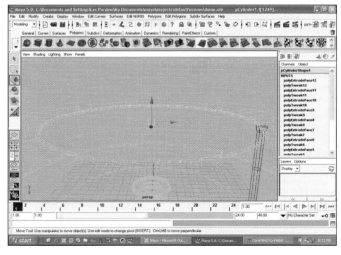

Figure 5.32 Select the faces at the edge of the balcony.

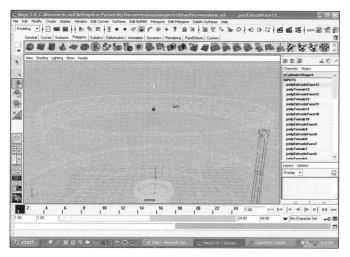

Figure 5.33 Extrude the faces upward.

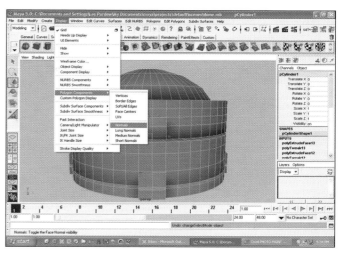

Figure 5.34 Select Normals from the menu.

The geometry for the room is almost complete, but you have one more thing to deal with before you move on to applying the textures. Because you created the room from a cylinder, all the faces are pointed in the wrong direction. If you exported this room into a game right now, you would be able to see the room from the outside but not from the inside because all the faces are pointing out.

You can see the direction of the faces in Maya by selecting Polygon Components, Normals from the Display menu, as shown in Figure 5.34.

Maya shows the direction a face is facing with a line coming out of the middle of the face, perpendicular to it. Notice in Figure 5.35 that the room looks like a porcupine, with all the face normals pointing outward.

You need to correct this problem. Maya has a tool that will reverse the normals of an object. Select Normals, Reverse from the Edit Polygons menu, as shown in Figure 5.36.

Now you will notice that there are almost no face normals visible from the outside of the room, except for the few around the top of the room where the face normal lines are showing through. These are actually pointing in the correct direction, but the lines are so long that the ends are poking through the room geometry.

To better understand how faces work in a game, select Backface Culling from the Shading menu, as shown in Figure 5.37.

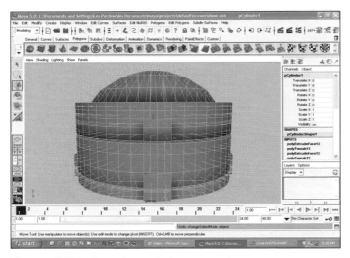

Figure 5.35 Normals are facing outward.

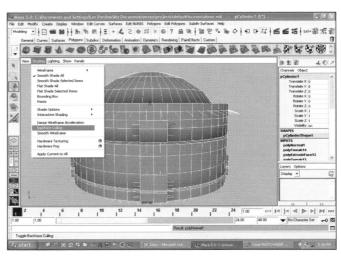

Figure 5.37 Turn on backface culling.

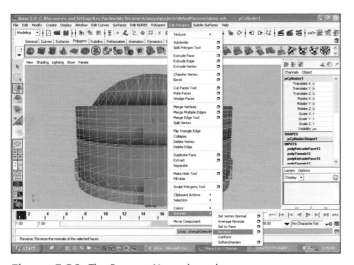

Figure 5.36 The Reverse Normals tool

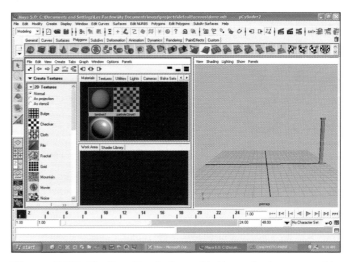

Figure 5.38 The Two-Panel view with Hypershade on one side and Perspective view on the other

As you can see, all the face normal lines are pointing inward. In a game, it takes processor time to render a polygonal face. Most game engines will automatically cull the back side of all faces to reduce rendering time.

Now that the room is built, it is time to see how it will look with some textures.

1. Start with the column. Change the view to Two-Panel, with Hypershade on one side and the Perspective view on the other.

2. Hide the room so only the column is showing, as in Figure 5.38.

3. All the textures for this project are on the CD. Create two new materials and load the bluemarble and base textures from the CD. (I covered creating and naming materials in Chapters 1 and 4; you can review those chapters if you need a refresher on this.)

4. Rename the new materials, as in Figure 5.39.

5. Apply the new materials to the model of the column by either dragging the material to the selected faces or right-clicking on the material and selecting Assign Material to Selection from the menu. Use the Cylindrical Mapping tool. Apply the bluemarble material to the column; apply the base to both the top and bottom of the column. Refer to Figure 5.40 to see how the column should look. Make sure to press the 6 key to turn on hardware texturing so you can see the textures.

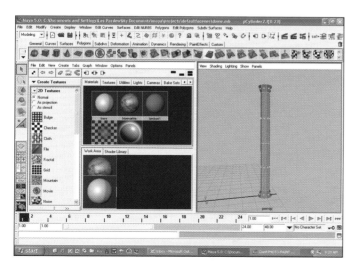

Figure 5.39 Rename the new materials.

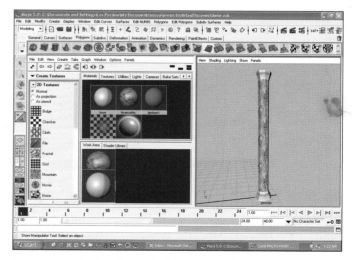

Figure 5.40 Map the materials to the column.

6. Notice that the column looks faceted; you want it to look round. You can give the column a rounded look without having to add more geometry. Go back to Object mode. In the Edit Polygons menu, select Normals, Soften/Harden, as shown in Figure 5.41.

7. Set the tool to all soft and then apply it to the object. All of the facets should disappear, and the column should look like Figure 5.42.

8. Now that the column is textured, you can duplicate it. Press Ctrl+G to group the column and center the pivot on the middle axis.

9. Next, duplicate the column and rotate it 45 degrees around the middle axis.

10. Continue duplicating the column and rotating it around the axis in 45-degree increments until you have eight columns supporting the balcony, as shown in Figure 5.43.

11. It would be easier to texture the rest of the room if you didn't have the columns obstructing your view of the interior faces. Go to Hypergraph in the Window menu and select all of the columns, as shown in Figure 5.44. Press Ctrl+H to hide the columns.

12. At this point save the file again. This time rename it *dome1*, as shown in Figure 5.45. I often save different versions of my work in progress. The advantage of saving in this manner is

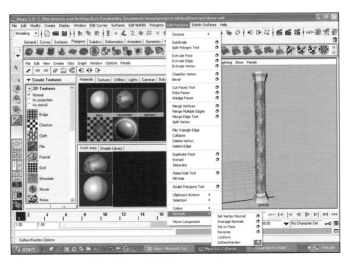

Figure 5.41 The Soften/Harden menu item

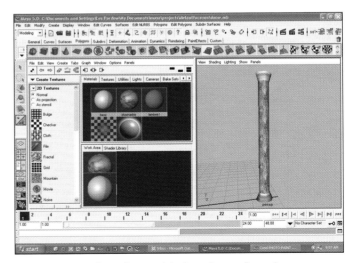

Figure 5.42 The column with the edges softened

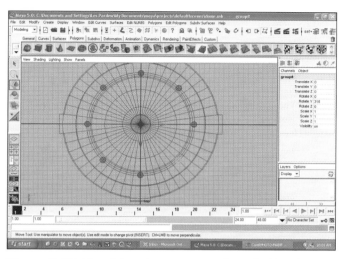

Figure 5.43 The eight columns, as seen from the Top view

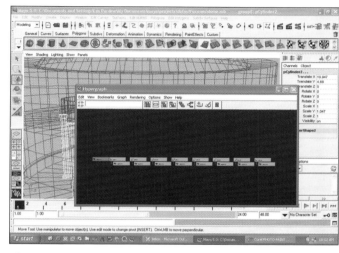

Figure 5.44 Select and hide the columns in Hypergraph.

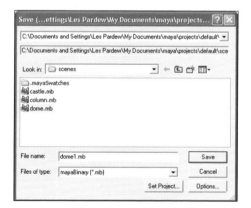

Figure 5.45 Save the file as *dome1*.

that if you don't like the work, you can always go back to an earlier version and take a different path.

13. You are now ready to apply materials to the room. Load all the remaining texture files for this lesson into Hypershade, creating materials for each one and naming each one, as shown in Figure 5.46.

14. The first thing to which you should apply a material is the pool. Change the view to Face mode and select all the pool's faces except the ones at the bottom of the pool, as shown in Figure 5.47.

15. Apply the white marble texture and use the Cylindrical Mapping tool to set the material on the surfaces (see Figure 5.48). Make sure the image scale is set to 2.

16. Select the faces at the bottom of the pool and apply the tile1 material using the Planar Mapping tool, as shown in Figure 5.49. Make sure to take note of the image scale.

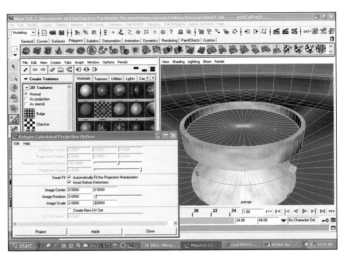

Figure 5.46 The textures loaded into Hypershade

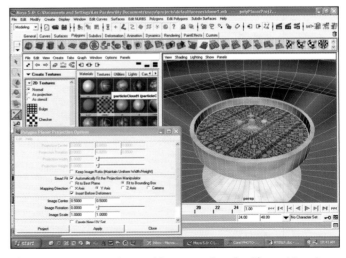

Figure 5.48 Use the Cylindrical Mapping tool to set the material on the surface.

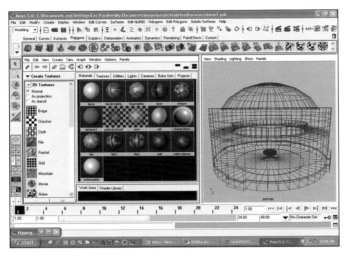

Figure 5.47 Select the faces of the pool.

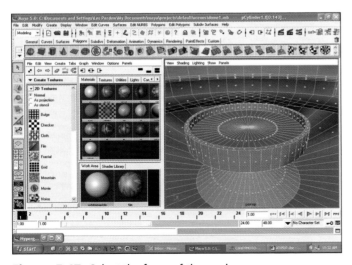

Figure 5.49 Map the pool bottom using the Planar Mapping tool.

17. The pool needs to contain some water. You create the water by selecting the faces at the bottom of the pool and duplicating them. The Duplicate Face function is in the Edit Polygons menu. Select the small square next to the Duplicate Face option to bring up the Duplicate Face Options dialog box.

18. Make sure the check box for Separate Duplicated Faces is unchecked and click on the Apply button.

19. Move the newly duplicated faces upward to the edge of the pool, as shown in Figure 5.50.

20. Apply the water material to the new faces.

21. You want to make the water transparent. In Hypershade, go to the water material and bring up its attribute editor by pressing Ctrl+A.

22. Find the Transparency slider bar and move it about halfway to the right, as shown in Figure 5.51.

23. Next work on the floor of the room. Select the ring of faces next to the pool and apply the tile material to them.

24. Unitize the faces. They should now look like Figure 5.52.

25. Now select the small ring of faces that you extruded earlier to form a platform around the pool.

26. Apply the tile material to the selected faces and unitize them, as shown in Figure 5.53.

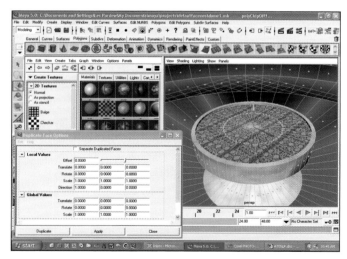

Figure 5.50 Raise the new faces to the top edge of the pool.

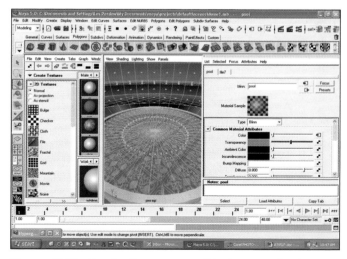

Figure 5.51 Use the Transparency slider bar to make the water material transparent.

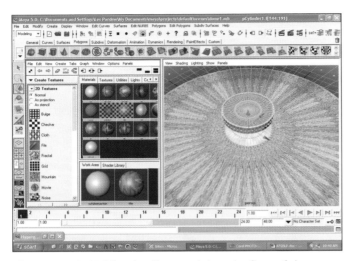

Figure 5.52 Unitize the tile material on the floor of the room.

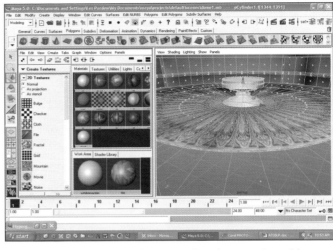

Figure 5.53 Apply the tile material to the next ring of faces.

27. You will use tile2 for the next ring of faces. Apply it and unitize it the same way you did for the other two rings. It should now look like Figure 5.54.

28. Notice that this texture is a little different. It is not a complete texture; rather, it is a half texture. To make it complete you need to flip some of the faces. Select every other face around the ring.

29. In the Edit Polygons menu, choose Texture, Flip UVs to

bring up the Polygon Force UV Options dialog box.

30. Set the options as shown in Figure 5.55 and click on Apply.

31. The last section of the floor is the area next to the doors. You will use the blockmarble material for this section of the floor. Later, you will use this material for most of the walls in the room. Select the faces next to one of the doors.

32. Apply the blockmarble material and use the Planar Mapping

tool to adjust the material so it looks like Figure 5.56.

33. Now repeat the process for the areas next to the other three doors.

34. Now that the floor is textured you can move on to the walls. Start with the doors. Select the faces that make up the doors to the room. Apply the door material to the selected faces and then use the Planar Mapping tool to project the material, as shown in Figure 5.57.

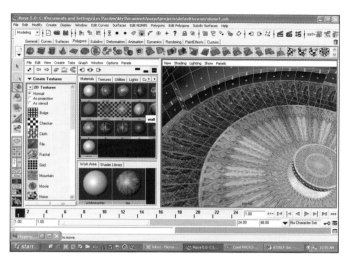

Figure 5.54 The next ring of faces with the tile2 material applied

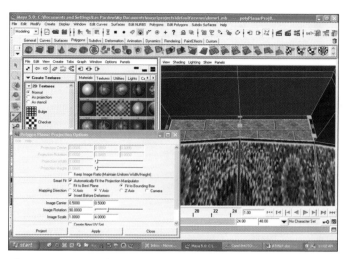

Figure 5.56 Apply the blockmarble material to the floor area near the door.

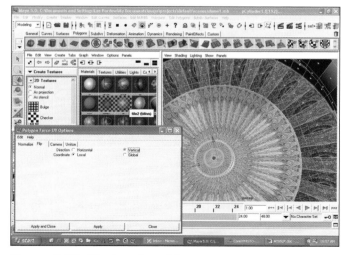

Figure 5.55 Flip the selected faces.

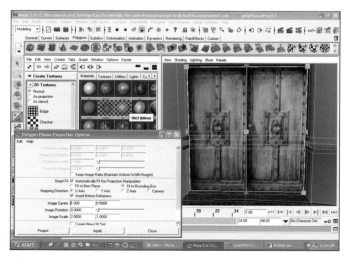

Figure 5.57 Apply the door material to the door faces.

35. Select the first row of faces at the base of the wall. Make sure you don't select the faces of the doors that you mapped earlier. Refer to Figure 5.58 to check your work.

36. Apply the wallsculpture material to the selected faces and unitize them.

37. You will notice that the material will be lying on its side. You need to rotate the faces so they are correct. To rotate them you first need to change the selection mode from Face to UVs.

You can do this without having to reselect them by changing your selection mode for the selected faces in the Edit Polygons menu. In the menu, choose Selection, Convert Selection to UVs, as shown in Figure 5.59.

38. Now bring up the Rotate UVs Options dialog box. It is located in the Edit Polygons menu under the Texture option.

39. Set the rotation amount to 90 and click on Apply until the

material is lined up correctly on the wall, as shown in Figure 5.60. Note that the materials near the doors will have to be rotated separately from the rest of the walls.

40. Now you must continue to move up the wall. Select the three rows of faces that form the top of the wainscoting on the wall, as shown in Figure 5.61. Apply the whitemarble material to the selected faces and unitize them as shown.

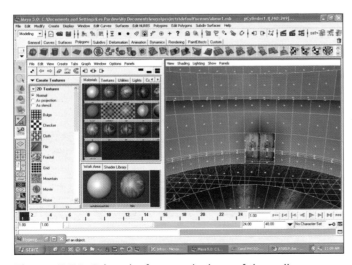

Figure 5.58 Select the faces at the base of the wall.

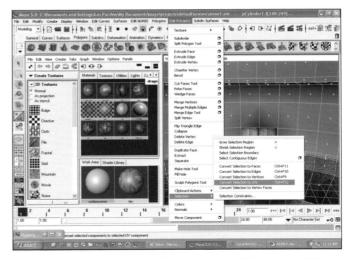

Figure 5.59 Convert the selection mode of the selected faces to UVs.

Figure 5.60 Rotate the texture until it is lined up correctly.

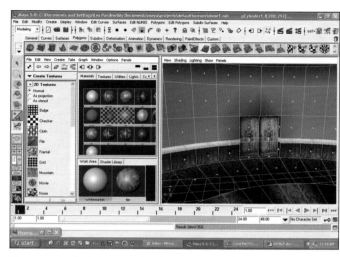

Figure 5.61 Select the faces of the top of the wainscoting.

41. Select the next two rows of the wall's faces, moving upward.

42. Apply the blockmarble material to these wall faces. Unitize and rotate the faces to match Figure 5.62.

43. Next, apply the dragon material to the top of the wall. Unitize the material and rotate it as needed. Refer to Figure 5.63 to check your work.

44. You will be applying the tile1 material to the bottom of the balcony. Select the faces for the bottom and the first row of faces on the inside lip of the balcony.

45. Apply the tile1 material and unitize all the selected faces. The room should now look like Figure 5.64.

46. The next step is to apply the rail material to the rail of the balcony. You use the Cylindrical Mapping tool for the job. Select all the faces for the balcony rails.

47. Apply the rail material and then use the Cylindrical Mapping tool, as shown in Figure 5.65.

48. Use the tile2 material to map the floor of the balcony, much like you did for the floor of the room. It should look like Figure 5.66.

49. You will again use the Cylindrical Mapping tool to map the wall above the balcony. Apply the blockmarble material to the wall using the Cylindrical Mapping tool, as shown in Figure 5.67.

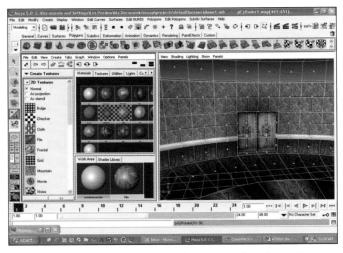

Figure 5.62 Apply the blockmarble material to the wall.

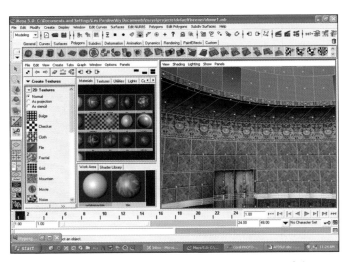

Figure 5.64 Apply the tile1 material to the bottom of the balcony.

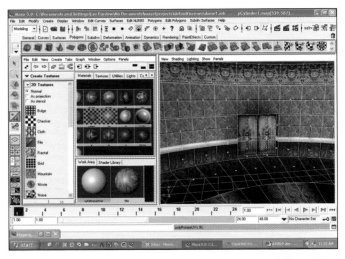

Figure 5.63 Add the dragon material to the top of the wall.

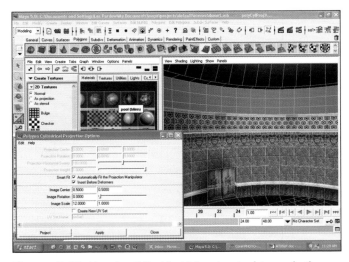

Figure 5.65 Use the Cylindrical Mapping tool to apply the material to the rail of the balcony.

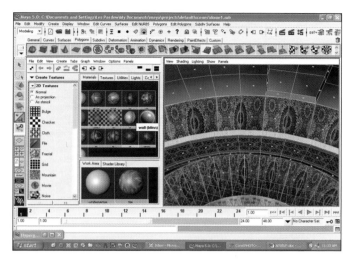

Figure 5.66 Apply the tile2 material to the floor of the balcony.

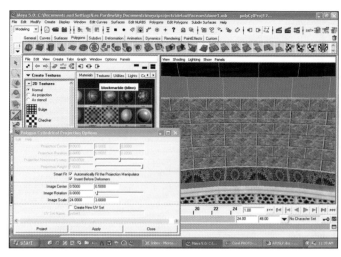

Figure 5.67 Apply the blockmarble material to the wall.

50. Now you will use the Planar Mapping tool to apply the blockmarble material to the walls around the door, as shown in Figure 5.68.

51. Now apply the blockmarble material to the floor area near the doors, much like you did for the floor on the ground floor of the room. See Figure 5.69 for reference.

52. Now apply the door material to the doors, as shown in Figure 5.70.

53. Next apply the dragon material to the top of the wall, much like you did on the lower section of the room.

54. Apply the tile1 material to the lower part of the roof, the same way you did for the bottom of the balcony. Refer to Figure 5.71 to check your work.

55. Select all the faces of the dome and apply the dome material to them.

56. Unitize the faces. Your design should now look like Figure 5.72.

The room is now textured. It looks a lot different with the textures than it did with just the geometry of the model. Unhide the columns you created earlier by selecting Show, Show Last Hidden from the Display menu. The geometry of the room should look like Figure 5.73.

The room will be much easier to view if you turn on backface culling, as shown in Figure 5.74.

Figures 5.75 and 5.76 show two more views of the finished room.

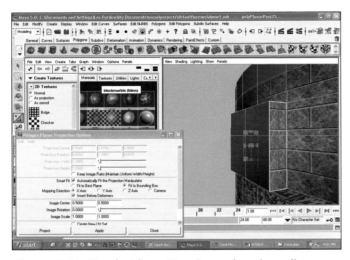

Figure 5.68 Use the Planar Mapping tool on the walls near the door.

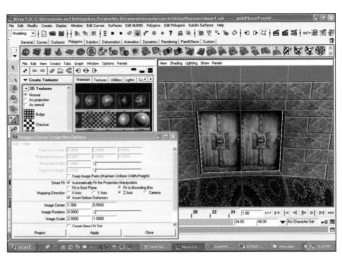

Figure 5.70 Apply the door material to the doors of the balcony.

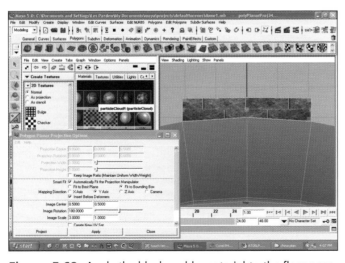

Figure 5.69 Apply the blockmarble material to the floor near the doors of the balcony.

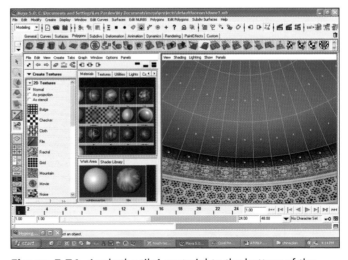

Figure 5.71 Apply the tile1 material to the bottom of the roof.

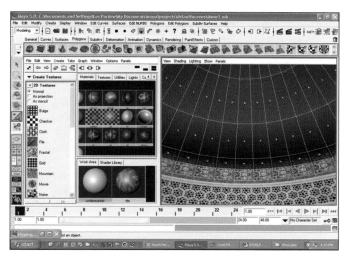

Figure 5.72 Apply the dome material to the faces of the dome.

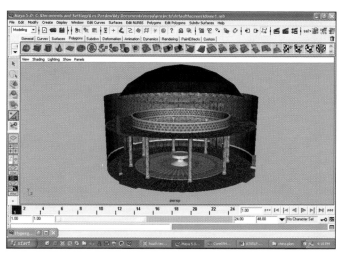

Figure 5.74 The finished room seen from a distance

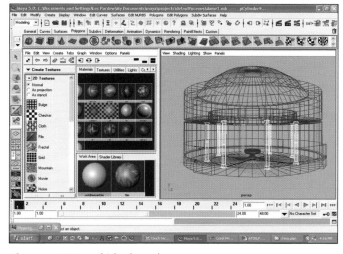

Figure 5.73 Unhide the columns.

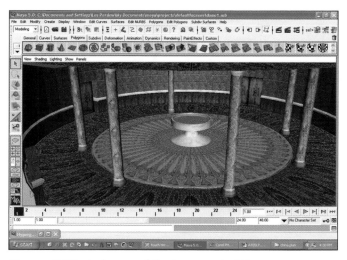

Figure 5.75 A closeup of the lower part of the room

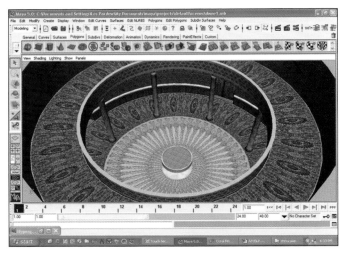

Figure 5.76 A view of the room from the balcony

Summary

In this chapter you learned some very important material. You learned how to create a domed two-story room with a balcony and a pool. You also learned how to apply materials and how to manipulate those materials to work correctly on the model.

Now that you have finished creating a room, try creating a few more. Add some rooms to this model, connecting the doors.

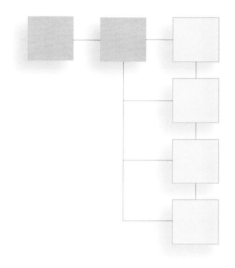

CHAPTER 6

LIGHTING AND REFLECTIONS

An important part of developing realistic game environments is developing qualities and attributes that you see in normal life. How an environment is lit will play a big role in how realistic that environment will look. Another important factor of an environment is its reflective nature. A shiny object should reflect what is around it.

Real-time lighting and reflections require intensive calculations. You must use them sparingly in games, or they will bog the game speed down and make the game difficult to play. In this chapter you will examine real-time lighting and reflections. In addition to real-time, you will also take a look at other methods of lighting and reflections that don't require as much calculation. These methods give the game a great look while freeing the processor to render more important game elements.

Real-Time Lighting

Real-time lighting is used in a game to illuminate the game geometry; it is updated every frame so it simulates the real world. Real-time lighting has traditionally been the realm of the programmer, but more and more artists are being asked to design the lighting for a game.

When designing the lighting for a game, you need to understand two important things—where and what. By where, I mean the location of the light. By what, I mean the type of light. Before you get into placing a light, you need to understand the types of lights used in games. They are

- Point light
- Directional light
- Ambient light
- Colored light

Point Light

A *point light* is similar to the light given off by a light bulb. The light projects in all directions and is brightest near the source. The light from a point light diminishes with distance. Look at the light in Figure 6.1. Notice that the light gives off a strong highlight on the ball. The area around the light is brightest; the areas on the corners of the plane are darker.

Point lights are good for lighting a room or a local area outside where artificial light is used, such as a streetlamp at night.

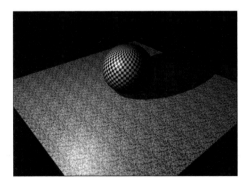

Figure 6.1 A point light is used to light a scene.

Directional Light

Directional lights simulate the light of the sun. The sun is a bright light source that is millions of miles away. Its light rays are almost exactly parallel to each other as they hit the Earth's surface. A directional light illuminates everything evenly. Look at Figure 6.2 and notice how the light on the plane is even. There is no darkening with distance from the light.

Directional light is the most widely used light source in games because it is one of the easiest to calculate. It is also a light that you are comfortable with because you see it every day in real life.

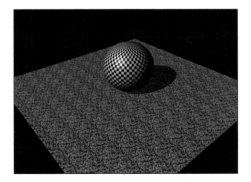

Figure 6.2 A directional light is used to light a scene.

Ambient Light

An *ambient light* is a general light source that lights all surfaces in all directions evenly. Ambient light is the result of light bouncing off one surface and then another. Most light in a home that comes through the windows is ambient light unless the sun is shining directly through the window. Because the nature of light is to bounce from one surface to another, shadows are not completely black. You might have noticed that the shadows in Figures 6.1 and 6.2 are almost completely black, which gives them a very unnatural look. In real life, light bounces off everything so almost all shadows have some light. Look at Figure 6.3, and notice that

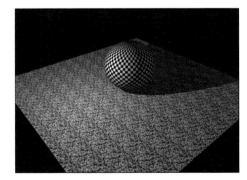

Figure 6.3 An ambient light is used to light the shadow areas.

the shadows are much softer and the ball looks three-dimensional. The ambient light simulates the reflected light normally seen in real life.

Almost every scene needs to have some ambient light to make it look realistic. The only exception is a game set in deep space, where there is little or no reflected light.

Colored Light

A *colored light* is not really a light; rather, it is an attribute of all the lights I have already discussed. Colored light is any light source that has a specific color. The scene in Figure 6.4 is lit with four separate colored lights. They are all point lights, but they each have a different color.

Figure 6.4 Four colored lights are used to light this scene.

Almost every light source is a colored light. A fluorescent light is usually slightly blue, while a normal incandescent light bulb is yellow. The rays of the sun tend to be a little on the yellow side unless it is setting, and then they can be very red. When you are lighting a scene, use a light that fits the nature of the scene. For example, when you are doing an interior room, give it a slightly yellow light.

Preset Lighting

Because real-time lighting is so processor intensive, most games use a system of lighting that is set up prior to the game running. This system is often referred to as *vertex lighting* because it is controlled from the vertices of the polygons. The concept behind vertex lighting is a simple one. The game engine can lighten and darken a texture based on information stored in the model. The lighting takes the form of a gradient, which is a ramp from one color to another. Figure 6.5 shows an example of a gradient. One corner is light blue, and the opposite corner is dark blue. The colors blend evenly from one corner to the other.

Figure 6.5 An example of a gradient

There are basically two ways to set up vertex lighting in a model—prelighting and applying a color directly to a vertex. *Prelighting* is a process in Maya where the lighting is calculated and applied to the vertices automatically. All the artist has to do is set up the lighting for the scene, and Maya will calculate the vertex lighting automatically. To apply color directly to vertices, the artist simply needs to select the vertices and then apply a color to them. Take a look at how both processes are used to create lighting for games.

For this example you will use the room you created in Chapter 5. Before you create the lights, however, you need to create some lamps and windows for the room. Bring up Maya and let's get started.

1. The first step is to create a cylinder. Bring up the Polygon Cylinder Options dialog box and adjust the attributes to those shown in Figure 6.6.

2. For this example you want the lamps to be six-sided, but you need more polygons so you need to subdivide the cylinder. The Polygon Subdivide Face Options dialog box can be accessed via the Edit Polygons menu. Bring up the dialog box and set the subdivision levels to 1, as shown in Figure 6.7.

3. Before you go any farther, you need to create a template so you can adjust the polygons of the cylinder to match those of the texture. A *template* is an object that is used as a guide for creating your model. It is not used as part of the model. There are many ways to create templates; I will go over some of them in this book. Create a polygon plane, as shown in Figure 6.8.

4. Now you are ready to load the texture for the lamp. Create a new material in Hypershade and load the lamp texture file, as shown in Figure 6.9.

5. Apply the lamp material to the texture template plane.

6. Press the 6 key so you can see the textures.

7. Under the Shading menu on the view screen, go to Shade Options. Turn on both the X-Ray and Wireframe on Shaded options, as shown in Figure 6.10.

8. Adjust the width of the template to match the panel size of the lamp, as shown in Figure 6.11.

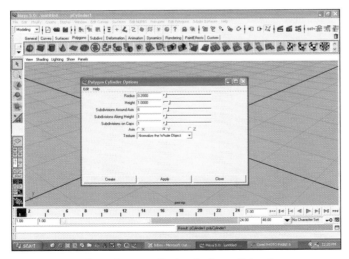

Figure 6.6 The Polygon Cylinder Options dialog box

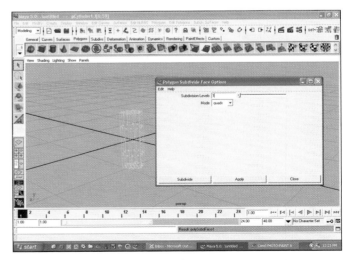

Figure 6.7 Subdivide the cylinder.

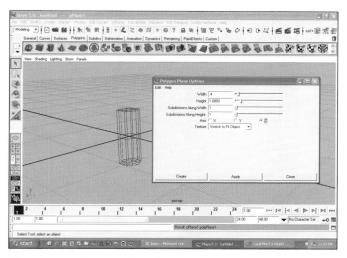

Figure 6.8 Create a plane for a texture template.

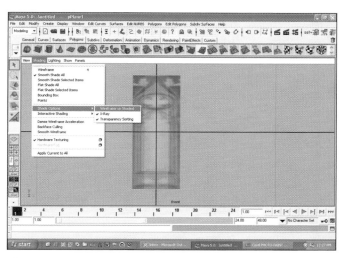

Figure 6.10 Turn on the options under Shade Options.

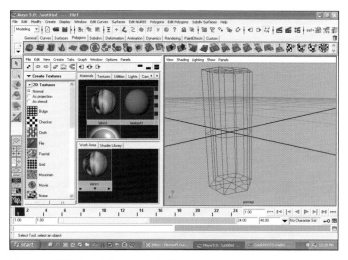

Figure 6.9 Load the lamp texture.

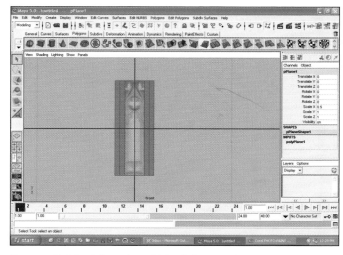

Figure 6.11 Adjust the width of the template.

9. Select the vertices of the cylinder and pull them up, as shown in Figure 6.12.

10. On the top of the cylinder, select all the interior vertices and the corner vertices on the edges, as shown in Figure 6.13.

11. Move the vertices down so they are even with the one you raised earlier. Your model should now look like Figure 6.14.

12. You don't need the template any longer, so hide it.

13. Apply the lamp material to the cylinder, as shown in Figure 6.15.

14. Now you need to project the material so it matches the template you created earlier. Select the faces of the lamp panel facing you in the Front view.

15. Project the material using the Planar Mapping tool, as shown in Figure 6.16.

16. Rotate the lamp cylinder around the y-axis 60 degrees, as shown in Figure 6.17.

17. Project the material to the panel facing you, the same way you did in Step 15.

18. Continue rotating and projecting the lamp material until it is projected on all sides, as shown in Figure 6.18.

19. Save the lamp to a file, as shown in Figure 6.19, so you can use it later.

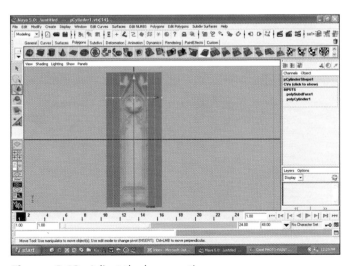

Figure 6.12 Adjust the lamp vertices.

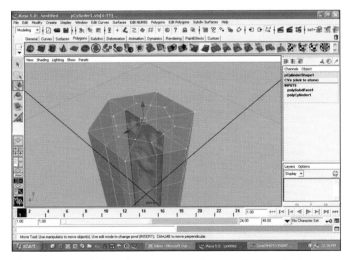

Figure 6.13 Select the vertices at the top of the cylinder.

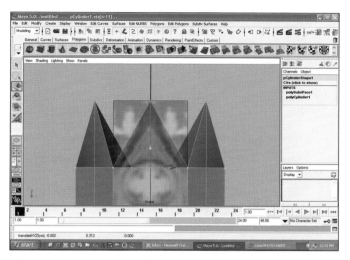

Figure 6.14 Move the selected vertices down.

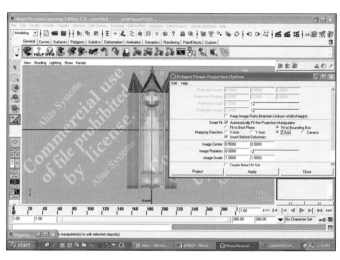

Figure 6.16 Project the material using the Planar Mapping tool.

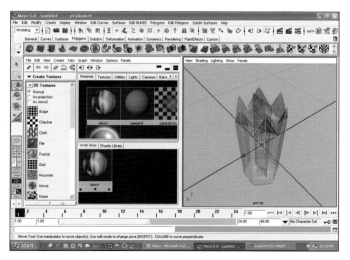

Figure 6.15 Apply the material to the cylinder.

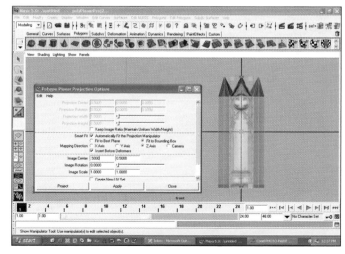

Figure 6.17 Rotate the cylinder.

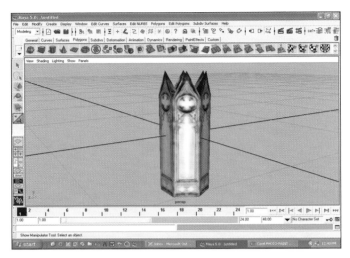

Figure 6.18 The finished lamp

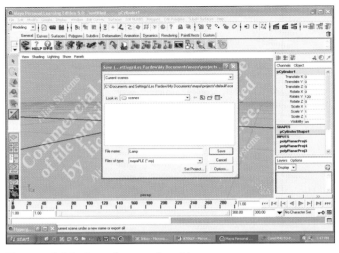

Figure 6.19 Save the completed lamp.

Now you have a lamp that you can add to the room you created earlier. Bring up the room from Chapter 5. You will add the lamp and create windows to the room for your light sources.

1. In the File menu, go to Import, as shown in Figure 6.20.

2. Import the lamp file you just saved.

3. Adjust the position of the lamp using the channel box, as shown in Figure 6.21.

4. Press Ctrl+G to center the pivot of the lamp and then duplicate it by pressing Ctrl+D.

5. Rotate the duplicated lamp –33 degrees around the y-axis to place it on the other side of the doorway, as shown in Figure 6.22.

6. Select both lamps.

7. Press Ctrl+G to center the pivot.

8. Duplicate the two lamps and rotate them 90 degrees to the next doorway, as shown in Figure 6.23.

9. Repeat the process of duplicating and rotating the lamps until they are in front of the other two doorways. The lamps should now be by each doorway, as shown in Figure 6.24.

10. Now create two windows in the room by the balcony. Go to the Side view and select the four faces in the center of the room. (You will actually be selecting eight faces because there are four faces on each side of the room.) Look at Figure 6.25 for reference.

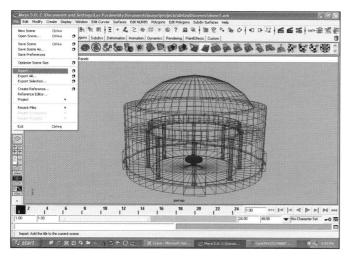

Figure 6.20 The Import menu item

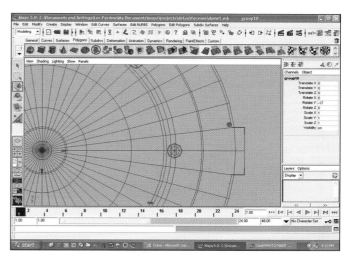

Figure 6.22 Rotate the duplicated lamp.

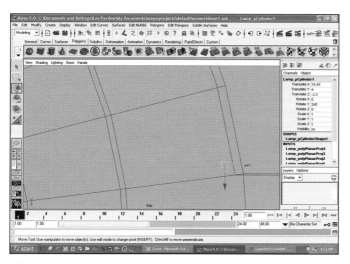

Figure 6.21 Move the position of the lamp using the channel box.

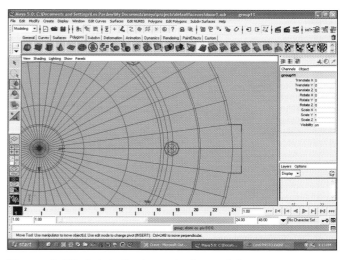

Figure 6.23 Rotate the lamps to the next doorway.

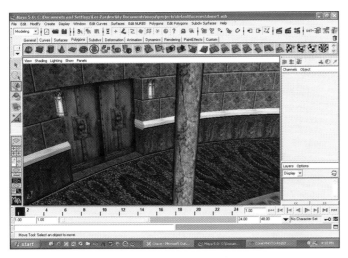

Figure 6.24 The lamps in place by the doorways

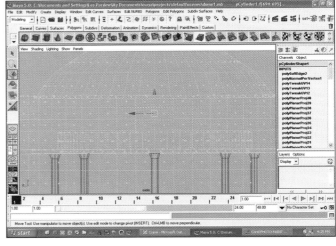

Figure 6.25 Select faces for a window.

11. Extrude the faces.

12. Use the Scale tool to size the extruded face outward, as shown in Figure 6.26.

13. Make a new material and load the window texture.

14. Apply the new material to the window faces and use the Planar Mapping tool to project the material onto the faces, as shown in Figure 6.27.

Now you have the geometry in place for your light sources. You are ready to add the vertex lighting to the scene.

1. You create lights in Maya the same way you create polygonal primitives. Bring up the Create Point Light Options dialog box by selecting Lights, Point Light from the Create menu, as shown in Figure 6.28.

2. Set the intensity of the light to 5 and the drop off (Decay Rate) to 2.

3. Click on the rectangle box next to Color to bring up the color palette.

4. Move the color selection circle in the palette to a warm yellow color, as shown in Figure 6.29.

5. Select a dark, cool blue color for the shadow color, as shown in Figure 6.30.

6. Click on Create to create a light in the scene. Lights are represented by a sunburst in Maya.

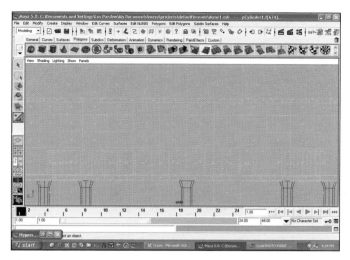

Figure 6.26 Size the windows outward.

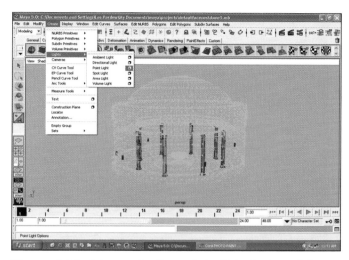

Figure 6.28 Bring up the Create Point Light Options dialog box.

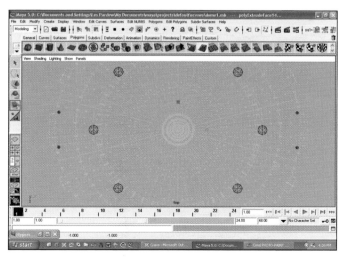

Figure 6.27 Project the window material on the faces of the window.

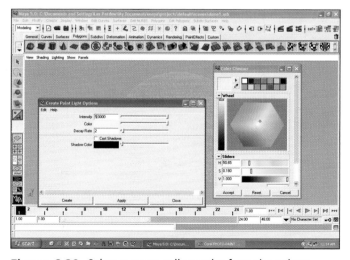

Figure 6.29 Select a warm yellow color from the palette.

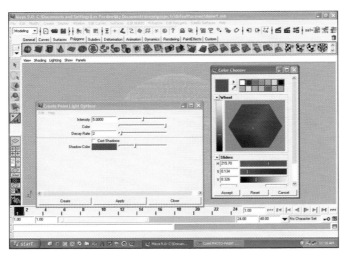

Figure 6.30 Select a dark blue color for the shadow.

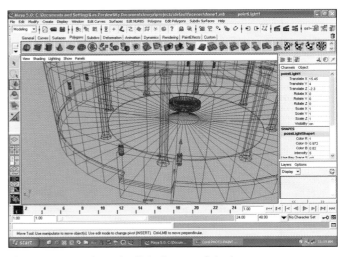

Figure 6.31 Place the light in one of the lamps.

7. Move the light to a lamp. You can use the channel box and type in the same coordinates you used earlier to place the lamp near the doorway. Refer to Figure 6.31.

8. Remember how you duplicated the lamps and placed them near the doorways? You can do the same thing with the point light. Place one light in each lamp.

9. Having the light inside each lamp will not give you the lighting effect you want. With each light selected, press Ctrl+G to group them.

10. Use the Scale tool to bring the lights just in front of the lamps, as shown in Figure 6.32.

11. You will also use the pool as a light source. A luminescent pool is a cool thing. Bring up the Create Point Light Options dialog box again.

12. Adjust the colors, intensity, and drop off to those shown in Figure 6.33.

13. Place the new light just above the pool, as shown in Figure 6.34.

14. Now you are ready to prelight the room. Bring up the Polygon Prelight Options dialog box by selecting Colors, Prelight from the Edit Polygons menu, as shown in Figure 6.35.

15. Check the options shown in Figure 6.36.

16. Click on the Prelight button. It will take Maya a few seconds to calculate the lighting.

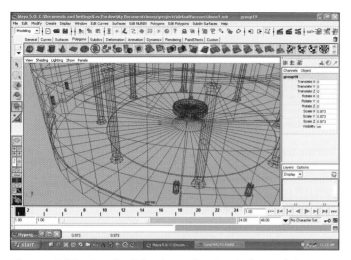

Figure 6.32 Size the lights inward to just in front of the lamps.

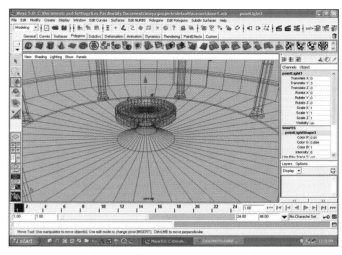

Figure 6.34 Place the light above the pool.

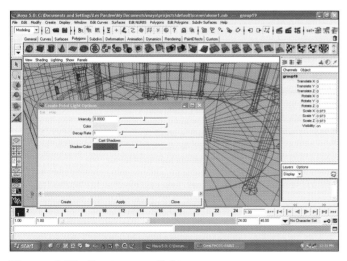

Figure 6.33 Create a new light.

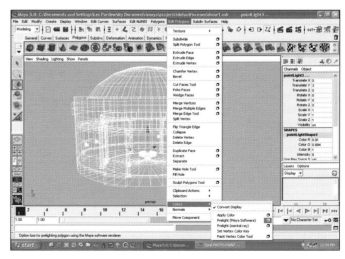

Figure 6.35 Bring up the Polygon Prelight Options dialog box.

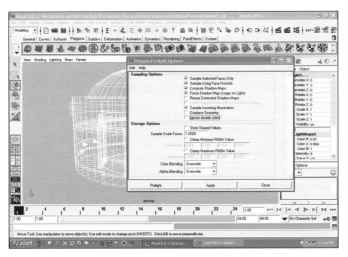

Figure 6.36 The Polygon Prelight Options dialog box

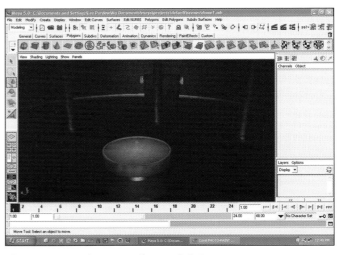

Figure 6.37 The room after prelighting

17. When Maya is finished calculating the lighting, the image will change from the Wire-Frame view to the Shaded view. If you want to see how the shading looks, go to the Lighting menu of the view screen and select Use No Lights. Your scene should look like Figure 6.37.

    The room will appear dark. This is because the prelighting is to establish shadows. When the room is in a game, real-time lighting will also illuminate the room.

18. You will want the lamps to be brighter, as if they are lighting the room. Select all the lamps and bring up the Polygon Apply Color Options dialog box, as shown in Figure 6.38.

19. Change the colors to those shown in Figure 6.39.

20. Click on the Apply Color button. The lamps should look bright, as shown in Figure 6.40.

21. Next you need to light the upper part of the room. Select the faces of the room from the balcony upward, as shown in Figure 6.41.

22. Use the View Selected function to only see those areas on which you want to work.

23. Now apply color evenly to the upper part of the room using the Apply Color tool. Change the selection mode to Vertices and select all the vertices.

24. Bring up the Polygon Apply Color Options dialog box and adjust it to match Figure 6.42.

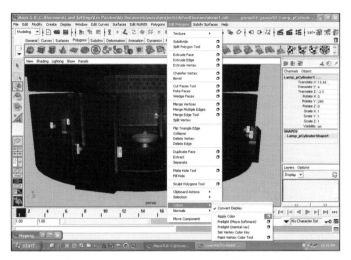

Figure 6.38 Bring up the Polygon Apply Color Options dialog box.

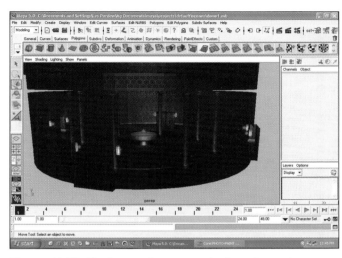

Figure 6.40 The lamps after you apply the color to the vertices

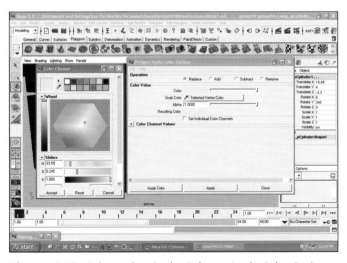

Figure 6.39 Select colors in the Polygon Apply Color Options dialog box.

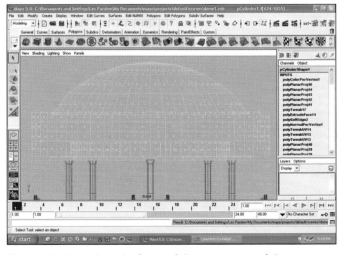

Figure 6.41 Select the faces of the upper part of the room.

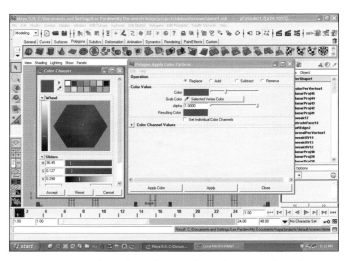

Figure 6.42 Adjust the values in the Polygon Apply Color Options dialog box.

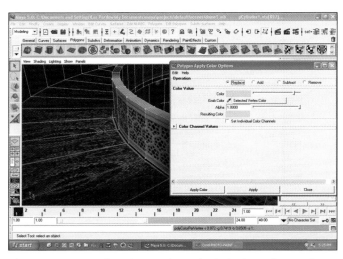

Figure 6.44 Apply color to where the light from the window falls.

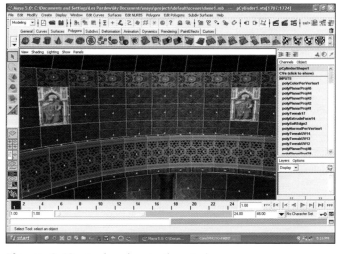

Figure 6.43 Apply colors to the window.

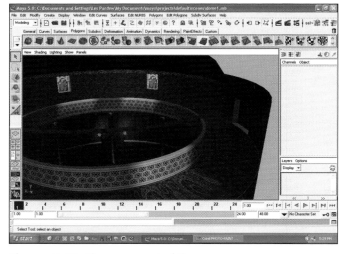

Figure 6.45 The upper part of the room

25. Once you have an even lighting on the room, you can go in and adjust individual vertices to give the lighting a more realistic look. Start with the windows. Select the vertices of the window.

26. Use the Apply Color tool and apply color to the selected vertices, as shown in Figure 6.43.

27. Usually a bright window will cast light into a room. The light will be brighter near the window. You can simulate this effect by selecting the vertices of the rail and floor where the light would fall and lightening them by applying a lighter color, as shown in Figure 6.44.

28. Repeat the process for the other window. The model should now look like Figure 6.45.

29. Bring back the lower part of the room to see how your lighting looks. Refer to Figure 6.46 to compare your room to the example.

You now have a basic understanding of lighting and prelighting. Experiment with the lighting tools in Maya to get more familiar with them. Try building a few simple rooms and lighting them in different ways.

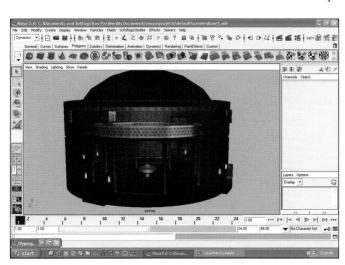

Figure 6.46 Finished room with lighting

Real-Time Reflections

A shiny surface looks shiny because it reflects its surroundings. The only way to get a true reflection on a surface in a game is to calculate it based on the angle of the surroundings and the game view, and then render the calculated image on the surface. This usually has to be done for each ray of light; the process is called *ray tracing*. Ray tracing is impractical for real-time game rendering because it takes up too much processor time. In the absence of true reflections, game developers have come up with a few tricks that simulate reflective surfaces.

Specularity

Specularity is a surface property that helps define an object as shiny or dull. Look at Figure 6.47. There are several slider bars for specular properties in the attribute editor of a blinn material. In Figure 6.47, I have moved the Specular Roll Off slider all the way to the left. Look at the image of the material—it is dull.

Now look at Figure 6.48, in which I have moved the slider bar all the way to the right, increasing the specular

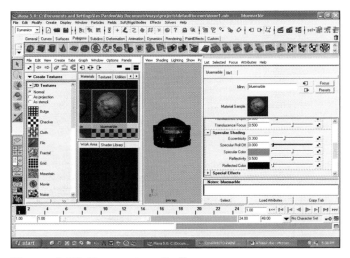

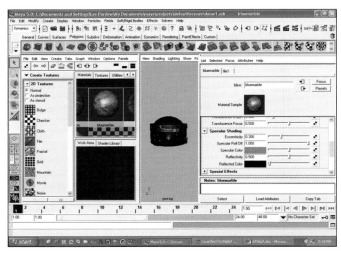

Figure 6.47 No specular roll off

Figure 6.48 High specular roll off

roll off. Notice how the material looks shiny.

The material is not reflecting its surroundings, but by changing the way the material reflects highlights, you can give it a simulated shiny look. Adjusting the specular qualities of the material is the basic way game developers add shininess to surfaces.

Environment Maps

Some surfaces need more than just a specular highlight to look right. A shiny car, for example, needs to reflect its surroundings. One way developers have created the look of reflections without the time-consuming process of ray tracing is by using an environment map. An *environment map* is a texture that gets rendered onto a surface as a reflection. The texture is usually a close approximation of the environment the object is in, and it can be changed from time to time as an object moves. Figure 6.49 shows an example of an environment map.

Figure 6.49 An environment map

Rendered Reflections

Another trick for achieving reflective qualities in games is to build the reflection geometry. This method only works on flat surfaces, such as floors, but it is very effective in giving a scene a realistic reflection. Take a look at how this is done.

1. In Maya, load the lamp model you created earlier.

2. Use the channel box to translate the model up .5 so the bottom of the lamp is flush with the grid, as shown in Figure 6.50.

3. Create a single polygon plane under the lamp, as shown in Figure 6.51.

4. Create a new blinn material and load the tile texture into that material.

5. Apply the new material to the plane (see Figure 6.52).

6. Project the material using the Planar Mapping tool in the y-axis.

7. Set the projection width and height to 1 in the channel box.

8. Bring up the tile material in the attribute editor.

9. Adjust the Transparency slider bar to the right, as shown in Figure 6.53.

10. Now select the lamp in Object mode.

11. Select Mirror Geometry from the Polygons menu, as shown in Figure 6.54. In the Polygon Mirror Options dialog box, select the –Y radio button.

12. Click on the Apply button, as shown in Figure 6.55.

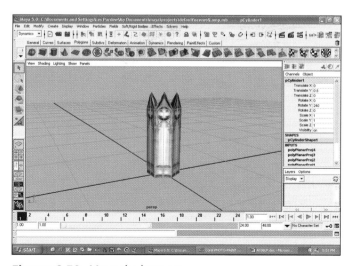

Figure 6.50 Move the lamp up.

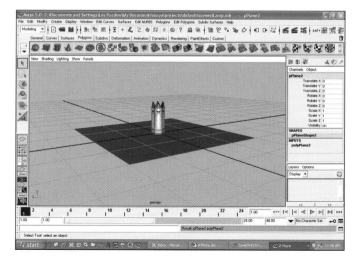

Figure 6.51 Create a polygon plane.

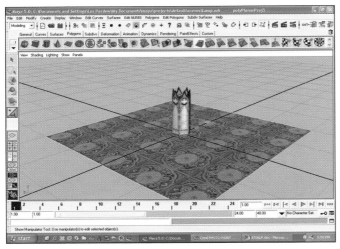

Figure 6.52 The tile material applied to the plane

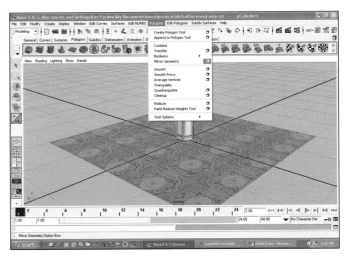

Figure 6.54 Select Mirror Geometry from the Polygons menu.

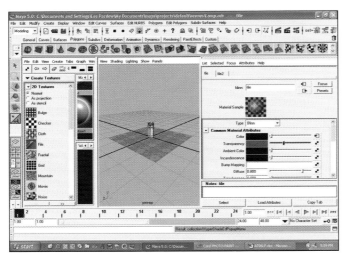

Figure 6.53 Give the tile material some transparency.

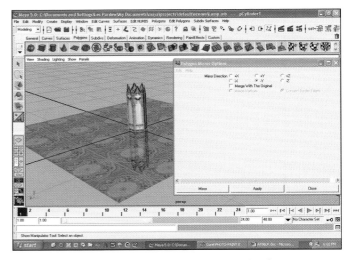

Figure 6.55 The Polygon Mirror Options dialog box

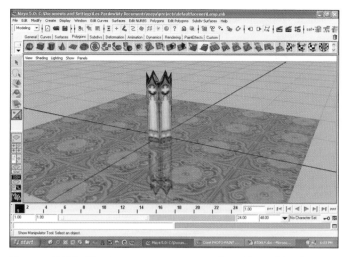

Figure 6.56 The lamp now appears to be reflected in the tiles.

The lamp now looks like it is reflecting off the surface of the plane (see Figure 6.56). This process is effective, but it is also costly because not only does the environment need to be duplicated, but all objects, characters, and special effects need to be mirrored as well. Usually the game artist will have to create a different model for the reflection that has substantially fewer polygons than the original for it to work well.

Summary

In this chapter you learned how game artists create reflections. You also learned about lighting a scene and differences in lights. These techniques are very useful for a game artist to create believable game worlds. Practice building a few game environments to experiment with the principles you have learned.

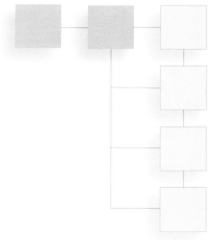

CHAPTER 7

BUILDING ENVIRONMENTS IN NURBS

So far you have built all your 3D models in polygons using polygon-modeling techniques. Polygons are the basic building units in 3D games. More advanced geometry, such as NURBS and subdivisional faces, is too slow when it comes to real-time rendering. You will have to convert any model you build using these other methods to run in the majority of game engines currently in use today. As processors get faster you will see other rendering systems for games.

Even though your end product has to be in polygons, this doesn't mean that using other methods of modeling is not useful. In this chapter you will explore some NURBS modeling techniques for building a racecourse. This chapter will by no means be an in-depth exploration of NURBS. It will, however, give you a starting point for exploring NURBS modeling on your own.

What Are NURBS?

NURBS stands for *Non-Uniform Rational B-Splines*, which is a technical way of saying curves. A *spline* is a curve that is calculated mathematically. Because it is a mathematical

curve, it can be manipulated using math. The nice part about 3D programs is that the computer does all the math, and all the artist has to do is manipulate a series of points called *control vertices* (CV, for short). A control vertex is an editable point in space that influences a curve. Control vertices make it very easy to manipulate complex geometry.

Creating a Racecourse

A racecourse for a game is a specialized type of terrain model. It needs to look like the player is traveling through a world that goes on forever, while at the same time using as little geometry as possible. In the following example you will build an oval outdoor course. You will be using Maya for this project.

1. In Maya there are two types of curves. For this example you will be working with an EP curve. EP stands for *edit point*—the point that separates two segments of a curve. The EP Curve tool is located in the Create menu, as shown in Figure 7.1.

2. Go to the Top view. When you select the EP Curve tool, the cursor will change. To use the tool all you have to do is click with the left mouse button in the work area. Go to the Top view and click the mouse three times in a line, as shown in Figure 7.2.

3. Continue placing edit points to form the shape of the track, as shown in Figure 7.3. When you are almost finished with the shape, press Enter on the keyboard to finish the curve.

4. Now you need to connect the two ends of the curve. Right-click on the curve and select Control Vertex from the marking menu.

5. Select one of the ends of the curve using the Move tool.

6. Hold down the V key and move the end of the curve toward the other end. (The V key is a shortcut key for snapping to a vertex.) The two ends should join, as shown in Figure 7.4. The two ends are not merged; they are simply occupying the

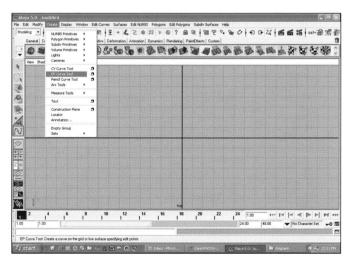

Figure 7.1 The EP Curve tool is located in the Create menu.

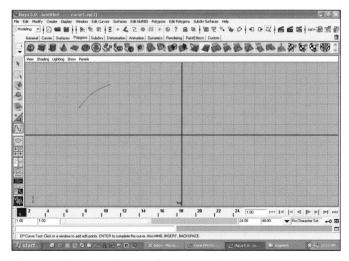

Figure 7.2 Start drawing the curve using the EP Curve tool.

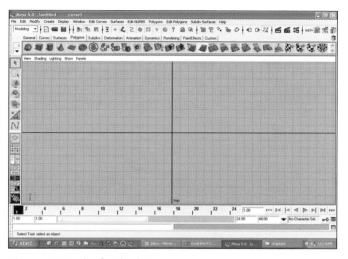

Figure 7.3 The finished EP curve

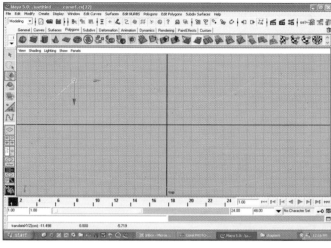

Figure 7.4 Join the two ends of the curve.

same space. This is important to remember when you are selecting them in the future. Always drag a selection box around both ends so you make sure to select them both.

7. Now that the ends are joined, take a few minutes and get used to moving control vertices. Notice all the small dots around the curve. Select one and move it using the Move tool. Watch how the curve moves with the control vertex. Move your curve

around until it looks like Figure 7.4.

8. Now that you have the desired shape, you need to rebuild the curve so that all your edit points are equal distances from each other. Maya has an automatic function for rebuilding curves. To bring up the tool, select Rebuild Curve in the Edit Curves menu, as shown in Figure 7.5.

9. The segment of a curve between edit points is called a *span*. Set the number of spans

for the curve to 30. Make sure all the check boxes in the Rebuild Curve Options dialog box are set exactly as shown in Figure 7.6, and then click on Apply.

10. The curve you have just built will be the outside of the road. Now you need to build the inside. Select the curve in Object mode and duplicate it.

11. Use the Scale tool to reduce the size of the duplicated curve, as shown in Figure 7.7.

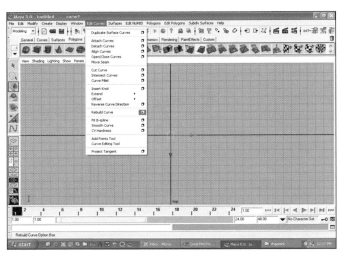

Figure 7.5 The Rebuild Curve menu item

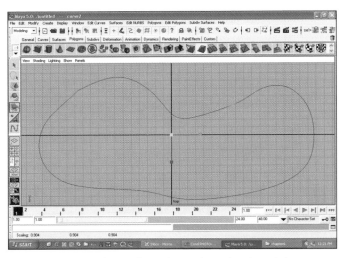

Figure 7.7 Use the Scale tool to reduce the size of the curve.

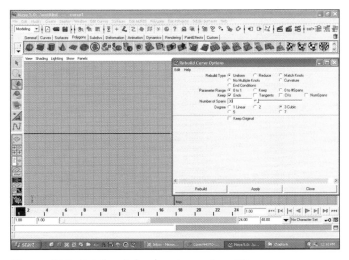

Figure 7.6 Set the dialog box to create a 3D-span curve.

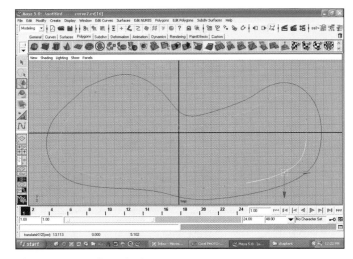

Figure 7.8 Adjust the inner curve.

12. The Scale tool will only work for part of the reduction process. To get the curve to follow the original curve like the two sides of a road, you will have to go in and adjust the curve using the control vertices, as shown in Figure 7.8.

13. Now that you have the sides of the road, you need to create the area around the road. Duplicate and resize two more curves. Place one outside of the road curves and one inside the road curves. Refer to Figure 7.9 for an example of the curves.

14. You will want the banks of the roadside areas to go up from the road. Select the inside and outside curves and move them up a little, as shown in Figure 7.10.

15. You now have the base shape for the road. It is time to add polygons to the areas between the curves. You add polygons using a process called *lofting*. Select the road curves and then select Loft from the Surfaces menu, as shown in Figure 7.11. This will bring up the Loft Options dialog box.

16. This dialog box is a little complicated because Maya allows for many different options when you are lofting. You can explore the many options later; for now, set the options exactly as shown in Figure 7.12. This will give you a set of polygons for the road that are two polygons wide by 100 polygons long.

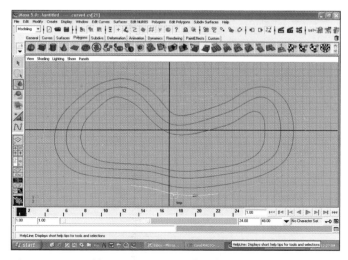

Figure 7.9 Add two more curves for the roadside areas.

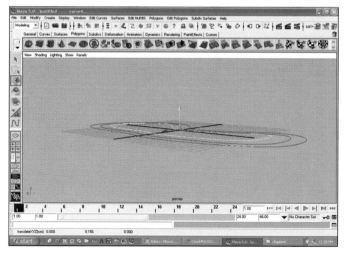

Figure 7.10 Move up the roadside curves.

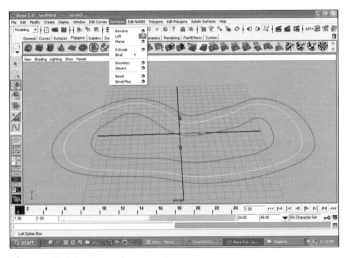

Figure 7.11 The Loft menu item

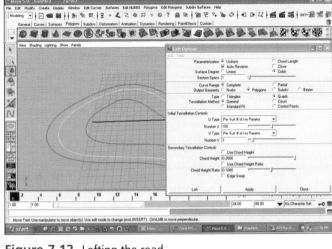

Figure 7.12 Lofting the road

17. You now need to create polygon sets for both of the roadsides. Loft these two areas the same way, but change the Number V option to 2 instead of 3 (see Figure 7.13). You want a polygon set that is only one polygon wide so it will be easier to texture the polygon later.

18. Loft both roadside areas. The model should now look like Figure 7.14. Notice that all the polygons line up with each other. This is important to avoid gaps or seams between sets of polygons.

19. Now that you have the polygons sets in place, you need to check the model for potential problems. In Figure 7.15 I have circled two areas where the model needs to be adjusted to eliminate diamond-shaped polygons, which are more difficult to render than square or rectangle polygons. The problem is compounded if the polygons are large. Diamond-shaped polygons also will create problems when you later try to apply textures to the models.

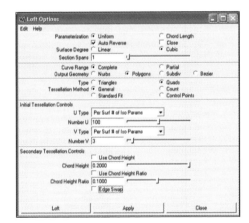

Figure 7.13 Change the Number V option in the dialog box to 2.

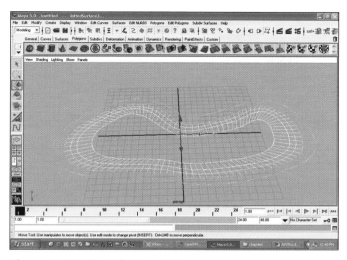

Figure 7.14 The lofted roadsides

Figure 7.15 Problem areas on the model

20. The nice part about working with curves in Maya is that as long as the history is not cleared, the polygons will stay attached to the curves. Moving a control vertex on a curve will move the polygon sets with it. All you have to do is adjust the control vertices, as shown in Figure 7.16, to adjust the underlying polygons.

21. Go through the entire model and adjust all the polygons to make them as square as possi-

ble. Refer to Figure 7.17 for how the model should look when you are finished.

22. Notice that while you adjusted the polygons, you also adjusted the control vertices to line up with each other from one curve to the next. You will now use that to add a hill to your racecourse. Select the control vertices on a corner of the racecourse, as shown in Figure 7.18.

23. Move the selected corner up slightly.

24. Deselect the first and last rows of control vertices along the road and then raise the remaining control vertices a little more, as shown in Figure 7.19. The more you raise each set of vertices, the steeper the grade of the road will be in the final model.

25. Continue to build the hill until you have it to your liking.

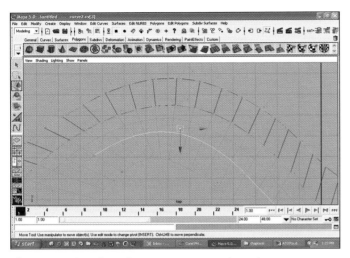

Figure 7.16 Adjust the curves to move the polygons.

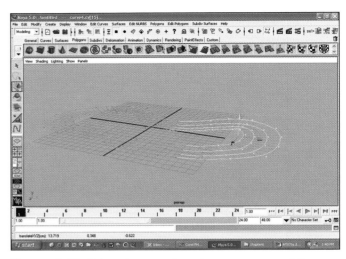

Figure 7.18 Select the control vertices on a corner of the racecourse.

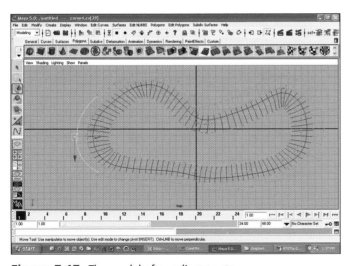

Figure 7.17 The model after adjustments

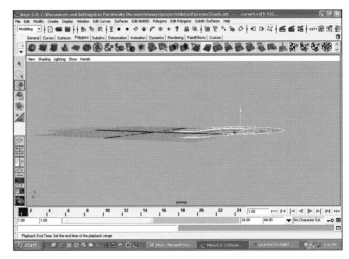

Figure 7.19 Continue raising the successive control vertices to build a hill.

Hint

Hills in racing games are deceiving. It only takes a little rise in elevation to make a big difference in the course. Most people consider a six-percent grade a steep road. Unless you are making an off-road rock climbing game, be careful how steep you make the roads in your models.

26. Racecourses are more fun if the outside of a curve is higher than the inside. In real life, these curves help to keep the car from sliding off the track or rolling while traveling at high speeds. If the racing game is using a simulated physics routine for the cars, the same thing will hold true for the game. Select the control vertices on the outside of a corner, as shown in Figure 7.20, and move them up a little. Do not move them too far or the curve will seem unnatural.

27. Go through each curve and raise the outside edge.

28. Now for a little excitement. What's the fun of racing if you can't catch any air? On a straighter section of the road, select a row of control vertices and move them up to form a small hill, as shown in Figure 7.21.

29. The layout of the road is now almost complete. The next thing you need to do is create the tree line. A *tree line* is the vertical area off the road that blocks your view. Most of the time this line is made up of trees, hence the name tree line. Tree lines are sometimes very complex, but for this game you will make a simple one. Select both the inside and outside curves of the model.

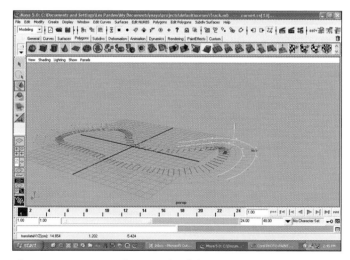

Figure 7.20 Raise the outside of the curve.

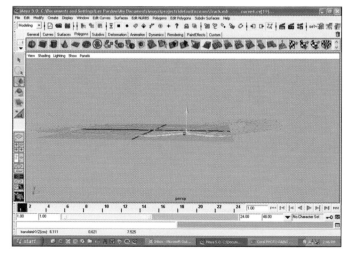

Figure 7.21 Make a small hill for catching air.

30. Next you will build a line of trees to block the view on the edges of the track. Duplicate the curves and move them up, as shown in Figure 7.22.

31. You also want a fence on either side of the road to keep your racecars from going off the track. Select the curves you used for the road.

32. Duplicate the curves and raise them. Don't raise them too far unless you want a huge fence. Figure 7.23 shows the correct height.

33. In the Loft Options dialog box, set the same values you used for the roadsides to loft between the new and old curves, as shown in Figure 7.24.

34. It is time to start adding some textures to your model. Open Hypershade and create new materials for the textures. All the texture files are on the CD in the directory for this chapter. Load all the .tga files, road.bmp, and side.bmp. Rename the materials to match the textures, as shown in Figure 7.25. The

black-and-white mask files go with the .tga files. The mask files are for use with some game engines that require a mask for transparency. I will not be using those files in this example, but they are included on the CD to help you with your projects.

35. Select the road polygon set.

36. Apply the road material to the selected polygons. Notice that the material looks distorted, as shown in Figure 7.26.

37. Unitize the material (see Figure 7.27). Many of the textures will

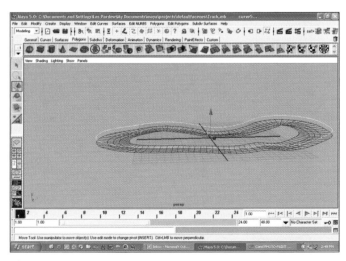

Figure 7.22 Duplicate and move up the new curves.

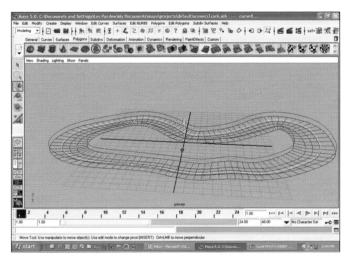

Figure 7.23 Raise the duplicated road curves.

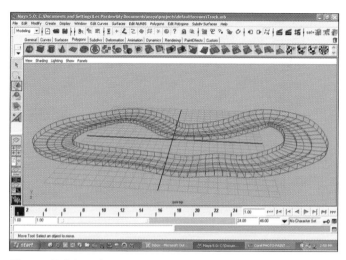

Figure 7.24 Loft polygon sets between the new and old curves.

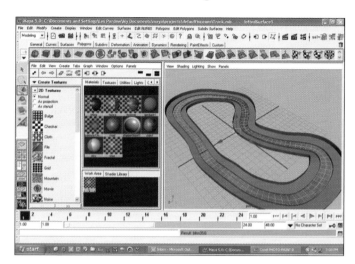

Figure 7.26 Apply the road texture to the model.

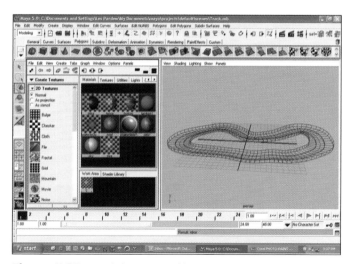

Figure 7.25 Load the texture files into Hypershade.

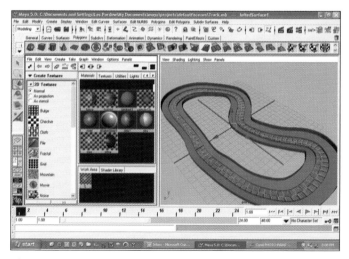

Figure 7.27 Unitize the road materials.

be rotated incorrectly. You can come back and fix the problem after you finish applying the rest of the materials.

38. Apply the side material to both sides of the road.

39. Unitize the material. It should now look like Figure 7.28. Notice that because you are using a polygon set that is only one polygon wide, the textures map correctly.

40. Apply the trline material to the tree line polygons and unitize those materials like you did the others. The model should now look like Figure 7.29.

Hint

The trline texture is a Targa file with an alpha channel. The alpha channel gives the texture a transparent area because it is set up with a mask. Take a look at the texture file in Corel Photo Paint to see how the alpha channel was made. You can see the channels in the Docker under the Channels tab.

41. Now apply the fence material to the fence polygon sets and unitize them, as shown in Figure 7.30.

42. Now you have to deal with the road textures. Go to the Top view and select the road polygons, as shown in Figure 7.31.

43. Convert the selection to UVs by selecting Selection, Convert to UVs from the Edit Polygons menu.

44. Rotate the UVs 90 degrees. You can access the Rotate UVs dialog box by selecting Textures, Rotate UVs from the Edit Polygons menu. The rotated UVs should look like Figure 7.32.

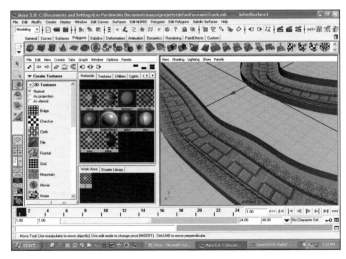

Figure 7.28 Apply the side material to the roadsides.

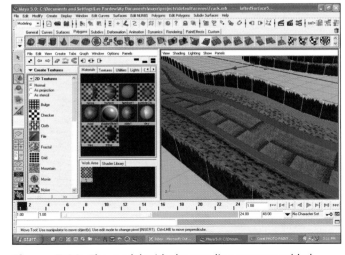

Figure 7.29 The model with the tree line textures added

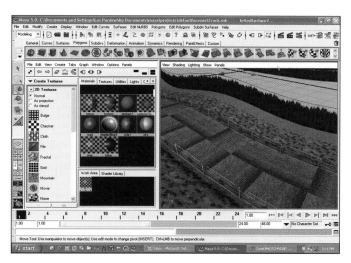

Figure 7.30 The fence material added

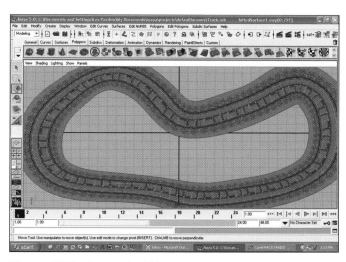

Figure 7.32 Rotate the UVs

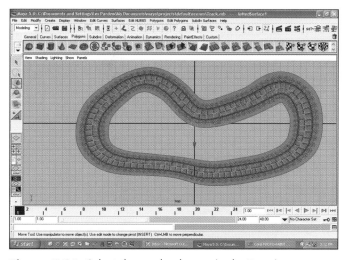

Figure 7.31 Select the road polygons in the Top view.

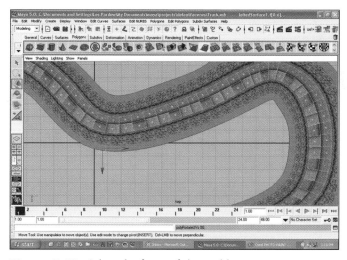

Figure 7.33 Select the faces of the problem textures.

45. You fixed a little more than half of the texture problems of the road. You need to select the remaining problem textures individually. Change the selection mode to Face and select the problem textures, as shown in Figure 7.33.

46. Convert the selected faces to UVs.

47. Rotate the selected UVs 270 degrees. You can either change the number in the Rotate UVs dialog box or simply hit the Apply button three times with the default 90 degrees option selected. The road should now look like Figure 7.34.

You now have a functioning track with textures. You could stop here, but this track doesn't look very good because there is nothing along the sides of the track to break up the scenery. In most racing games, the artist puts many interesting elements along the course to give the game personality. These elements can include buildings, people, parked cars, signs, and more often than not, trees. For this exercise you will add a number of trees because they are the most common sideline element.

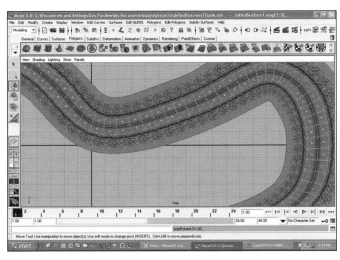

Figure 7.34 The corrected textures on the road

Adding Scenery Elements to the Racecourse

You are going to build a simple tree to put in the racecourse as a background scenery element. There are three basic approaches to building trees for games—billboards, fans, and geometry.

The most basic approach is to create what is sometimes called a billboard. A *billboard* is a single polygon with a picture of a tree, character, or other background element. The billboard is rotated so that it always faces the camera. This system has the advantage of using the least number of polygons (one), so you can add a maximum number of trees to the game. The disadvantage is that the flat nature of the tree is very noticeable.

A tree *fan* is similar to a billboard in that a texture of a tree is applied to a single polygon, but rather than rotating the image to the camera, the polygon is duplicated and rotated once or twice to form a fan. It is kind of like taking a couple cardboard cutouts and intersecting them in the middle. This method has the advantage of not using very many polygons and still giving the tree a 3D look. The problem with this method is that the fans sometimes cast weird shadows that reveal the artificial nature of the tree.

The final method is to build a tree (leaves and all) out of polygons. This method will give the trees in the game the most realistic look possible. The problem with this method is that trees are organic elements, and organic elements usually require many polygons to look right. Imagine how many polygons it would take to build a tree

if you only used one polygon for each leaf. It is somewhat impractical for a high-speed racing game.

For this racing game you will use the second method—creating fans and planting the trees along the sides of the racecourse. You should hide the racecourse by pressing Ctrl+H so it will be easier to build the tree model.

1. You start with a single polygon. Create one that is twice as high as it is wide, as shown in Figure 7.35.

2. Move the polygon up one unit so the base is even with the origin point.

3. Apply the tree texture to the polygon, as shown in Figure 7.36. If you were using the billboard method, you would be finished at this point.

4. Duplicate the polygon. As I stated earlier, normals only face in one direction. You need to see this polygon from both sides. You duplicate the polygon for exactly that purpose.

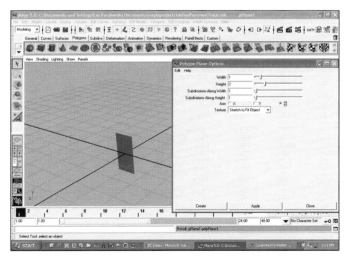

Figure 7.35 Create a single polygon.

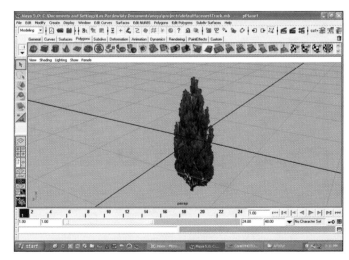

Figure 7.36 Apply the tree texture to the polygon.

5. With the duplicate polygon selected, reverse the normals, as shown in Figure 7.37.

6. Combine the two polygons into the same object. You will find the Combine function under the Polygons menu.

7. Now duplicate the new object and rotate the duplicate 60 degrees.

8. Repeat Step 7, but this time rotate the new duplicate 120 degrees. The tree should now look like Figure 7.38.

9. Combine the three objects into a single object.

10. Now you need to size the tree so it is the same height as the tree line. Bring back the model of the racecourse by selecting Show, Show Last Hidden from the Display menu, and move the tree so the bottom is level with the bottom of the tree line.

11. Size the tree so it is the same height as the tree line, as shown in Figure 7.39.

Hint

Maya sometimes has difficulty sorting scenes with multiple transparent textures. You might find that when you are placing objects like the tree you just created, they appear behind the tree line when they should be in front of it. This can sometimes get very confusing. Hang in there—it is only a sorting problem. The guys at Alias are working on it and should have it fixed in their next edition.

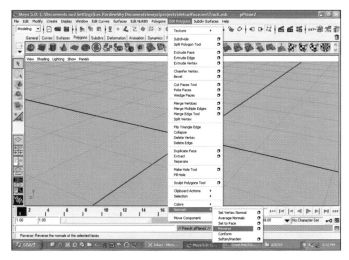

Figure 7.37 Reverse the normals of the duplicate polygon.

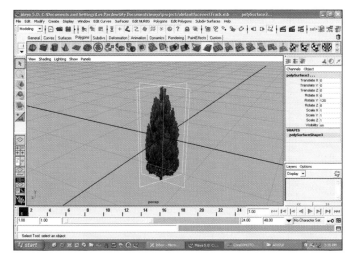

Figure 7.38 The tree fan

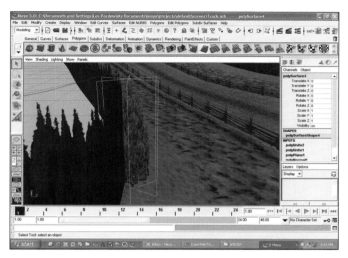

Figure 7.39 Size the tree to fit the model.

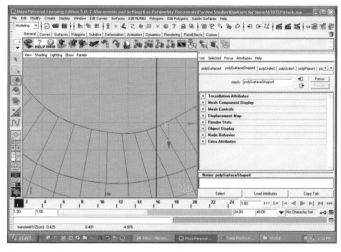

Figure 7.40 Move the tree to the edge of the model.

12. Next you need to plant some trees. Go to the Top view. Make sure you have Wire-Frame Shaded turned on.

13. The critical areas for the tree are on the inside of the curves near the tree line. You need to plant trees coming out of the tree line so the player doesn't see a flat polygon edge as he comes around the corner. Place the tree so that it intersects the tree line, as shown in Figure 7.40.

14. Place several trees along the tree line to break up the edge that will be seen by the player. Create each new tree by duplicating the first tree. Refer to Figure 7.41 for spacing.

15. Continue to duplicate and plant trees throughout the course. Pay attention to the inside curves. When you are finished, your model should look similar to Figure 7.42.

16. Now go to the Perspective view. As shown in Figure 7.43, you will notice that many of the trees are either floating above the ground or sunk below the ground. It is easiest to see this in the Flat Shaded mode.

17. Select each tree and move it so that it intersects the ground correctly, as shown in Figure 7.44.

18. When you are finished, go to Shaded mode. Your model should now look similar to Figure 7.45.

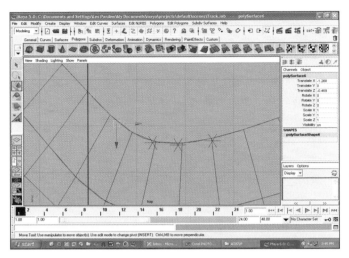

Figure 7.41 Space the trees along the edge of the model.

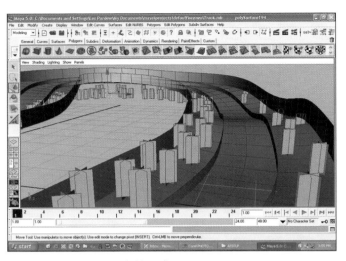

Figure 7.43 The model has floating trees.

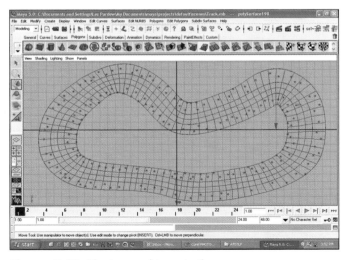

Figure 7.42 Plant several trees in the scene.

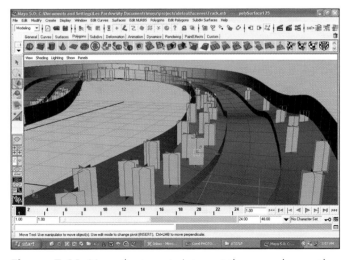

Figure 7.44 Move the trees to intersect the ground correctly.

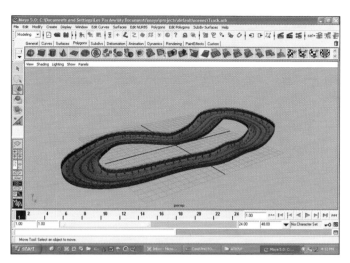

Figure 7.45 The trees after being moved

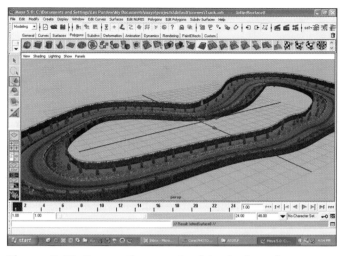

Figure 7.46 Reverse the normals of the duplicate fences.

19. Remember how you duplicated and reversed the normals on the tree polygon? You need to do the same thing with the polygons forming the fence. Otherwise, the fence will disappear if it is seen from the back side. Select the fence polygon sets and duplicate the polygons.

20. Reverse the normals of the duplicate fences, as shown in Figure 7.46.

21. While you're at it, you need to check the direction of the nor-mals for the rest of the track. Turn on backface culling.

22. Reverse the normals of any polygon set that is facing the wrong direction.

23. Save the current model.

Level of Detail

The current model you have is okay, but it might not look good on close scrutiny. It is what you would call a *base* or *low-resolution* model. In many racing games, several versions of a course model are used. These differ-ent models represent *levels of detail*, or LOD, as they are sometimes referred to in the industry. The way it works is that one model is substituted for another depending on an object's dis-tance from the player. For example, a more detailed high-resolution model is used near the player for maximum detail. Farther away from the player, a low-resolution model is used because the detail is lost in the distance.

The higher-resolution model has more polygons and larger textures than the lower-resolution model. I won't go into a lot of detail about

LOD in this book, but I'll give you a quick look at how to create a higher-resolution model from the base low-resolution model.

1. Select the polygon face set that makes up the road.

2. Change the selection mode to Face and select all the faces of the road set, as shown in Figure 7.47.

3. Select Subdivide in the Edit Polygons menu to access the Subdivide dialog box.

4. Set the subdivisions to 1 and click on Apply.

5. Repeat the process to subdivide the other polygon sets in the model. When you are finished, the model should look similar to Figure 7.48.

6. The next step for creating a high-resolution model is to adjust individual vertices to add more interesting terrain features. The adjustments should be small so that the high-

resolution model does not change dramatically from the base model.

7. After you finish the geometry adjustments, the last step is to replace the low-resolution textures with higher-resolution textures. You can change the textures by simply loading the new texture files into the material in Hypershade.

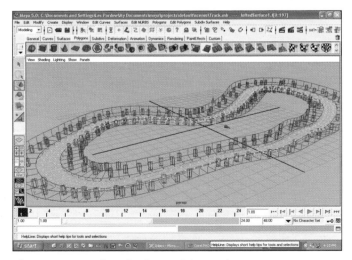

Figure 7.47 Select the faces of the road.

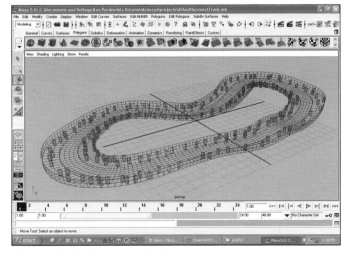

Figure 7.48 The subdivided model

Prelighting the Racecourse

As you learned in the previous chapter, the higher the model's resolution, the better prelighting will work. Now that you have a higher-resolution version of the model, you can set up the lighting. If you want more detail in the lighting you can subdivide the model further. Just remember that game engines have polygon limits, so be careful how many times you subdivide.

1. Create a directional light. Set the intensity to 5 and make the light a little yellow.

2. Adjust the position of the light so it shines on the course from an angle, as shown in Figure 7.49.

3. Select the light and the entire model, as shown in Figure 7.50.

4. Prelight the model with the same setting you used to prelight the room in Chapter 6. Figure 7.51 shows the model after prelighting.

Building Skyboxes

A *skybox* is a model used for the sky and distant terrain features. It is a separate model from the racecourse, and it is rendered differently than the racecourse model. The game engine renders the skybox last, after everything else is finished rendering. This keeps the distant terrain features in the back, behind the rest of the course. Because it is rendered last, you don't need to build the skybox large enough to cover the entire course. In fact, most skyboxes are relatively small compared to the world geometry.

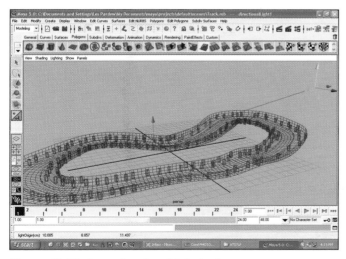

Figure 7.49 Put a directional light in the scene.

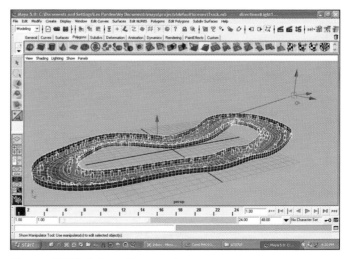

Figure 7.50 Select all scene elements.

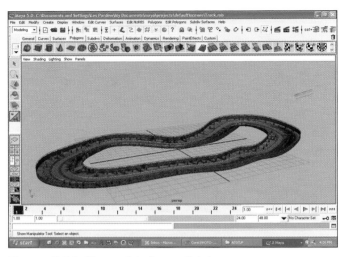

Figure 7.51 The model after prelighting

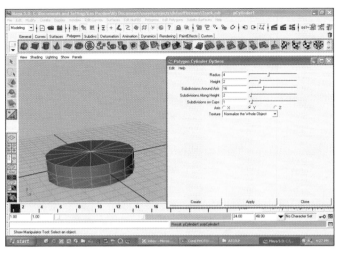

Figure 7.52 Create a cylinder.

You will build a simple skybox for the racecourse. Hide the current scene so it will be easier to work on the skybox.

1. Create a polygon cylinder, as shown in Figure 7.52.

2. Delete the top and bottom faces.

3. Apply the horizon material using the Cylindrical Mapping tool, as shown in Figure 7.53.

4. Create a polygon sphere slightly larger than the cylinder, as shown in Figure 7.54.

5. Go to the Side view.

6. Delete the lower five rows of faces from the sphere.

7. Apply the sky material using the Cylindrical Mapping tool, as shown in Figure 7.55.

8. Turn on backface culling to see the inside of the skybox. It should look like Figure 7.56.

The skybox is now finished. Figure 7.57 shows how it will work for the horizon of the game.

For this example you used a clear blue sky and a mountain horizon. You can experiment with different sky textures and horizons to get different looks. Some games have very complex systems for developing skyboxes, including cloud-generation programs and the movement of the sun across the sky.

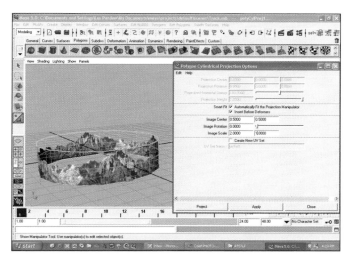

Figure 7.53 Apply the horizon material.

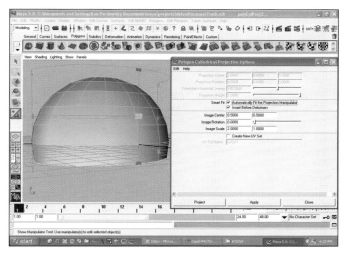

Figure 7.55 Apply the sky material to the sphere.

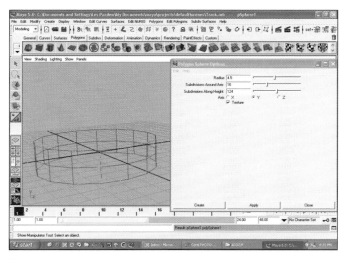

Figure 7.54 Create a polygon sphere.

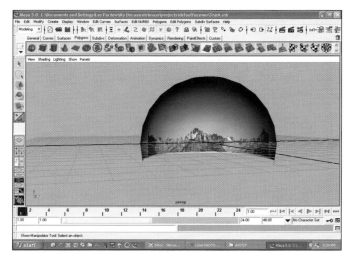

Figure 7.56 The completed skybox

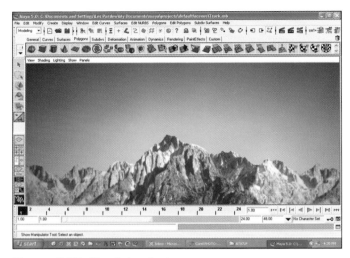

Figure 7.57 The skybox horizon

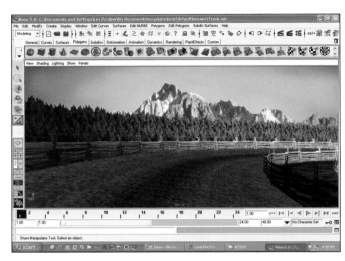

Figure 7.58 View of the finished racecourse

Summary

Congratulations! You have just fin-ished building a racecourse. Figure 7.58 shows a mockup of how the race-course will look in a game.

In this chapter I covered some very basic NURBS modeling techniques. As you can see, NURBS modeling is a very powerful way to create models. Continue to experiment with NURBS to see other ways in which they might be helpful in your modeling efforts.

I also covered techniques for building specialized terrain models, such as racecourses, as well as level of detail and building skyboxes. Many of the techniques you learned are used in other types of games too, such as adventure games of and first-person shooters. Try to build some other environments using the same techniques.

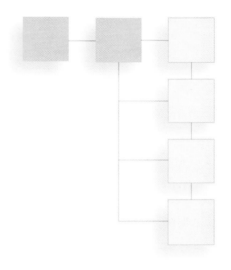

CHAPTER 8

BUILDING GAME OBJECTS

Objects in games are non-character game elements that are separate from the environment geometry. An *object* is something that can be moved or manipulated in the game. When you build a set, items such as walls, columns, floors, mountains, and so on, do not move and are built into the set geometry. Items such as swords or guns are things that a player can pick up. Because they can be moved, these items are defined as *game objects*. Although characters could be defined as game objects, they are typically more complex than objects and there-fore have their own designation as characters.

The trend in games is to have more and more objects. Like in real life, in a game you can interact with your environment. In real life, you can pick up a rock and throw it. You can break windows if you want. You can get in a car and drive. Players want to do the same things in a game environment.

When they are setting up a game environment, the development team needs to designate the items that are part of the environment and those that are separate objects. Objects take more programming and processor time than scene elements. As an artist, you have to be constantly aware of the limitations of the game engine. Usually the development team will give you some guidelines on the number and scale of objects possible in the game.

Types of Objects

A game object can be almost any-thing. Some objects are very simple, such as a rock or a piece of paper. Other objects are complex, such as cars or helicopters. The types of objects in a game depend on the type of game. For example, a racing game might have cars or some other vehicles. An adventure game might have clue items, such as notes or keys. A first-person shooter might have weapons or ammunition lying around. Most objects will fall into the following categories:

- Pick-ups (objects the player collects)

- Power-ups (objects that give the player an advantage in speed, strength, and so on)

- Movable items (objects such as doors, chests, furniture, and so on)

- Destructible items (objects such as barrels, windows, walls, and so on)

- Controllable items (objects such as cars, trucks, tanks, and so on)

- Animated items (objects such as water fountains, torches, fires, and so on)

Naming Conventions

Each of these object types is used differently in game development. Most games have a naming convention for designating the role the object will play in the game. For example, a door might have a file name of drsl04, where the "dr" means door, the "sl" refers to the type of door (in this case sliding), and the "04" means that it is the fourth door created for the game. It is often wise to set up the naming conventions at the beginning of a project so the art files are well organized.

Building a Game Object

In the project for this chapter, you will build an ATV (*All-Terrain Vehicle*). You will build the ATV so it is ready for animation, with all the moving parts as separate pieces. Bring up Maya so you can get started.

1. You will be using a template to help you build the ATV. Create a single polygon plane, as shown in Figure 8.1.

2. Create a new material and load the ATV texture from Chapter 8 directory on the CD.

3. Apply the new material to the plane, as shown in Figure 8.2.

Hint

The ATV texture is called a blanket texture. In a *blanket texture,* most (if not all) of the textures used on an object are on one piece of art. The advantage of a blanket texture is that there is only one file for the game to keep track of. It is also easier for the artist to edit the texture's UVs. It is common for some objects and almost all characters to use blanket textures.

4. Duplicate the plane and rotate it 90 degrees around the x-axis so it is perpendicular to the first plane.

5. Now duplicate the plane again and rotate it 90 degrees around the y-axis, as shown in Figure 8.3.

6. Now you need to move and rescale the textures so they line up with each other in your template. You will use the Planar Mapping tool to accomplish this. Select the horizontal plane and go to the Overhead view.

7. Use the Planar Mapping tool to project the image on the selected plane in the y-direction.

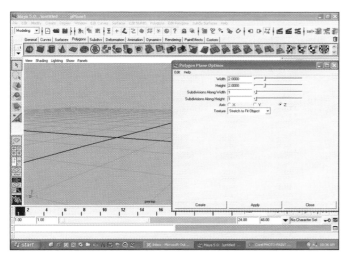

Figure 8.1 Create a single polygon plane.

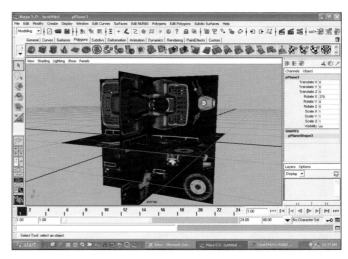

Figure 8.3 Duplicate and rotate the plane.

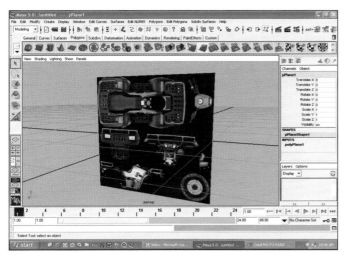

Figure 8.2 Apply the texture to the plane.

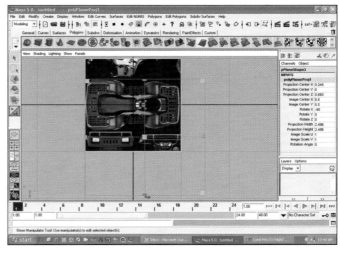

Figure 8.4 Scale and center the Top view image.

8. The Planar Mapping tool has several manipulators. The light blue boxes on the corners are for sizing objects equally. You can use these manipulators to keep your object scales correct. Select one of the corner manipulators and expand the texture image until the Top view of the ATV is about the width of the polygon.

9. Use either the center light-blue box or the lines extending from it to move the rescaled texture

so it is centered over the midpoint of the scene, as shown in Figure 8.4.

10. Now go to the Front view and scale the side image of the ATV the same way you did the Top view. It should look like Figure 8.5.

11. Go to the remaining plane from the Side view and line up the Front view image with the other two images. You will need to go back and forth between the Side and Perspective views

to get it right. Refer to Figure 8.6 for an example of how it should look.

12. Your template is now finished and ready to be used in modeling the ATV. Activate the X-ray view mode. Start with the body. Create a polygon cube, as shown in Figure 8.7.

13. Scale the cube using the Scale tool so that it approximates the scale of the body, as shown in Figure 8.8.

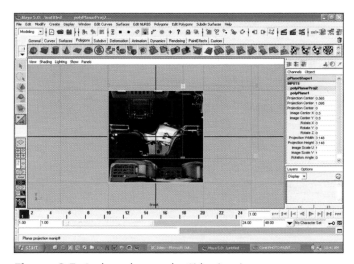

Figure 8.5 Scale and move the Side view image.

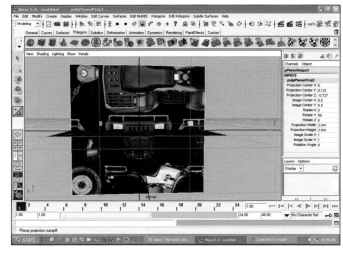

Figure 8.6 Scale and move the Front view image.

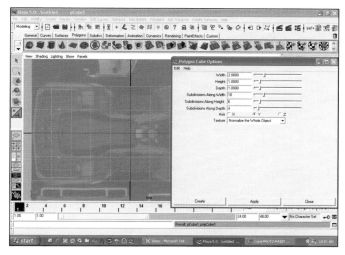

Figure 8.7 Create a polygon cube for the body of the ATV.

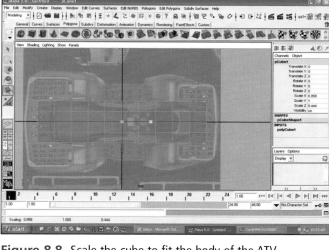

Figure 8.8 Scale the cube to fit the body of the ATV.

14. Use the Scale tool to shape the contour of the vertices, as shown in Figure 8.9.

15. Continue scaling each row of vertices until the cube conforms to the contour of the body as seen from the Top view. The cube should now look like Figure 8.10.

16. Go to the Front view and shape the contours of the cube from that direction, as shown in Figure 8.11. Don't get confused by the fact that you are looking at the side of the ATV in the Front view. I usually put the most complex view in the Front view.

17. Now you need to shape the body of the ATV from the Side view. Notice that the Side view template does not help you here because the radiator obscures the body. Just follow the example in Figure 8.12.

18. Shaping in the three Orthographic views will only do part of the work. You must do the rest in the Perspective view. You need to round many of the corners, especially around the seat and gas tank. Do this by adjusting the vertices.

19. Now you need to extend the body in the front and back to where the axles are. Use Figure 8.13 as a guide to how the body should be shaped.

20. Now you will work on the fenders. Create another cube, as shown in Figure 8.14.

21. Adjust the vertices of the cube so it follows the contour of the fender, as shown in Figure 8.15.

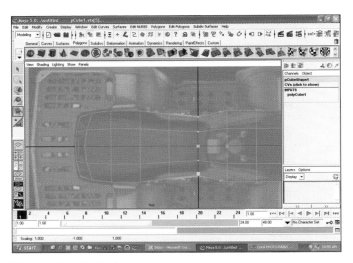

Figure 8.9 Scale the vertices.

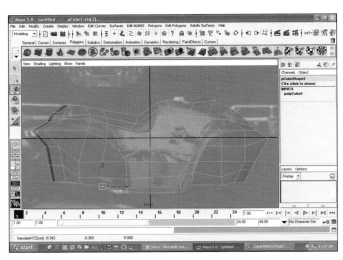

Figure 8.11 Shape the contours of the side of the ATV.

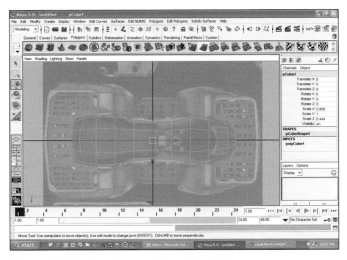

Figure 8.10 The shaped sides of the ATV

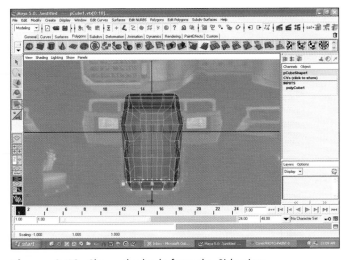

Figure 8.12 Shape the body from the Side view.

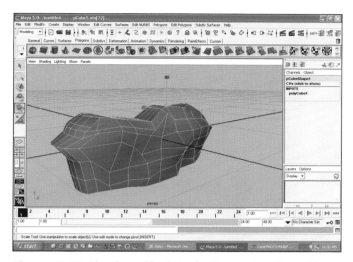

Figure 8.13 The shaped body in the Perspective view with templates hidden

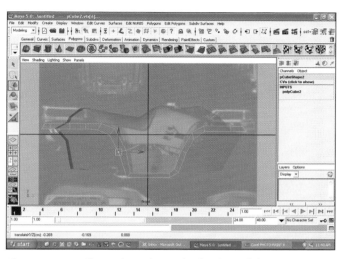

Figure 8.15 Shape the cube to the fenders of the ATV.

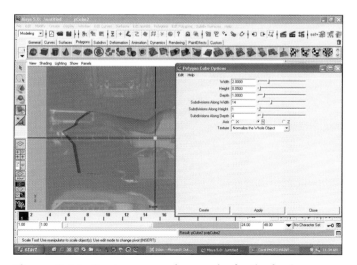

Figure 8.14 Create a new polygon cube for the fender.

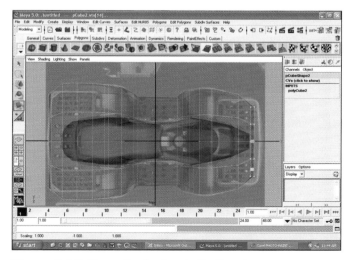

Figure 8.16 Shape the fenders in the Top view.

22. In the Top view, adjust the vertices to follow the shape of the fenders, as shown in Figure 8.16.

23. Touch up the shape of the fenders in the Perspective view.

24. Create a new polygon cube, as shown in Figure 8.17.

25. Move and fit the new cube to the tray behind the seat, as shown in Figure 8.18.

26. Shape the tray from the top, as shown in Figure 8.19.

27. Duplicate the tray and move the duplicate to the front tray of the ATV.

28. Adjust the front tray to fit the template, as shown in Figure 8.20.

29. The front tray is smaller than the rear tray, so make sure you shape it from the Top view as well.

30. Now you need to make the rail bars for the trays. Create a new polygon cube, as shown in Figure 8.21.

31. Move the new cube to the rails on the back of the ATV.

32. Adjust the vertices so the geometry conforms to the shape of the back rail, as shown in Figure 8.22.

33. Select the faces of the two ends of the rail.

34. Extrude the faces to form the side rails, as shown in Figure 8.23.

35. Extrude the rails two more times, rotating and moving them to form the anchor of the rails, as shown in Figure 8.24.

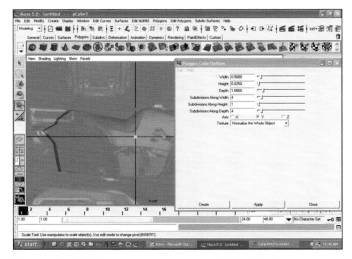

Figure 8.17 Create a new polygon cube for the tray.

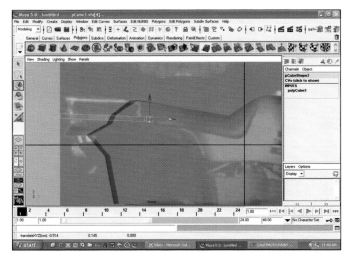

Figure 8.18 Scale the cube to fit the rear tray of the ATV.

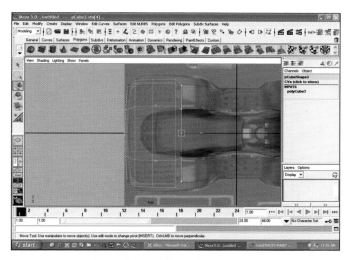

Figure 8.19 Shape the tray from the Top view.

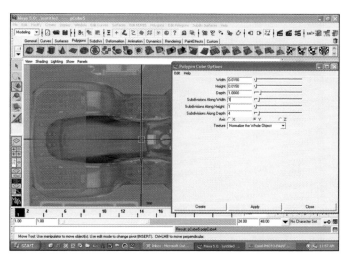

Figure 8.21 Create a new polygon cube for the rail bars.

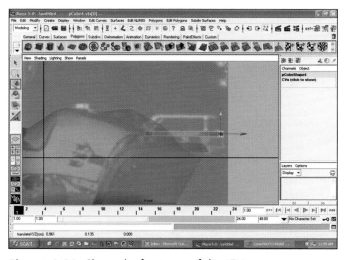

Figure 8.20 Shape the front tray of the ATV.

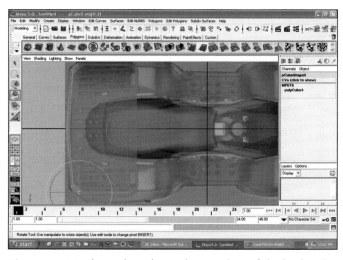

Figure 8.22 Shape the cube to the template of the back rail.

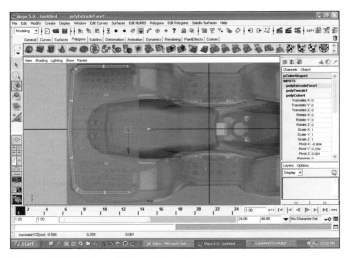

Figure 8.23 Extrude the side rails.

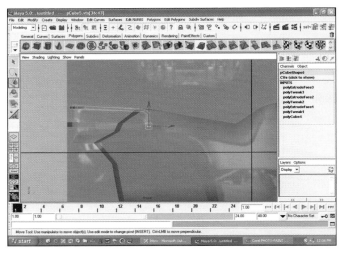

Figure 8.24 Extrude the rails to form the anchor into the tray.

36. Duplicate the finished rail and move it to the front tray.

37. Rotate and scale the rail to fit the front tray.

38. Create a new polygon cube for the front grill, as shown in Figure 8.25.

39. Shape the new cube to fit the grill of the ATV, as shown in Figure 8.26.

40. Now create another box for the radiator, as shown in Figure 8.27.

41. Shape the box to fit the radiator. This will be easy from the front, but there is no reference from the side. Use Figure 8.28 as a guide for how it should look.

42. Now select all the objects you have created so far and combine them into a single object, as shown in Figure 8.29. Hide the templates.

43. Apply the ATV material to the ATV model, as shown in Figure 8.30.

44. In the Front view, select all the faces that are facing directly toward or directly away from the view, as in Figure 8.31. You will need to look at several views to make sure you get all of them.

45. Use the Planar Mapping tool to project the material in the z-direction.

46. Move and scale the material until the texture is placed correctly, as shown in Figure 8.32.

47. Now select the faces on the top of the model.

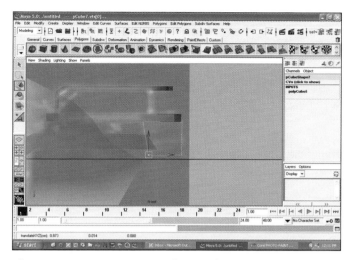

Figure 8.25 Create a new polygon cube.

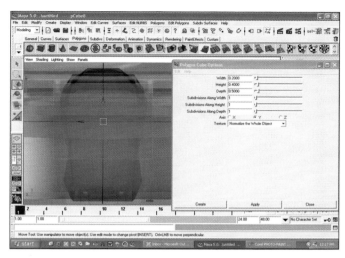

Figure 8.27 Create another new polygon cube.

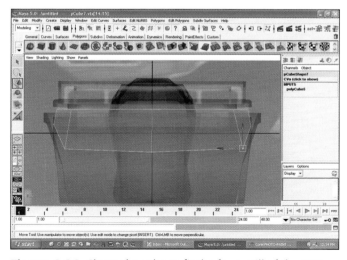

Figure 8.26 Shape the cube to fit the front grill of the ATV.

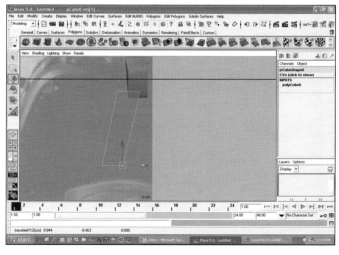

Figure 8.28 Shape the cube for the radiator.

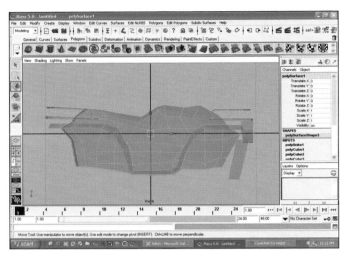

Figure 8.29 Combine all the objects into a single object.

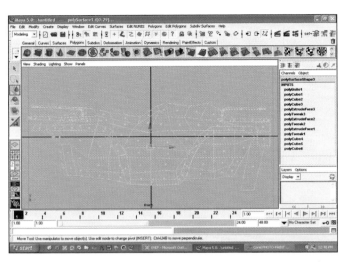

Figure 8.31 Select the faces that will make up the sides of the ATV.

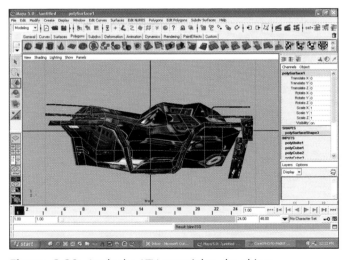

Figure 8.30 Apply the ATV material to the object.

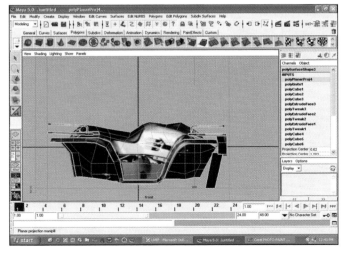

Figure 8.32 Fit the texture to the model.

48. Project and fit the material so the Top view image fits correctly to the model, as shown in Figure 8.33.

49. Select the faces on the front of the ATV and project the Front view image onto them, as shown in Figure 8.34.

50. Now select the faces on the back of the body, below the fenders, and project the taillight image, as shown in Figure 8.35.

51. If you rotate the ATV, you will notice that there are some seams between projections. For example, the side images don't line up with the top images. You can use the Texture Editor to adjust the UVs. Bring up the Two-Panel Side-by-Side view.

52. Change the left panel to Panel, UV Texture Editor in the Panels menu.

53. Change the selection type to UVs for both windows.

54. It will be much easier to adjust UVs if you are only seeing the UVs that are immediately around the work area. In the View menu of the Texture Editor, select View Connected Faces, as shown in Figure 8.36.

55. Now you can use the Move tool to adjust the UVs so they match up with each other. Look at Figure 8.37 to see how I moved the UVs.

56. Now I've spotted another problem that can't be fixed by moving UVs. In Figure 8.38, notice where the rail texture is projected on the trays. I have circled the problem in red.

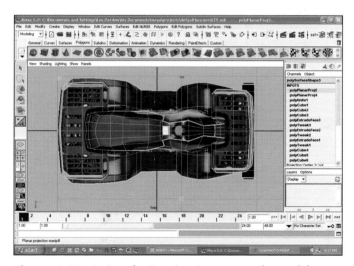

Figure 8.33 Project the Top view image onto the model.

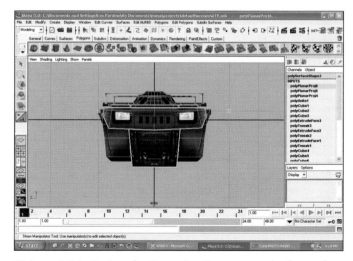

Figure 8.34 Project the Front view image onto the front of the ATV.

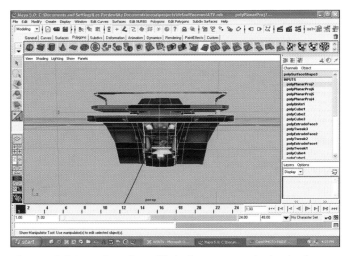

Figure 8.35 Project the taillight image onto the back of the ATV.

Figure 8.37 The adjusted UVs

Figure 8.36 Select View Connected Faces from the View menu.

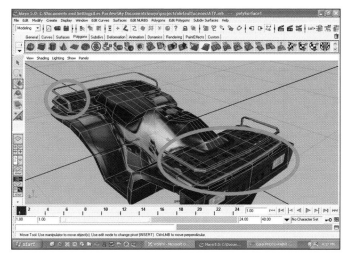

Figure 8.38 Problems in the texture

Figure 8.39 Paint out the rails on the texture.

You can only fix this problem in the texture itself. Open the texture in a paint program and paint out the rails on the Top view of the ATV (see Figure 8.39).

57. Save the new texture as ATV1.

58. The CD contains a texture named ATV1. Load it into the ATV material in place of ATV.

59. You no longer need the model as a single object. Separate the objects, as shown in Figure 8.40.

60. You will need two more materials, but you will be using colors instead of texture files. Bring up Hypershade and create a new material. Name the new material *gray*.

61. Instead of clicking on the checkerboard icon to the right of the color slider, click on the gray solid square on the left side to bring up the color palette.

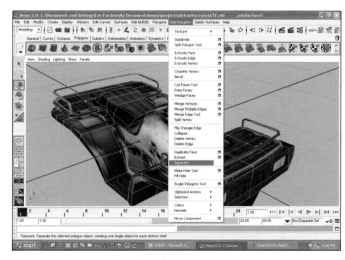

Figure 8.40 Separate the objects.

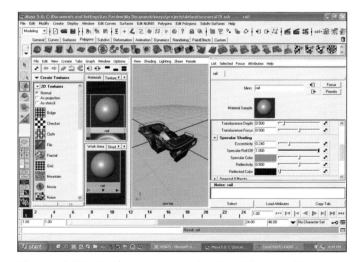

Figure 8.41 Set the new material so it will have a shiny appearance.

62. For this example you want a cool, light gray color, so move the color selection toward blue and increase the value to lighten the color.

63. Set the Specular Roll Off and Eccentricity options as shown in Figure 8.41.

64. Make a new material and name it *black*.

65. Move the color slider so the color square is completely black.

66. This color needs to be a matte black. Set the Specular Roll Off and Reflectivity options as shown in Figure 8.42.

67. Select the rails and apply the gray material to them.

68. Soften the edges of the rails. They should now look similar to Figure 8.43.

69. Select the faces on the underside of the fenders.

70. Apply the black material to the selected faces, as shown in Figure 8.44.

71. Select the faces on the bottom of the ATV body, as shown in Figure 8.45. Apply the black material to the selected faces.

You now have the main body elements of the ATV. You still need to complete a lot of texture cleanup for the model, though. Go over the model in detail to fix any areas that have seams or don't look right.

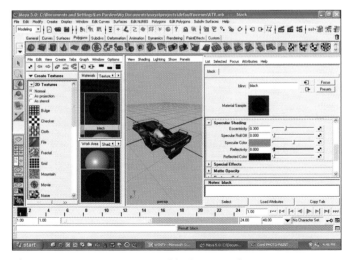

Figure 8.42 Create a matte black material.

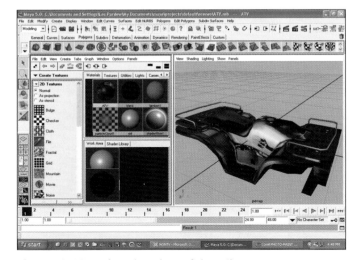

Figure 8.43 Soften the edges of the rails.

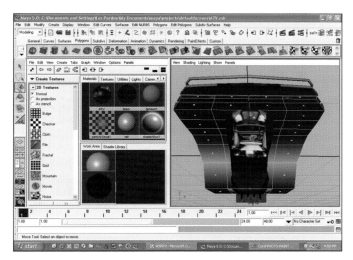

Figure 8.44 Apply black to the underside of the fenders.

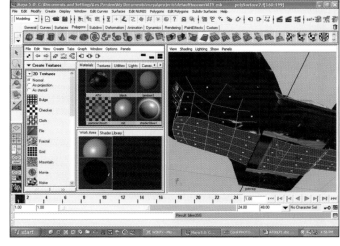

Figure 8.45 Select the faces that intersect the front tray.

Moving Parts

The ATV is meant to be an animated object. You must create separately the parts of the model that move so they can be animated. These parts include the handlebars, the rear struts, and the tires. You can start by creating the tires.

1. Create a cylinder with the attributes shown in Figure 8.46.

2. The texture for the side of the tire is located on the ATV blanket. Apply that texture to the sides of the tire geometry, as shown in Figure 8.47.

3. Now use the Planar Mapping tool to scale and move the texture to fit the tire, as shown in Figure 8.48.

4. Select the inside center vertices and scale them in to form the shape of the tire rims. Look at Figure 8.49 for reference.

5. Cylindrical mapping is difficult with a blanket texture. Create a new material and load the tire texture.

6. Use the Cylindrical Mapping tool to project the tire texture onto the tire, as shown in Fig-

ure 8.50. Pay attention to the setting on the tool.

7. Move the tires into the wheel wells of the ATV, as shown in Figure 8.51. Duplicate the tire as needed. Notice that the tires are small. I enlarged the front tires by 115 percent and the rear tires by 125 percent

8. Now you will build the struts. Create a polygon cylinder, as shown in Figure 8.52.

9. Bring up the templates and shape the cylinder to fit the axle, as shown in Figure 8.53.

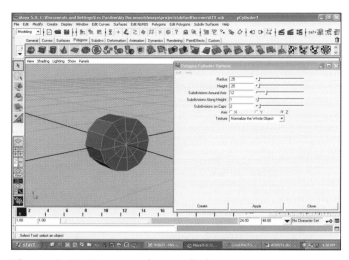

Figure 8.46 Create a polygon cylinder.

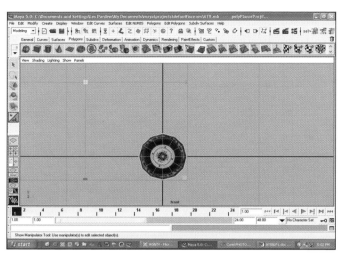

Figure 8.48 Scale and fit the tire texture to the tire model.

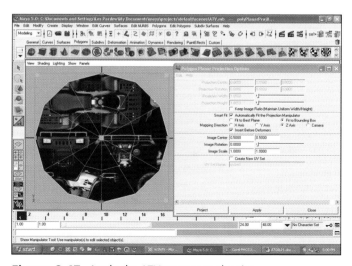

Figure 8.47 Apply the ATV texture to the tire.

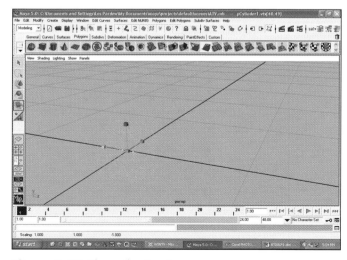

Figure 8.49 Shape the tire rims.

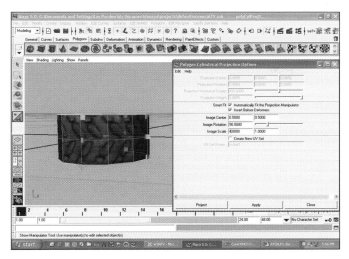

Figure 8.50 Project the tire texture using the Cylindrical Mapping tool.

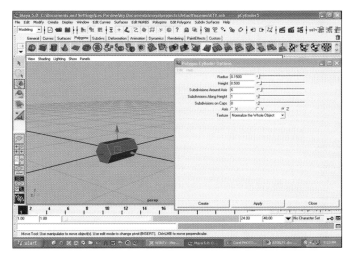

Figure 8.52 Create a polygon cylinder for the struts.

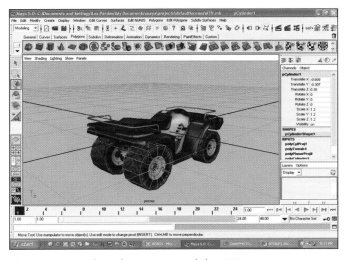

Figure 8.51 Place the tires around the ATV.

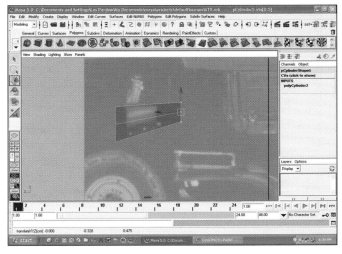

Figure 8.53 Shape the axle.

10. Now duplicate the cylinder and use it for the vertical strut.

11. Extrude the top of the duplicated cylinder's edges to form an additional horizontal strut, as shown in Figure 8.54.

12. Apply the ATV texture and fit the texture to the model, as shown in Figure 8.55.

13. Place the finished model so it intersects with the wheel and the ATV, as shown in Figure 8.56.

14. Now for the handlebars. Hide all of the current models. Create a polygonal cube, as shown in Figure 8.57.

15. Shape the cube to match the shape of the base of the handlebars. Use the template as a guide. Also refer to Figure 8.58 for an example of how the model should look.

16. Create a small, single-polygon-per-side cube for the handlebars.

17. Use the template as a guide to scale and place the cube.

18. Extrude the faces to create the handlebar for one side and then the other.

19. Use the Extrude Face tool to create a handbrake on the left handlebar. The model should now look like Figure 8.59.

20. Apply the ATV material to the model, as shown in Figure 8.60.

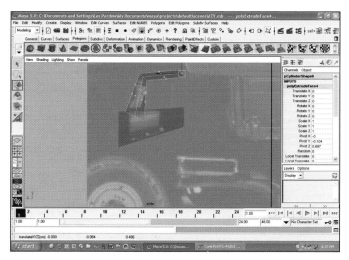

Figure 8.54 Create the struts as guided by the template.

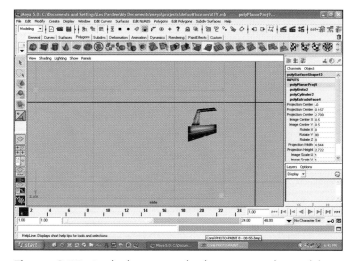

Figure 8.55 Apply the strut and axle texture to the model.

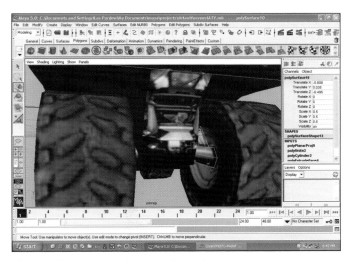

Figure 8.56 Move the struts into place.

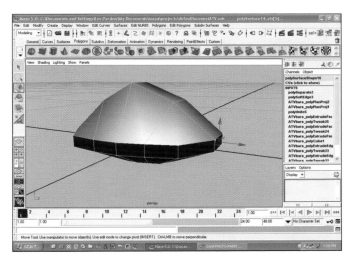

Figure 8.58 Shape the vertices to create the handlebar base.

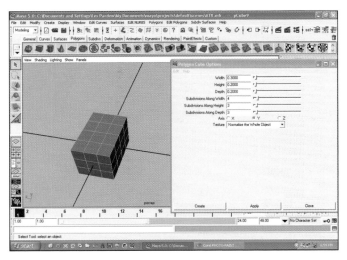

Figure 8.57 Create a polygonal cube for the handlebars.

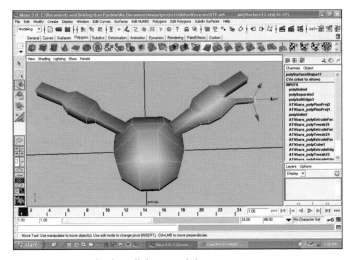

Figure 8.59 The handlebar model

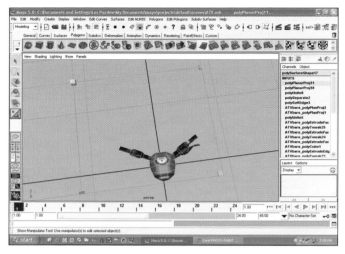

Figure 8.60 Apply the material to the model.

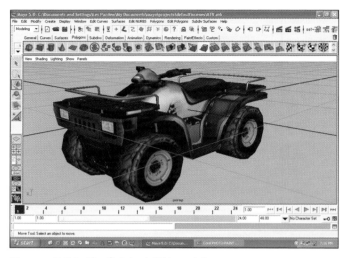

Figure 8.61 The finished ATV model

21. Use the Planar Mapping tool to project and fit the texture to the model.

22. Now move the handlebars into place, and you are done. The model should look similar to Figure 8.61.

Summary

In this chapter I explained how objects are different than environment models. I indicated the reasons why you need to make objects separately. I also covered the different types of objects used in games. You then created a model of a game object. In this case, it was an ATV model.

Try to think of a scene from a game that you want to create. Make a list of all the objects that your game will need, and then practice making the objects.

CHAPTER 9

BUILDING CHARACTERS
PART 1: THE HEAD

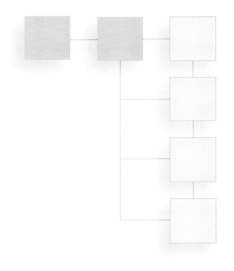

Characters are some of the most complex models in games for a couple of reasons. First, a game character is the focal point of the game. Players will be looking at the character more intently than any other element in the game. The second reason is that characters tend to be organic rather than mechanical. A human character, for example, is made up of many curves, which are difficult to create from flat polygons. Because of their complexity I will be devoting two chapters to building characters.

In this first chapter, you will explore creating a human head. Chapter 10, "Building Characters Part 2: The Body," will cover building and texturing the rest of the human character. I chose a human character because it is the most common character in games, but more importantly, it is the measure by which art directors choose who they will hire. Learning how to build great characters will go farther in helping you get a job in the game industry than knowing how to build any other game element.

The Human Head

We humans are fixated on our heads. When we talk with other people, we tend to focus on their faces. We look at ourselves in the mirror. We worry about moles or zits on our faces. We admire those who have great beauty and feel sorry for those who are less than beautiful. We spend considerable time and money trying to make ourselves look better. If it were not for this preoccupation with the way we look, the cosmetic and plastic surgery industries would be in real trouble (not to mention the publishers of the many magazines devoted to helping us look better). We can even recognize our friends from a distance even though the differences in our faces are sometimes very minor.

Our familiarity with the human head presents a significant challenge to an artist. If you are creating a tree and you move a branch up or down one or two feet, it isn't going to make much difference. On the other hand, if you move a character's eye up or down even a few fractions of an inch, everyone will notice.

Even though the human head is challenging to draw, it is still possible for even a beginning artist to create believable models of heads. The secret to building great heads is understanding their structure. Beginning artists should study the muscles and bones of the head, as well as the features. When I first started in art, one of my art teachers had us fill pages in our sketchbooks with drawings of noses, eyes, ears, and mouths. He had us draw them from every angle so we learned how they looked in three dimensions. I suggest you try doing the same thing. Get a good sketchbook and fill it with pictures of faces,

features, and heads. The more you draw the head, the more you will understand it.

Building the Head

Before you build the head, you need to create a template. In the last chapter you used the textures as a template for building an ATV. In this chapter you will be using a drawing of a head. Figure 9.1 shows a simple sketch of a head from the front and side. The drawings are done to scale so that the features line up straight across.

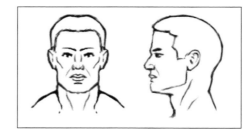

Figure 9.1 Drawings of the head from the front and side

These drawing are deliberately simple to help you model the head. For beginners it is easier to focus on the major features. If you were to use a photograph or a more detailed draw-

ing, it would only make the template more confusing.

You can use the two drawings in this exercise or you can draw two of your own. A texture file of each drawing is on the CD under the resource directory for this chapter.

1. In Maya, create two materials and load the drawings of the head, as shown in Figure 9.2.

2. Create a template with two polygons, as shown in Figure 9.3.

3. You will start by creating a simple plane in the z-axis, as shown in Figure 9.4.

4. From the Side view, move the vertices so they follow the contour of the face. For now ignore the nose; you will build it later. Right now you want the basic contour of the face itself. Refer to Figure 9.5 to see how I set up the plane.

5. Now turn on the X-ray view mode and size the plane to fit the contours of the face from the Front view, as shown in Figure 9.6. Don't worry about the ears at this stage.

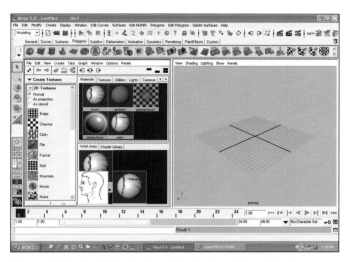

Figure 9.2 Load the textures for the head template into Hypershade.

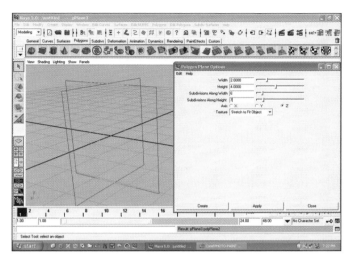

Figure 9.4 Create a plane facing the z-direction.

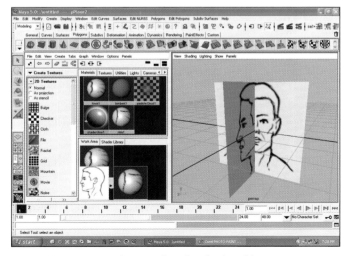

Figure 9.3 Set up the template for the head in Maya.

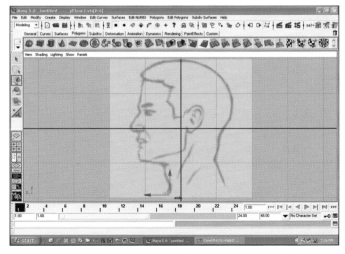

Figure 9.5 Move the vertices to fit the contour of the face.

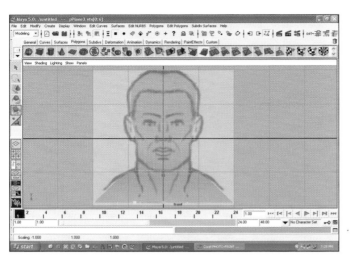

Figure 9.6 Size the plane from the Front view.

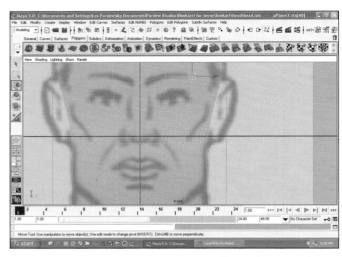

Figure 9.7 Move the vertices to better fit the features of the face.

6. Take the internal vertices and start to move them around to better fit the facial features, as shown in Figure 9.7.

Hint

When you are building complex symmetrical objects, it is easier to only work on one side of the object and then use Maya's mirror function to build the other side. A human head is a good example of a complex symmetrical object. I usually work on one side of the head and delete the polygons on the other side.

7. Use the Split Polygon tool to start creating polygons that follow the features of the face in more detail. The Split Polygon tool is used to manually divide polygons. When it is activated, the cursor will turn into an arrow. Position the arrow over the edge of a polygon and click with the left mouse button. A small green dot will appear. Now select another edge on the same polygon and click there.

Press Enter and the polygon will be split between the two points you selected. Most game engines will only support polygons with three or four vertices, so make sure that when you are splitting polygons you don't leave any with more vertices than that. To get the polygon edges in the right place, sometimes you will need to create support polygons, as shown in Figure 9.8.

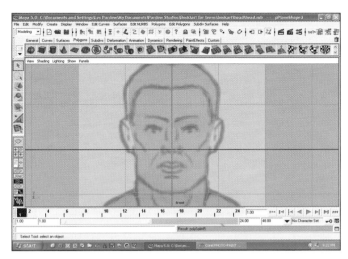

Figure 9.8 Create new polygons that follow the facial features.

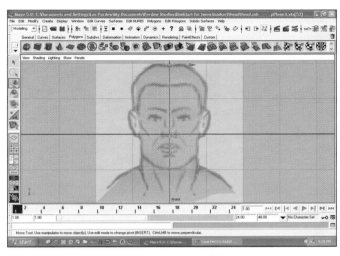

Figure 9.9 Polygon placement around the mouth

8. Place the polygons around the mouth in concentric circles radiating out from the lips. When you are placing new polygons, it is important to follow the shape of the face. When a face is animated, many of these polygons will stretch. Notice the placement of the polygons around the mouth in Figure 9.9. The concentric circles of polygons around the mouth are a good way to model the mouth for proper animation.

9. Continue splitting the polygons until you have defined all the features of the face. Figure 9.10 shows how I split the polygons for my model. Notice that the more detailed the facial feature, the more polygons I created.

10. Now you need to take your plane and move the polygons so that you create a three-dimensional face. Select the vertices on the outside edge of the plane, as shown in Figure 9.11.

11. Size the vertices in the z-axis so they all line up with each other in a straight line.

12. Move the vertices to the mid-point of the grid, as shown in Figure 9.12.

13. Now all you have to do is move the vertices in the z-direction until they are in the proper position. Figure 9.13 shows how the vertices around the nose are moved to fit the template. Select each vertex and move it along the z-axis to shape the nose.

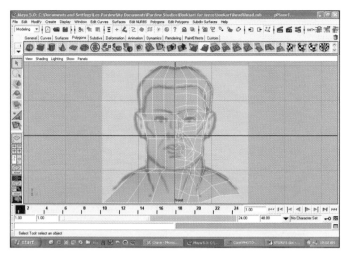

Figure 9.10 The new polygons of the face

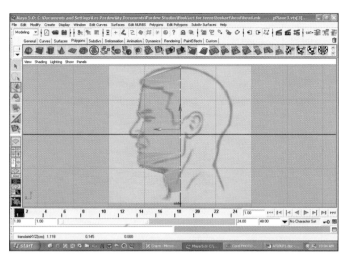

Figure 9.12 Move the vertices to the midpoint.

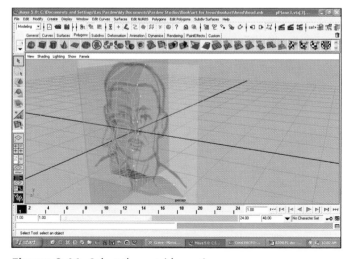

Figure 9.11 Select the outside vertices.

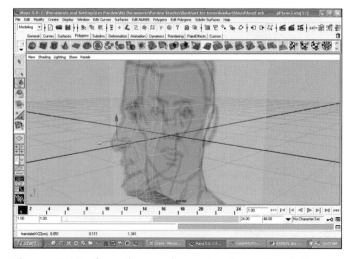

Figure 9.13 Shape the nose by moving the vertices in the z-axis.

14. Continue to move the vertices in the z-axis to round out the cheeks, forehead, mouth, and other areas of the face. Your model should look similar to Figure 9.14.

15. You will notice that not all of the features from the Side view will work. You might need to split some of the polygons to get things to work from that view. In Figure 9.15, notice how I created additional polygons at the top of the head to better follow its shape.

16. Sometimes the polygons will not work correctly. Figure 9.16 shows a more developed head model. Notice that I have created a few new polygons around the nose and hair.

17. Now it is time to create the back of the head. Bring up the Polygon Sphere Options dialog box and create a sphere, as shown in Figure 9.17.

18. From the Top or Front view, size the width of the sphere to the head, as shown in Figure 9.18.

19. From the Side view, move and size the sphere to fit around the back of the head, as shown in Figure 9.19.

20. You only need part of the sphere. Select the faces, as shown in Figure 9.20, and delete them so you only have the part of the sphere that forms the back of the head.

21. Adjust the shape of the back of the head from the Side view by moving the vertices to fit the outline of the drawing.

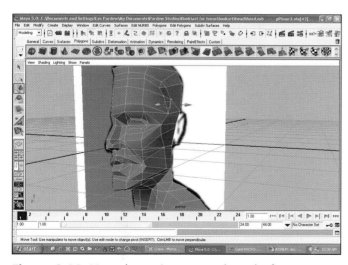

Figure 9.14 Move the vertices to round out the face.

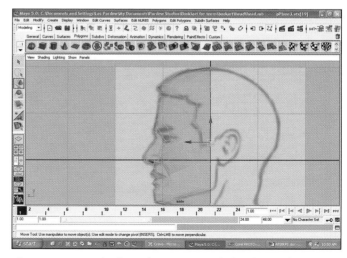

Figure 9.15 Split the polygons as needed to better follow the shape of the head.

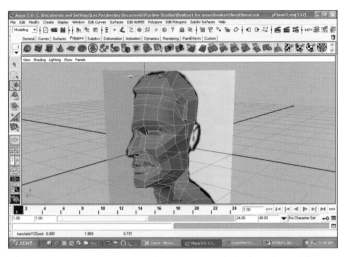

Figure 9.16 A more complete version of the head model

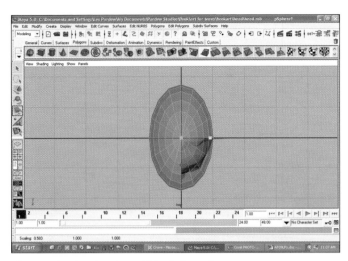

Figure 9.18 Size the width of the sphere.

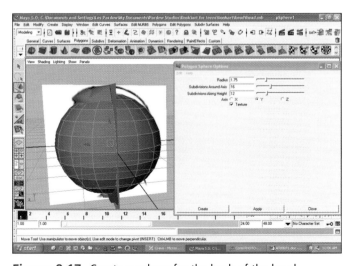

Figure 9.17 Create a sphere for the back of the head.

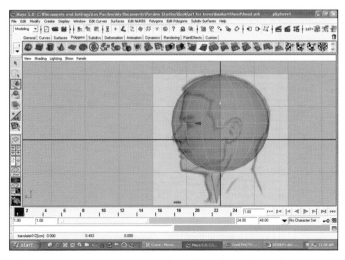

Figure 9.19 Move and size the sphere from the Side view.

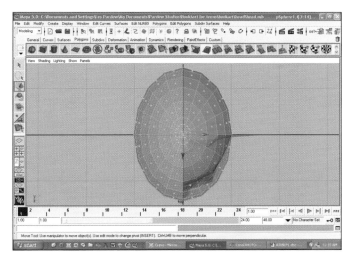

Figure 9.20 Delete the unneeded faces.

Figure 9.21 Delete the faces at the bottom of the sphere.

22. Delete the faces at the bottom of the sphere, as shown in Figure 9.21.

23. Size the lower part of the new geometry to fit the back of the neck, as shown in Figure 9.22.

24. Press the V key to snap to vertex. Snap the vertices of the new geometry to the vertices that border the face geometry. The vertices of the two pieces will not match up exactly; simply choose the ones that match closest, as shown in Figure 9.23.

25. Where the vertices don't match, create new ones by splitting the polygons in the new geometry (see Figure 9.24).

26. Snap the new vertices to the remaining vertices in the face geometry.

27. Select both pieces of geometry and combine them, as shown in Figure 9.25.

28. Select all the vertices that you snapped together earlier.

29. Merge the selected vertices, as shown in Figure 9.26.

30. The new geometry for the back of the head should now be adjusted to more closely match a human head. You will need to move many of the vertices to shape the head (see Figure 9.27).

31. From the Side view, you will notice that the vertices around the ear, jaw, and neck need to be adjusted to match the drawing. Move the vertices, as shown in Figure 9.28.

32. Now it's time to create the ear. Start to move some of the vertices around the ear so the edges of the polygons better follow the shape of the ear, as shown in Figure 9.29.

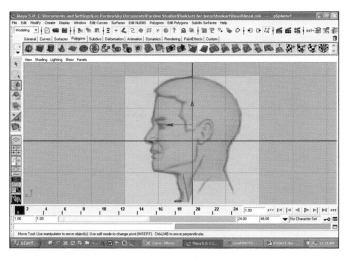

Figure 9.22 Size the lower part of the new geometry to fit the neck.

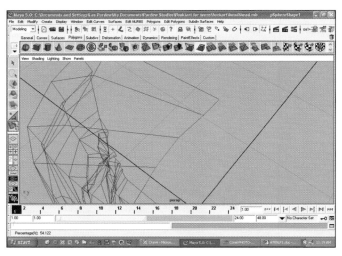

Figure 9.24 Split the polygons where necessary.

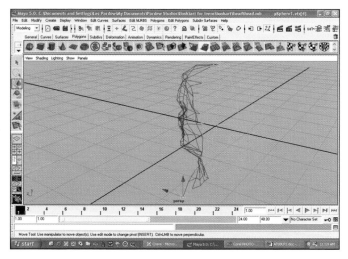

Figure 9.23 Snap the vertices of the new geometry to the vertices in the face geometry.

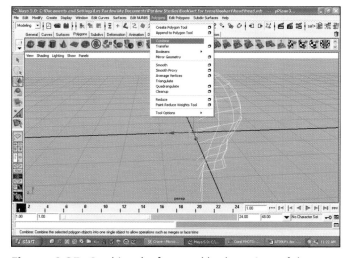

Figure 9.25 Combine the front and back portions of the head.

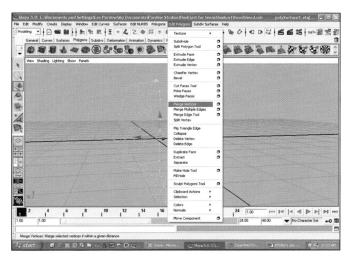

Figure 9.26 Merge the vertices.

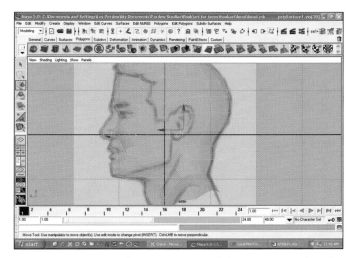

Figure 9.28 Move the vertices around the ear, jaw, and neck.

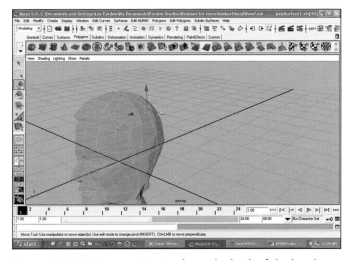

Figure 9.27 Move vertices to shape the back of the head.

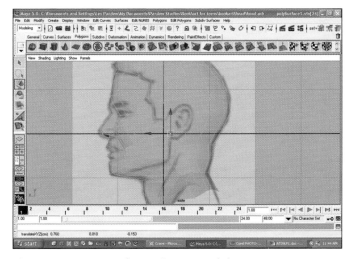

Figure 9.29 Move the vertices around the ear.

33. Split the polygons around the ear to follow its shape. Refer to Figure 9.30 for an example of how to split the polygons.

34. Select the faces that make up the ear and extrude them, as shown in Figure 9.31.

35. Extrude the faces a second time.

36. Shape the ear by moving and merging vertices, as shown in Figure 9.32.

37. Select the faces on the inside of the ear and extrude them inward, as shown in Figure 9.33, to finish shaping the ear.

38. Select the faces that form the eye and extrude them inward, as shown in Figure 9.34. You will build the eyeball later.

39. Now it is time to form the inside of the mouth. Select the faces that are between the lips and extrude them inward, as shown in Figure 9.35.

40. Now extrude the faces again and then size them vertically to form the inside of the mouth just behind the lips (refer to Figure 9.36).

41. The shape will not be correct from just sizing it. Move the vertices so they fit better as the inside of the mouth, as shown in Figure 9.37.

42. Select the adjusted faces and extrude them in to form the inside of the mouth, as shown in Figure 9.38.

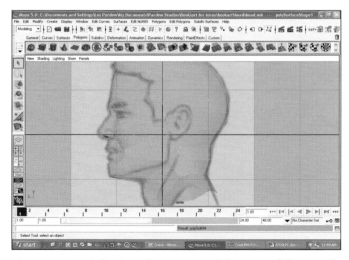

Figure 9.30 Split the polygons around the ear to follow its shape.

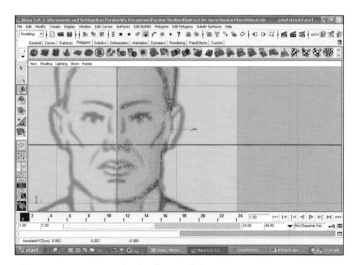

Figure 9.31 Extrude the faces of the ear.

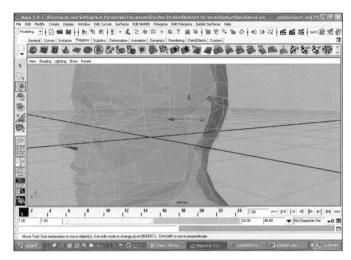

Figure 9.32 Shape the ear.

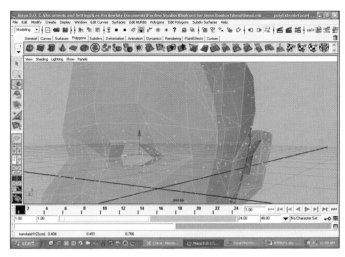

Figure 9.34 Extrude the eye faces inward.

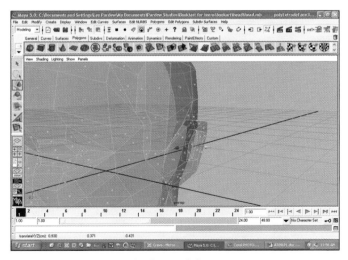

Figure 9.33 Extrude the faces of the inner ear.

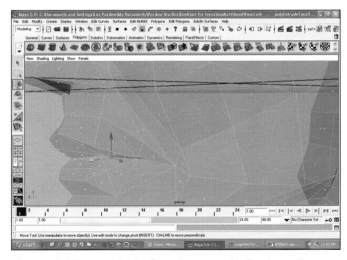

Figure 9.35 Extrude the faces between the lips inward.

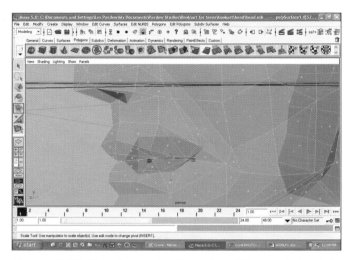

Figure 9.36 Extrude and size the inside of the mouth behind the lips.

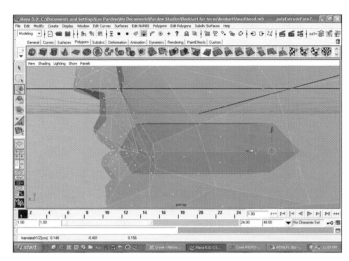

Figure 9.38 Extrude the faces to form the mouth.

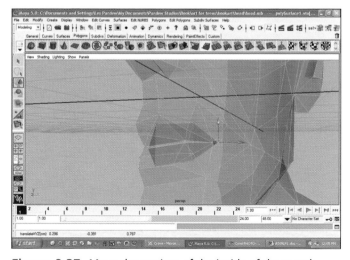

Figure 9.37 Move the vertices of the inside of the mouth.

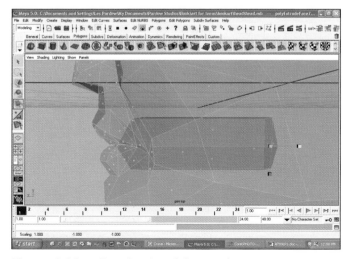

Figure 9.39 Adjust the size of the mouth.

43. Use the Scale tool to adjust the mouth, as shown in Figure 9.39.

44. The geometry of the face is starting to get in the way of the mouth. Select the faces of the mouth from the lips back and choose View Selected from the Show menu of the view screen. As shown in Figure 9.40, now you can see the mouth better.

45. Expand the size of the mouth vertically, as shown in Figure 9.41. You need to make room for teeth and a tongue.

46. Delete the faces on the inside wall of the mouth, as shown in Figure 9.42.

47. Restore the model to see how nice your head is starting to look. It should look similar to Figure 9.43.

There, that wasn't so hard, was it? You now have a polygonal model of a head. (Well, at least half a head; you will form the other half later.) You now need to focus on building some other elements of the face, such as eyeballs, teeth, and the tongue. You will start with the teeth.

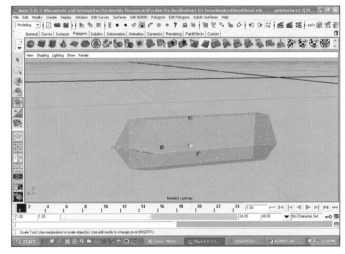

Figure 9.40 Isolate the faces of the mouth.

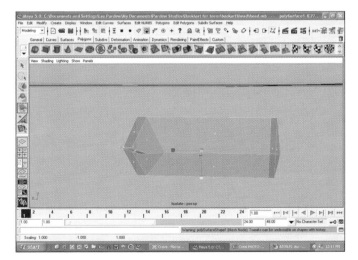

Figure 9.41 Expand the size of the mouth.

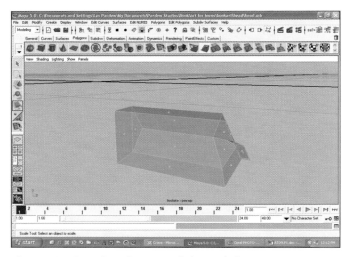

Figure 9.42 Delete the unneeded mouth faces.

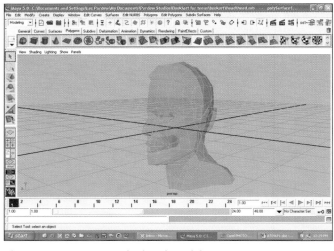

Figure 9.43 Restore the head model.

Facial Animation Elements

When you are building a face, you need to take into account whether the face will be animated. The face you are building is for animation, which is why you have not given your head any eyeballs. You want the character's eyes to be able to move independently of the head. You have not built the teeth and tongue for the same reason. You can create these elements now.

1. Hide the head geometry so you can focus on the new model elements.

2. Create a polygon torus by selecting Polygon Primitives, Torus from the Create menu (see Figure 9.44).

3. Set the options in the Polygon Torus Options dialog box, as shown in Figure 9.45.

4. You only need part of the torus for the teeth. Delete the unneeded faces so you only have a quarter of the torus left, as shown in Figure 9.46.

5. Now move and merge the vertices to adjust the torus to fit the shape of the teeth, as shown in Figure 9.47.

6. Split the polygons on the inside of the teeth to finish the teeth, as shown in Figure 9.48.

7. For the tongue, create a polygon sphere, as shown in Figure 9.49.

8. Size the sphere vertically to flatten it into a tongue shape, as shown in Figure 9.50.

9. As with the teeth, you only need a quarter of the sphere for the tongue. Delete the unneeded faces.

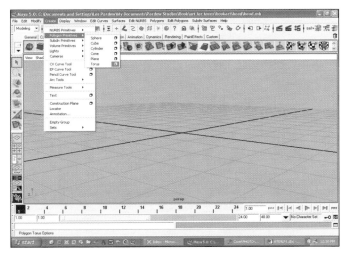

Figure 9.44 Select Polygon Primitives, Torus from the Create menu.

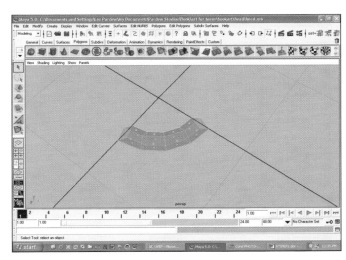

Figure 9.46 Delete the unneeded teeth faces.

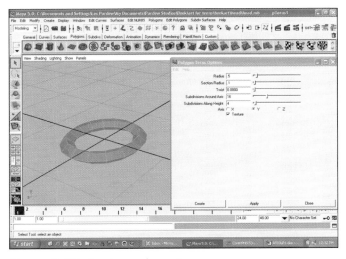

Figure 9.45 Create a polygon torus.

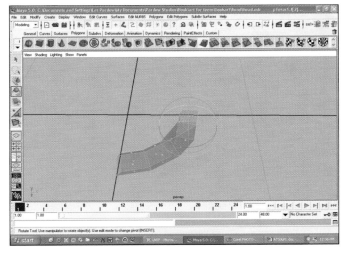

Figure 9.47 Shape the geometry to the teeth.

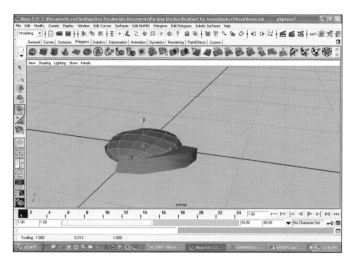

Figure 9.48 Split the polygons to finish the teeth.

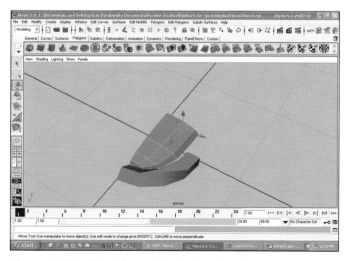

Figure 9.50 Shape the tongue.

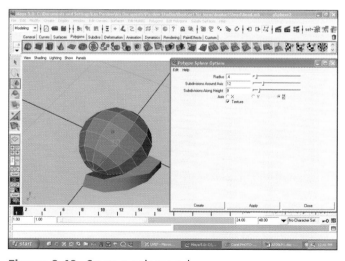

Figure 9.49 Create a polygon sphere.

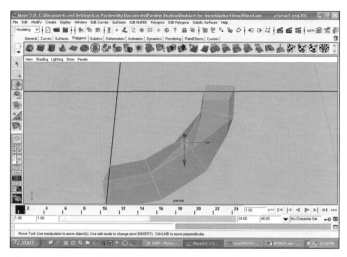

Figure 9.51 Move the vertices to lengthen the tongue.

10. Select the faces at the back of the tongue and move them to elongate the shape of the tongue, as shown in Figure 9.51.

11. Now bring back the face geometry.

12. Move the teeth and tongue so they fit into the inside of the mouth you built earlier.

13. You only have the bottom teeth. Use the Mirror tool in the Polygons menu to bring up the Polygon Mirror Options dialog box. Use the settings shown in Figure 9.52 to create the top teeth.

14. From the Edit Polygons menu, select Separate to make the upper and lower teeth separate objects.

15. Select the upper teeth and move them up slightly.

16. Move the tongue up so it is halfway between the upper and lower teeth.

17. Select the teeth and tongue and group them into a single group.

18. From the Top view, size the teeth and tongue so they fit inside the mouth, as shown in Figure 9.53.

19. Now you can create an eyeball by creating a new polygon sphere, as shown in Figure 9.54.

20. Move the eyeball into position, as shown in Figure 9.55. You might need to move some face vertices to get the eye in the right place without it showing through the skin of the face.

You have finished all the elements of the head!

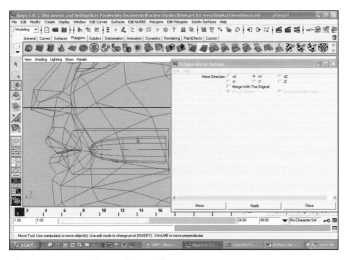

Figure 9.52 Mirror the teeth.

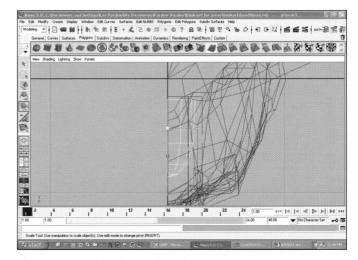

Figure 9.53 Size the teeth and tongue.

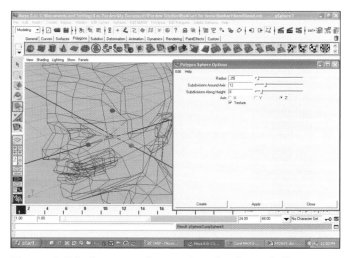

Figure 9.54 Create a polygon sphere for the eyeball.

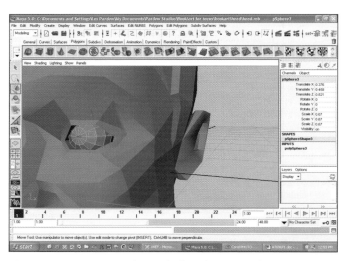

Figure 9.55 Position the eyeball in the eye socket.

Finishing the Head

The model of the head is now ready to be finished. You can do so by mirroring the geometry to create the other half. Start by mirroring the geometry of the head. Select the head in Object mode and bring up the Mirror tool's dialog box. Set the mirror, as shown in Figure 9.56. Make sure the Merge with the Original check box is checked, and then click on Apply.

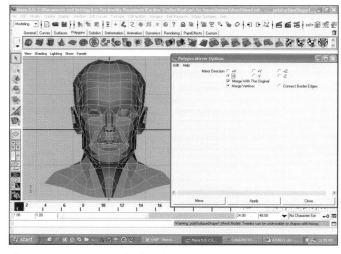

Figure 9.56 Mirror the head.

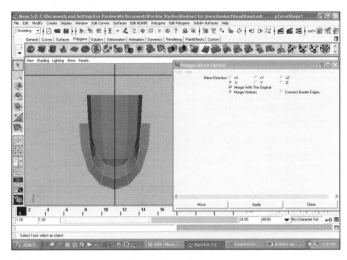

Figure 9.57 Mirror the teeth and tongue.

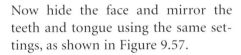

Figure 9.58 Move the duplicate eyeball into the empty eye socket.

Now hide the face and mirror the teeth and tongue using the same settings, as shown in Figure 9.57.

Bring back the face. All you have left to do is give your character another eyeball. Duplicate the eyeball. Move the new eyeball to the empty eye socket, as shown in Figure 9.58.

And there you have it, a nice human head for your superhero character. You should be proud of yourself! You have just finished what is possibly the most difficult type of model to create. Give yourself a pat on the back.

Summary

In this chapter you learned one method of creating a human head in polygons. But this is only one method—there are several methods to create heads. The one you used in this chapter will work well for most game modeling needs.

Now that you have created a human head, try creating some non-human heads. Build a creature of your own design. Try using the method you learned in this chapter to create animal heads. The more you practice, the better you will become.

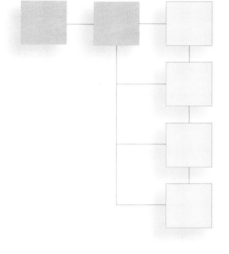

CHAPTER 10

BUILDING CHARACTERS
PART 2: THE BODY

In this chapter you will finish building your character. You have the head, so now you need to build the rest of the body. You will also set up the textures and apply them to your character. For this example, your character is a powerful superhero that we will call Polyman.

Like the design of the head, the design of the human body is very complex and intimidating to beginning artists. However, it does not need to be as difficult a task as you might imagine. The key to building good characters is starting with a good drawing as a template. The drawing will define the character, so spend some time on your drawings. Mistakes in the drawing will transfer to the model. Figure 10.1 shows a simple line drawing of your Polyman character.

Notice that you have front, back, and side views of the character. You also have a Top view of your character's arm. You need to set up your character's template a little differently than you have the other templates in this book. In this template, you need to have a Front and a Back view. If you use the X-ray view, the front and back pictures will become confusing. Instead of

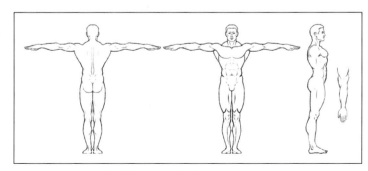

Figure 10.1 Multiple views of Polyman

213

using the X-ray feature, in this example you'll apply a semi-transparent material to the model. Let's get started.

1. Create a single plane polygon, as shown in Figure 10.2.

2. Translate the polygon .025 in the z-axis.

3. Now create another polygon the same scale as the first one.

4. Reverse the normal so it is facing the opposite direction of the first polygon.

5. Move the new polygon –.025 in the z-axis, as shown in Figure 10.3.

6. Create a third polygon the same scale as the first two.

7. Rotate the polygon 90 degrees on the y-axis.

8. Now the polygons are set up for the textures. In the Chapter 10 directory on the CD, there are textures for the template. Create three new materials and apply them to the template, as shown

in Figure 10.4, with the front picture facing forward and the back picture facing backward.

Now that the template is in position, you can start to model your character. You will start with a simple polygon cube. From that box you will build the torso.

1. Create a polygon cube of the dimensions shown in Figure 10.5.

2. Now create a new blinn material.

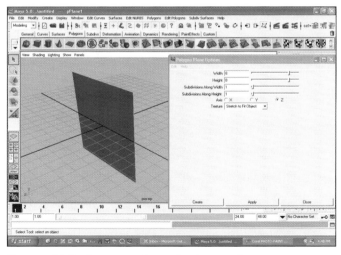

Figure 10.2 Create a polygon for the template.

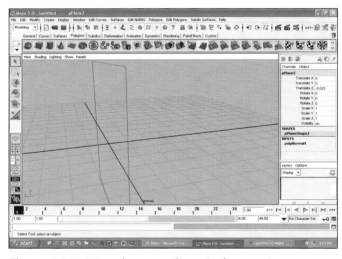

Figure 10.3 Move the new polygon in the negative z-direction.

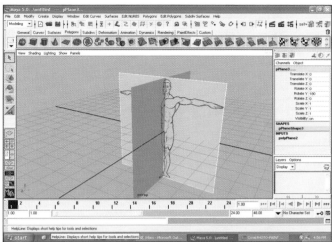

Figure 10.4 Apply the template textures to the template.

Figure 10.5 Create a cube for the torso.

3. Adjust the Transparency slider, as shown in Figure 10.6, and label the new material *xray*. Apply the xray material to the cube.

4. From the Front view, use the Move tool to line up the vertices with the major features of the character's body.

5. Use the Scale tool to adjust the scale of the cube to fit the body, as shown in Figure 10.7.

6. From the Side view, scale the rows of polygons to fit the template from that direction. You

will need to use the Scale tool as well as the Move tool to position the vertices correctly on the template. Use Figure 10.8 as a reference.

7. Now you need to work on the edges of the cube. Select the vertices of the vertical corners of the cube and snap them to the first row of vertices on the sides of the cube, as shown in Figure 10.9.

8. Go through each corner, snapping vertices.

9. Once you have finished snapping all the corners, select all

the vertices of the model and merge them by selecting Merge Vertices from the Edit Polygons menu. From the Top view, your model should now look like Figure 10.10.

10. You will see that the cube is starting to take the shape of a human torso. Like with the head, you don't need to build all of the body; you only need to build half. You can mirror the model later. Delete the unneeded polygons, as shown in Figure 10.11.

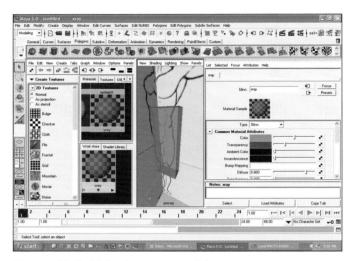

Figure 10.6 Make the new material transparent.

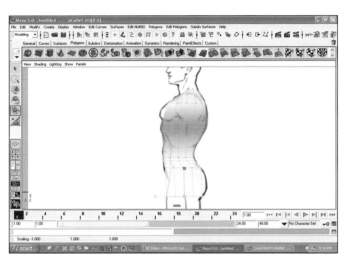

Figure 10.8 Scale the rows of vertices in the Side view.

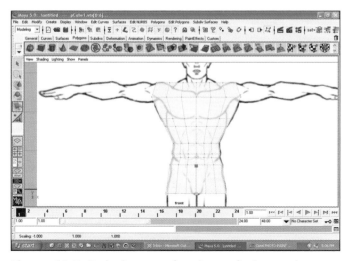

Figure 10.7 Scale the rows of vertices to fit the template.

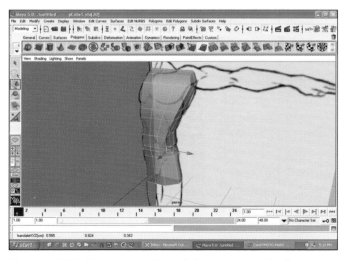

Figure 10.9 Snap the vertices of the corners to the first row on the sides of the cube.

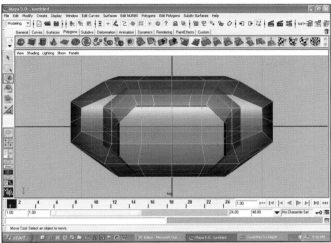

Figure 10.10 The model as seen from the Top view

Figure 10.11 Delete the unneeded polygons.

11. Now use the Split Polygon tool to fine-tune your torso model. However, you only want to do it one side at a time. You need to get rid of the extra polygons so they will not get in the way. Select the front-facing poly-gons, as shown in Figure 10.12, and then select View Selected from the View menu. You also need to select the front-facing template; otherwise, it will dis-appear, too.

12. Now you can move the vertices in the Front view without

adjusting the ones in the back. Move the vertices to more closely follow the shape of the body, as shown in Figure 10.13.

13. Split the polygons the same way you did for the face in Chapter 9, so they give you the geome-try you need to create the details of the torso, as shown in Figure 10.14.

14. Once you have the geometry that you need on the front, you must do the same thing on the back. Select View Selected to

bring the entire model back into the view screen.

15. Select the back-facing polygons of the torso along with the back-facing template and use View Selected to remove the rest of the model from the view.

16. You will notice that there is not a Back view in the Ortho-graphic view selection menu. You will have to create one. Select Orthographic, New, Front from the Panels menu, as shown in Figure 10.15.

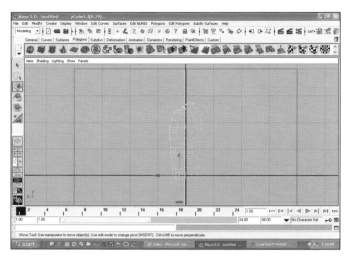

Figure 10.12 Select the front-facing polygons.

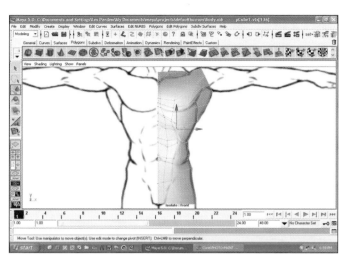

Figure 10.14 Split the polygons for the needed geometry.

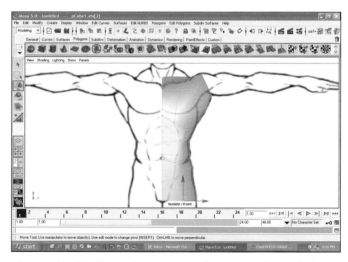

Figure 10.13 Move the vertices to follow the shape of the body.

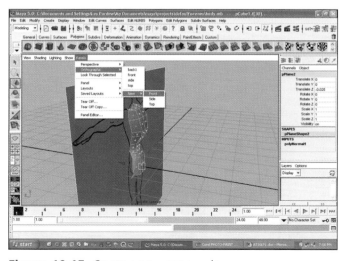

Figure 10.15 Create a new camera view.

17. You can adjust the new Front view to a Back view by typing the numbers in the channel box, as shown in Figure 10.16. Name the new view *Back1*. Be careful not to click in the view window until you have finished entering and naming the view.

18. Now you can adjust the vertices and split the polygons to fit the back of your character, as shown in Figure 10.17.

19. Adjust the vertices of the front of the model to create the muscles and contours of the torso, as shown in Figure 10.18.

20. Now go to the back and adjust those vertices as well, as shown Figure 10.19.

21. Now you need to adjust the vertices of the hips so you can create the legs later. Move the vertices of the hip area up, as shown in Figure 10.20.

22. You will need some more geometry to get the ribs to flow from the front to the back. Split the polygons in that area and adjust them to match the model in Figure 10.21.

23. Next you need to create the legs of your character, but before you can do that you need to adjust the vertices of the character's crotch, as shown in Figure 10.22.

24. You will be extruding the leg from the torso geometry. Select the faces, as shown in Figure 10.23. You will use these faces to extrude the leg.

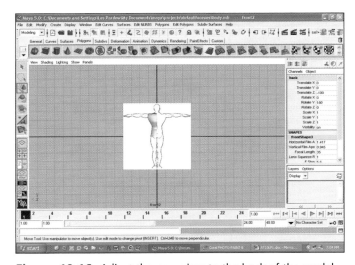

Figure 10.16 Adjust the new view to the back of the model.

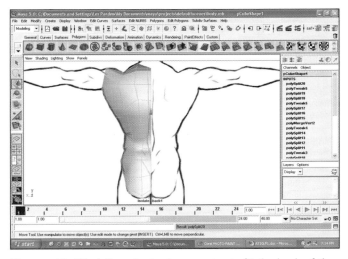

Figure 10.17 Adjust the back geometry to fit the back of the model.

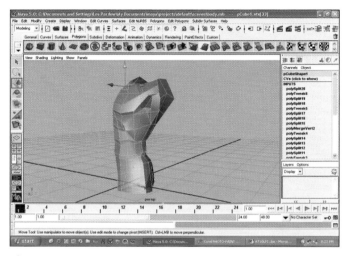

Figure 10.18 Adjust the vertices of the model.

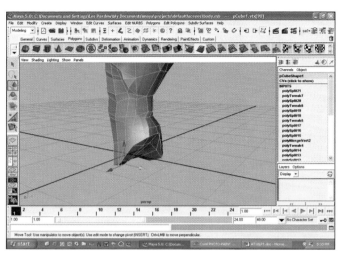

Figure 10.20 Adjust the vertices of the hip area of the model.

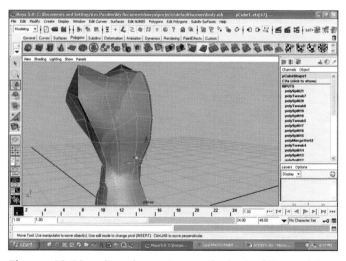

Figure 10.19 Adjust the vertices on the back of the model.

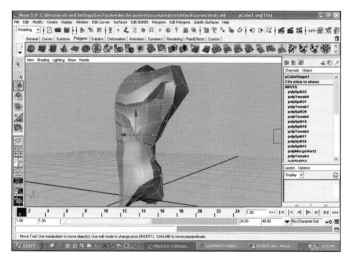

Figure 10.21 Create new polygons for the rib area.

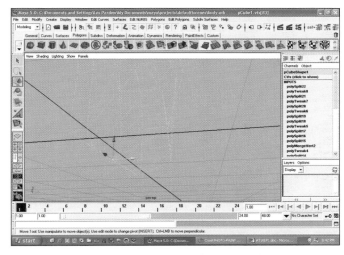

Figure 10.22 Adjust the vertices of the model's crotch.

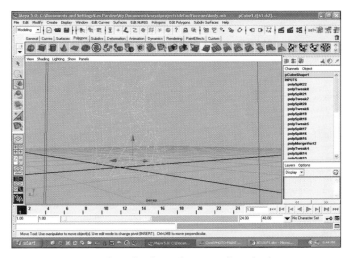

Figure 10.23 Select the faces for extruding the leg.

25. Extrude the faces and move them down following the template from the Front view. Use the Scale tool to adjust the faces, as shown in Figure 10.24. Scale the vertices in the y-axis so they flatten. This will create a better-animating hip area.

26. Extrude the faces again. This time, scale the faces so they flatten out perpendicular to the leg, as shown in Figure 10.25.

27. Continue extruding the faces until you reach the ankle, scaling them as you go (see Figure 10.26). When you are finished, delete the extruded faces on the end.

28. Change the selection mode to Vertices and from the Side view, adjust the rows of vertices to fit the template, as shown in Figure 10.27.

29. Now you need to extrude the arm. Select the faces of the shoulder where the arm is supposed to be.

30. Extrude the faces and scale them, as shown in Figure 10.28. When you are finished, delete the extruded faces at the end of the arm.

31. Continue extruding the faces to the wrist of the arm, as shown in Figure 10.29. Size the faces as you go.

32. There is one template picture that you have not used yet. It is of the arm. Create a new polygon the same scale as the original template polygons.

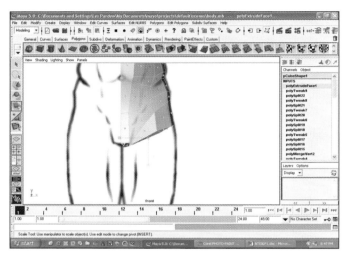

Figure 10.24 Extrude the faces and adjust them to fit the template.

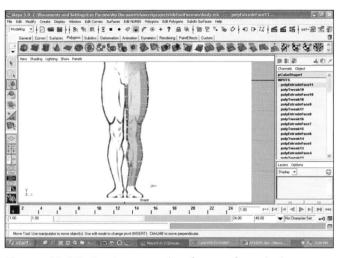

Figure 10.26 Continue extruding faces to form the leg.

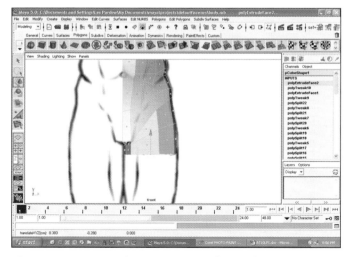

Figure 10.25 Extrude and adjust the faces of the leg to fit the template.

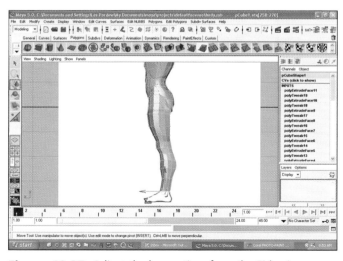

Figure 10.27 Adjust the leg vertices from the Side view.

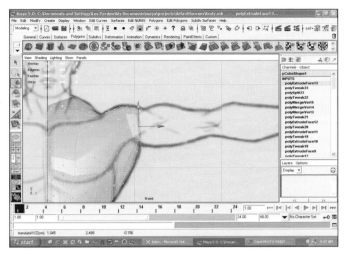

Figure 10.28 Start extruding the faces for the arm.

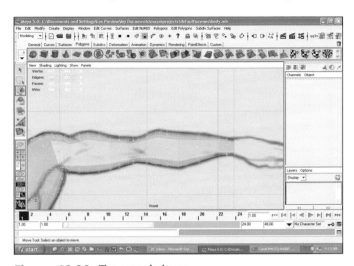

Figure 10.29 The extruded arm

Make sure that the Y check box is checked.

33. Create a new material and load the arm texture.

34. Apply the arm texture to the new polygon, as shown in Figure 10.30.

35. Rotate the new template 90 degrees in the y-axis and move it into position, as shown in Figure 10.31.

36. Adjust the vertices to fit the template, as shown in Figure 10.32.

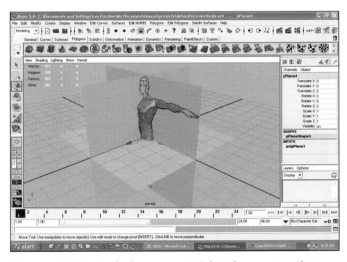

Figure 10.30 Apply the arm material to the new template polygon.

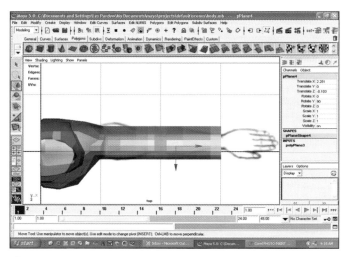

Figure 10.31 Move the arm template into position.

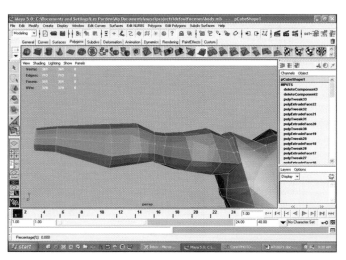

Figure 10.33 Split the polygons on the back of the arm.

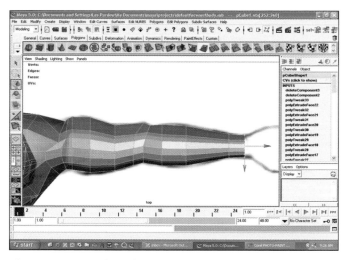

Figure 10.32 Adjust the vertices of the arm.

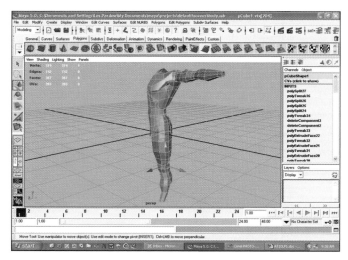

Figure 10.34 Adjust the vertices of the arm and leg.

37. The arm is not very well rounded, so split the polygons along the back of the arm, as shown in Figure 10.33.

38. Now shape the arm and leg to better match human anatomy. Use Figure 10.34 as a guide.

Building Hands and Feet

You now have the beginnings of the body of your superhero. You are missing only the extremities and the head you created earlier. You will create the hands and feet separately and then attach them to the body model.

1. Create a polygon cube, as shown in Figure 10.35.

2. Apply the xray material to the cube.

3. Move the cube into position at the end of the arm you created earlier.

4. Adjust the vertices of the cube to fit the template, as shown in Figure 10.36.

5. Extrude the fingers and thumb similar to the way you extruded the leg and arm earlier. Scale the fingers and thumb to fit the template. The resulting model should look similar to Figure 10.37.

6. Now adjust vertices to shape the hand. Remember that a hand is thicker by the thumb than by the little finger. Use Figure 10.38 as a guide.

7. Select the hand model and then the body model.

8. Combine the models.

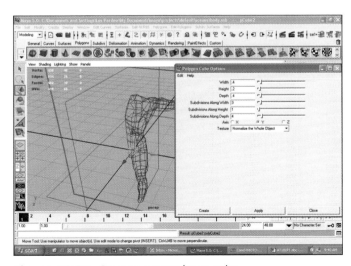

Figure 10.35 Create a new polygon cube.

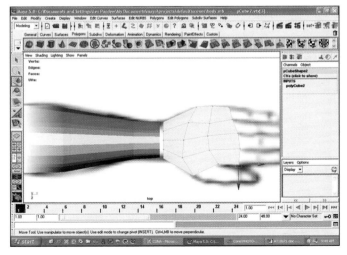

Figure 10.36 Adjust the vertices of the hand.

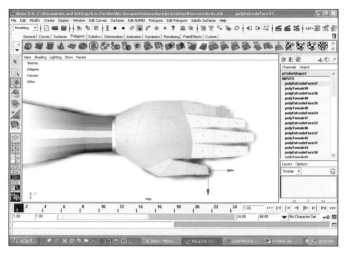

Figure 10.37 Extrude the thumb and fingers.

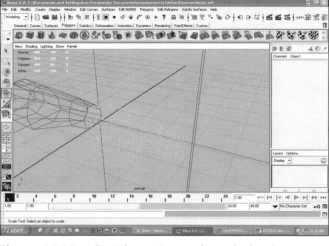

Figure 10.38 Adjust the vertices to shape the hand.

9. Snap the vertices of the arm to the hand. You will need to split some of the polygons to get the two models to match with each other. Look at Figure 10.39 as a guide.

10. Merge the vertices.

11. Now you will create the foot. Again, start with a polygon cube. Create a new cube, as shown in Figure 10.40.

12. Move the cube into position at the end of the leg.

13. Move the vertices of the cube to match the shape of the foot from the Side view, as shown in Figure 10.41.

14. Now adjust the vertices from the Front view, as shown in Figure 10.42.

15. Hide the rest of the body so it will be easier to work on the foot. Your model should look similar to Figure 10.43.

16. With the exception of the toe area, snap vertices from the corners to the next row of vertices, as shown in Figure 10.44.

17. You don't need so many polygons down the middle of the model (except for the toes). Snap the inside rows of vertices together, as shown in Figure 10.45.

18. Now you are ready to extrude the toes. Select the face where the big toe goes and extrude it.

19. Move the extruded face out from the foot and rotate the foot, as shown in Figure 10.46.

20. Extrude and scale the face twice more to form the big toe, as shown in Figure 10.47.

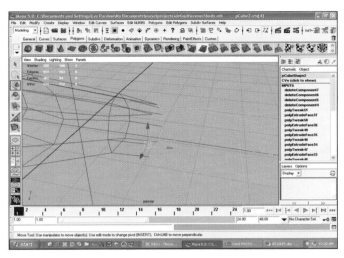

Figure 10.39 Snap the vertices of the arm to the hand.

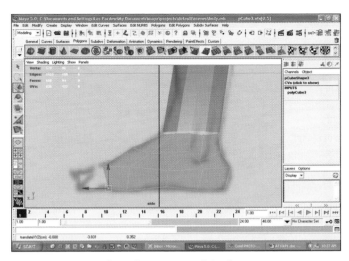

Figure 10.41 Adjust the vertices of the foot.

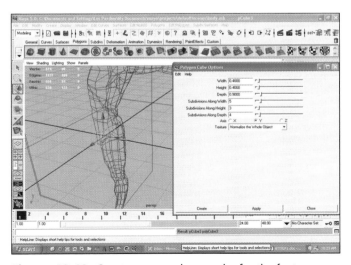

Figure 10.40 Create a new polygon cube for the foot.

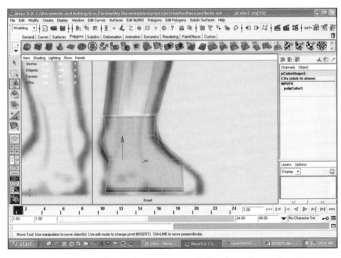

Figure 10.42 Adjust the vertices of the foot from the Front view.

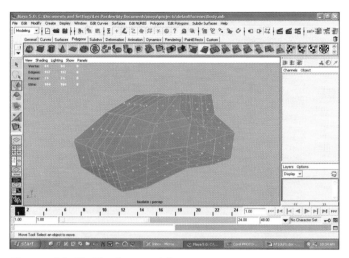

Figure 10.43 The foot model

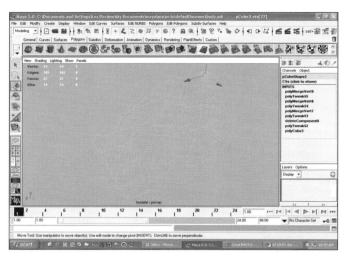

Figure 10.45 Snap the inside vertices together.

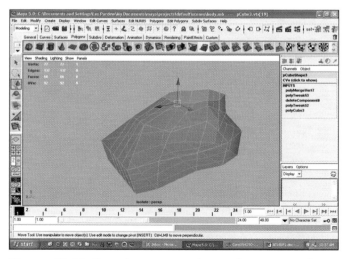

Figure 10.44 Snap the corner vertices to the next row of vertices.

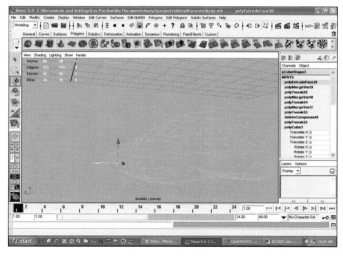

Figure 10.46 Rotate the extruded face.

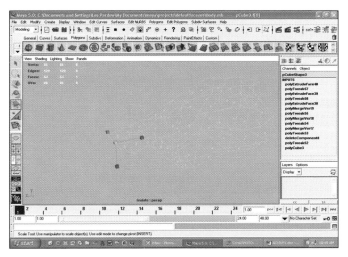

Figure 10.47 Extrude and scale the faces of the big toe.

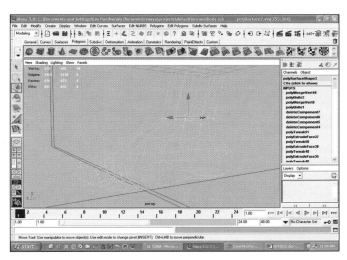

Figure 10.49 Attach the foot to the leg.

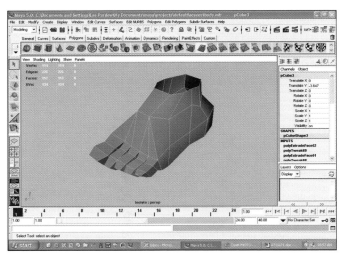

Figure 10.48 Extrude the remaining toes of the foot.

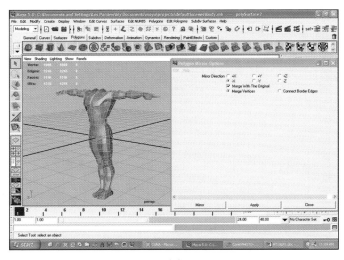

Figure 10.50 Mirror the model.

21. Repeat Steps 18 through 20 for each toe. The resulting model should look similar to Figure 10.48.

22. Now bring back the body model and attach the foot to the leg the same way you attached the hand to the arm. There will be more vertices on the foot model than on the arm model, so snap the extra vertices together, as shown in Figure 10.49.

23. With the foot and the hand attached to the model, now you can mirror your character's body so he is no longer just half a man. Mirror the model, as shown in Figure 10.50.

Adding the Head

You now have a pretty good model of your character, Polyman. He is lacking a head, so you had better fix that. Import the head model you created in

Chapter 9 into the scene, as shown in Figure 10.51.

Notice that the head is too large. You need to scale the head to the body and then attach it.

1. Turn on the X-ray view mode.

2. Scale and move the head to match the template, as shown in Figure 10.52.

3. This next step will be a little complicated, so I will take it slow. You need to combine the

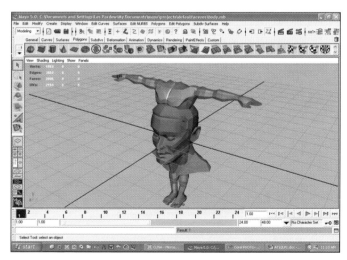

Figure 10.51 Import the head model into the scene.

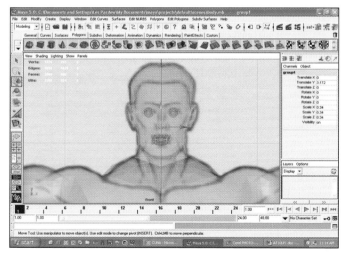

Figure 10.52 Scale the head to fit the template.

two models and attach the head to the body. The problem is that there are a lot more vertices in the head model than in the body at the point where the two attach. Starting at the back of the model, begin snapping the vertices of the head model to the vertices of the body model, as shown in Figure 10.53.

4. As you work your way around the back of the model, you will notice that there are problems with the way the two models match up. You need to split a couple of the polygons on the shoulders so they will match the head model.

5. You will also need to split the polygons for the front of the shoulders to match with the polygons on the head. You must split the shoulder polygons diagonally to follow the geometry of the head model. Use Figure 10.54 as a guide.

6. Now snap the vertices of the head model to the body model, as shown in Figure 10.55.

7. When all the vertices are snapped together, go into Face view and select the unneeded faces of the body model where the two models meet, as shown in Figure 10.56. You need to delete these faces.

8. Combine the two models and merge the vertices so you have one complete model, as shown in Figure 10.57.

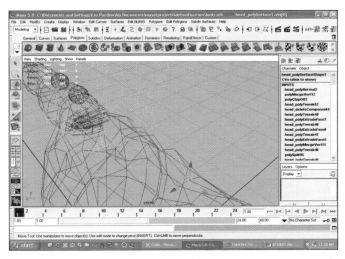

Figure 10.53 Snap the vertices of the head to the vertices of the body.

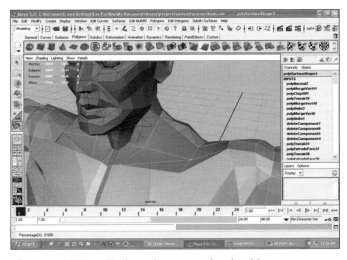

Figure 10.54 Split the polygons on the shoulders.

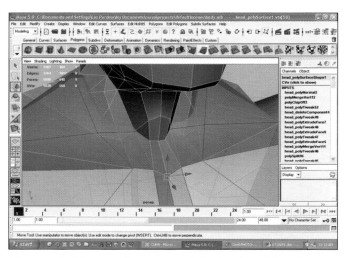

Figure 10.55 Snap the vertices of the head model to the body model.

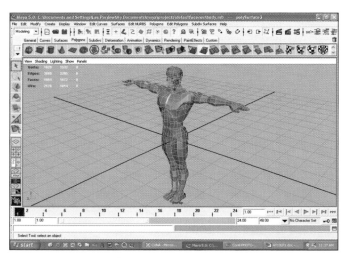

Figure 10.57 The finished character model with the head

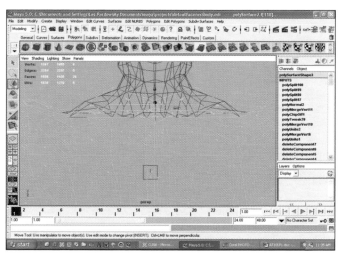

Figure 10.56 Select the unneeded faces of the body.

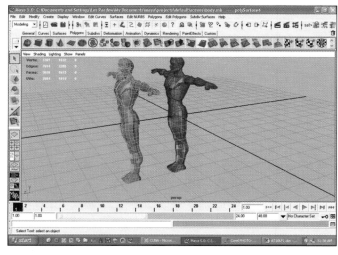

Figure 10.58 Duplicate the model and move it forward.

UV Mapping a Character

You now have a character model. The polygon count of the model is approximately 2,000 polygons, which is about right for many of the games on the more popular game systems today. Some games with multiple characters require characters with lower polygon counts, while others might let you have greater polygon counts. The number will depend on the game and the game engine.

Your model is finished, but you need to do one more thing before you are done. You need to add textures to your character to make him into Polyman. You will create a texture blanket similar to the one you used to build the ATV earlier. This time, though, you will be working from the model rather than making a blanket and applying it to the model.

1. Duplicate the model, as shown in Figure 10.58. You will be adjusting the geometry of the model to better set up the UVs, and then transferring the UVs from the duplicate to the original model.

2. The head is sometimes the hardest part of the body to map correctly. The problem is that the areas around the nose and ears have overlapping polygons. To correct this problem, select the polygons around the end of the nose and then select Average Vertices from the Polygons menu (see Figure 10.59). Apply the tool twice. This will smooth out those areas for better mapping.

3. Repeat Step 2 for each ear.

4. Now select the faces of the head and neck, excluding those at the top of the head and the inside of the mouth.

5. Use the Cylindrical Mapping tool to project the UVs on the head.

6. Go to the Two-Panel view with the right-hand panel having the UV Editor.

7. You will notice that the UVs of the head are mapped in a flat set in the UV Editor. You will want to keep the UVs within a 1:1 area on the UV Editor. Under the Edit Polygons menu,

choose Selection, Change Selection to UVs. The UV set will change to white, with the UVs as green dots.

8. You can use the Scale and Move tools in the UV Editor the same way you use them in the model views. You can also scale and move the view in the Editor the same way you do in the model views. Scale and move the UV set to the upper-left corner of the dark gray square in the Editor. Use Figure 10.60 as a guide.

9. Now select the faces of the torso (with the exception of the top of the shoulders) and use the Cylindrical Mapping tool on them the same way you did on the face.

10. Scale and move the UV set to the position shown in Figure 10.61.

11. Now select the faces on the top of the head that you left out earlier. Use the Planar Mapping tool to create a UV set.

12. Scale and move the UV set into the position shown in Figure 10.62.

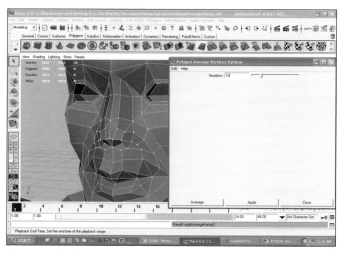

Figure 10.59 Average the vertices around the nose.

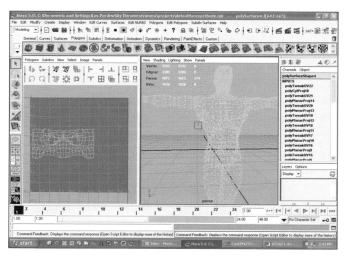

Figure 10.61 Scale and move the UV set for the body.

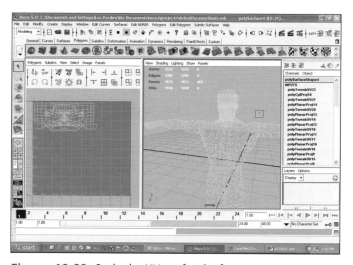

Figure 10.60 Scale the UV set for the face.

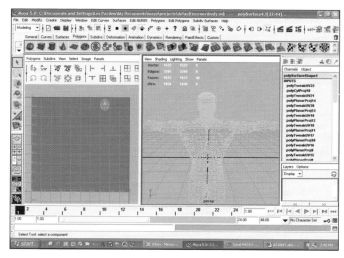

Figure 10.62 Scale and move the UV set for the top of the head.

13. It is difficult to get the Cylindrical Mapping tool to work correctly on a horizontal set of polygons such as the model's arms. I find it easier to simply rotate the model. Rotate the model of the body 90 degrees around the z-axis.

14. Cylindrical-map the UVs of the arm and position them in the Editor, as shown in Figure 10.63.

15. While the model is rotated, map the other arm and place the UV set next to the first arm set in the Editor.

16. Rotate the model back to the original position.

17. Use the Planar Mapping tool to map the inside of the mouth.

18. Scale and place the UV set, as shown in Figure 10.64.

19. Now select the faces on the top of the shoulders that were not selected when you mapped the faces of the face and torso.

20. Use the Planar Mapping tool to project a UV set.

21. Scale and move the UV set into the position shown in Figure 10.65.

22. Now select the faces on the top and sides of the hand.

23. Use the Planar Mapping tool to project the UV set of the hand.

24. Scale and move the UV set, as shown in Figure 10.66.

25. Now select the faces on the bottom of the hand and repeat Steps 23 and 24. Use Figure 10.67 as a guide for where to place the UV set.

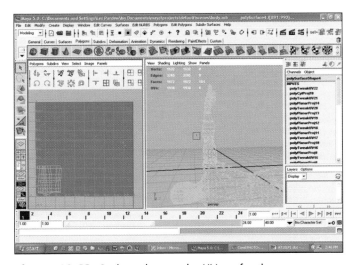

Figure 10.63 Scale and move the UV set for the arm.

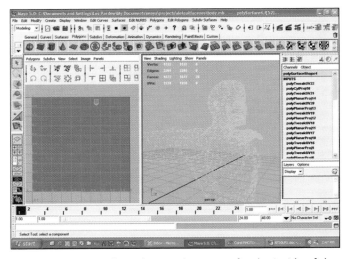

Figure 10.64 Scale and move the UV set for the inside of the mouth.

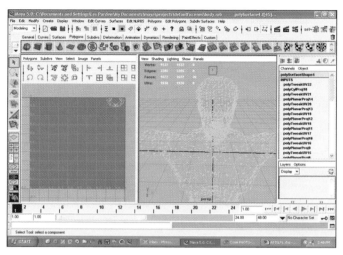

Figure 10.65 Scale and move the UV set for the shoulders.

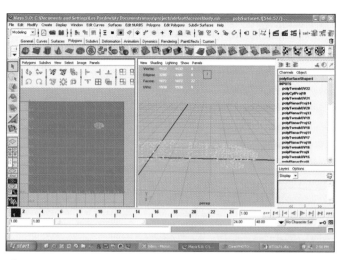

Figure 10.67 Scale and move the UV set for the bottom of the hand.

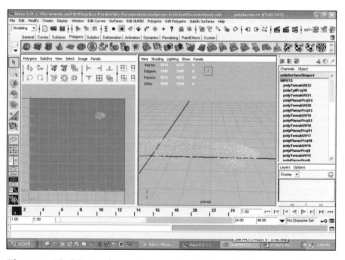

Figure 10.66 Scale and move the UV set for the top of the hand.

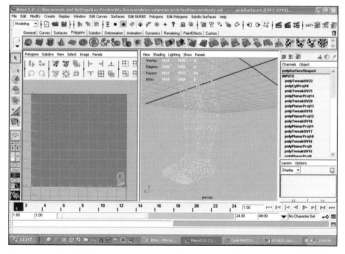

Figure 10.68 Scale and move the UV set for the top of the foot.

26. Repeat Steps 22 through 24 for the top and bottom of the right hand of the model. Place the UV sets just to the right of the left hand in the UV editor.

27. Now you need to map the feet. Use the Planar Mapping tool to map the top of the foot and place it in the Editor, as shown in Figure 10.68.

28. Now map and place the UVs for the bottom of the foot to the left of the top of the foot.

29. Repeat the mapping process for the right foot and place the UVs to the left of the left foot in the Editor.

30. Use the Cylindrical Mapping tool to map and place the UVs of the leg in the Editor. You will need to do the leg in two parts. Do the hip to knee and then do the knee to ankle. This will help keep the UVs from distorting.

Hint

Maya has a feature for joining UV maps. They call it *sewing*. If you have the two pieces of the leg UVs, you can sew them together by selecting the edges of the UVs that join the two parts. You have to be in Edge Selection mode. Select an edge of one leg piece that joins with the other piece. Notice that both edges are highlighted. That is because they are the same edge. Select the rest of the edges, and then select Texture, Move and Sew from the Edit Polygons menu. The two pieces will then be one.

31. Figure 10.69 shows the completed UV set for the model of the character's body. Use it as a guide to place the UV sets for the legs and crotch area of the body.

32. Now you need to transfer the UVs from the duplicate model to the original model. Select the duplicate in Object mode and then select the original model.

33. Use the Polygon Transfer tool in the Polygons menu to transfer the UVs of the duplicate to the original, as shown in Figure 10.70.

34. Now you need to map the UVs of the eyes, teeth, and tongue. Use the Planar Mapping tool for the eye, as shown in Figure 10.71.

35. You really don't need all the polygons on the back of the eyes, so delete them.

36. Map the UVs of the other eye the same way you did for the first. Place both UV sets in an open space on the UV map in the Editor.

37. Use the Planar Mapping tool to map the tongue and place the UV set in an open spot in the Editor.

38. You will use the Cylindrical Mapping tool to do the teeth; however, you need to change them because they are only half a cylinder. Mirror the teeth in the negative z-axis to make a full cylinder.

39. Project first the top teeth and then the bottom using the Cylindrical Mapping tool, as shown in Figure 10.72.

40. Delete the mirrored teeth.

41. Scale and place the UV sets for the teeth into an open spot in the UV Editor.

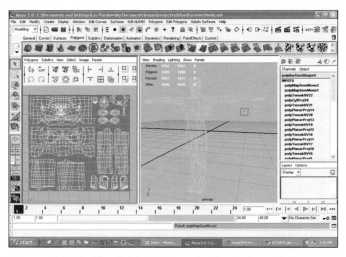

Figure 10.69 The finished UV set for the body model

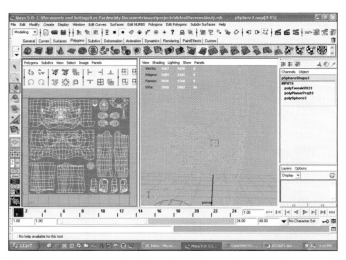

Figure 10.71 Use the Planar Mapping tool to map the UVs of the eye.

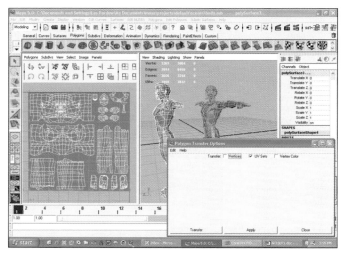

Figure 10.70 Transfer the UVs from the duplicate to the original model.

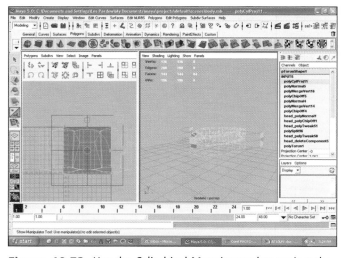

Figure 10.72 Use the Cylindrical Mapping tool to project the UVs of the teeth.

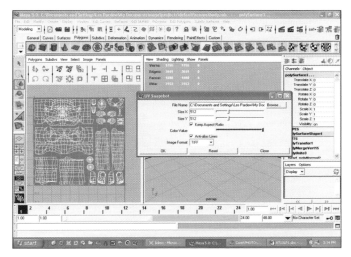

Figure 10.73 Take a snapshot of the texture blanket.

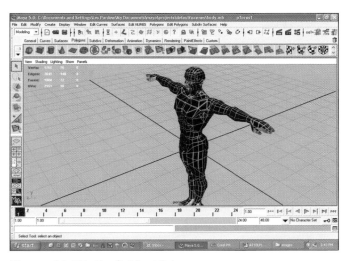

Figure 10.75 The finished Polyman

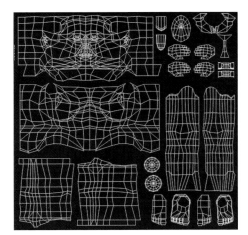

Figure 10.74 The snapshot of the texture blanket

42. Now you have everything set up for all the UVs in your model. It is time to create your texture blanket. In the UV Editor, choose UV Snapshot from the Polygons menu.

43. Set up the UV Snapshot dialog box as shown in Figure 10.73.

44. The resulting texture blanket will look like Figure 10.74. Because you are using the Personal Learning Edition of Maya, the snapshot will have an Alias watermark on it.

If you were creating this character for a real game, you would paint the texture for the model directly on the texture blanket and use the UV sets as a guide. For this exercise, you will use the snapshot as Polyman's texture to illustrate the point.

Create a new material in Hypershade and load the texture blanket into the material. Now assign the new material to the character model. The result will be Polyman. Notice how the lines on the texture line up perfectly with the polygons. See Figure 10.75 for an example.

Summary

This was a complex chapter, so if you were able to follow all the examples, congratulations. You have just created your first game character. If this chapter was a little confusing or your model didn't turn out quite the way it should have, try going through the steps again.

You learned quite a few concepts in this chapter, such as building character models and texture blankets. Use the texture blanket you created for Polyman and paint in your own textures. If you save them as separate files, you can create multiple textures for the single character model. This is one way that game artists create multiple characters from a single character model. Of course, it will only work for characters of similar builds, but it is a big timesaver in game development.

Try building a character of your own design. Perhaps create a villain character for Polyman to fight in your game.

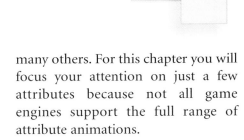

CHAPTER 11

3D ANIMATION

Now that you have a character model, it is time to learn how to get your character to move. For this process you will use 3D animation. 3D animation differs from 2D animation because in 3D animation, you will be moving an object or character in a three-dimensional environment, similar to how things move in real life.

Before 3D graphics became popular in games, all animation had to be drawn one frame at a time in 2D. With the advent of 3D graphics, a whole new world opened for animators. Now they could create animation in a 3D environment and view the animation from any angle. Animations became separate elements from the art, making it possible to do one animation and apply it to multiple characters.

How 3D Animation Works in Games

Unlike 2D animation that is stored as picture files in a game, 3D graphics are stored as motion files. Motion files can contain data on almost every attribute of a 3D model, including translation, rotation, size, color, and many others. For this chapter you will focus your attention on just a few attributes because not all game engines support the full range of attribute animations.

First take a look at how animation is controlled in Maya. From there, you will work on understanding how to get things to move around and react in a 3D environment. Figure 11.1 shows the animation controls in Maya.

- **Current Frame.** Indicates the current animation frame that is shown in the view screen.

241

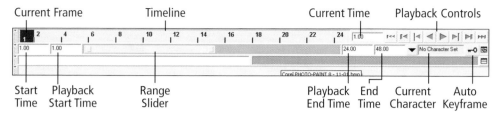

Figure 11.1 Maya's animation controls

- **Timeline.** Shows in a visual sequence the available frames in an animation. The Current Frame indicator slides along the Timeline.

- **Start Time.** Indicates the beginning frame of an animation. Note that the start time does not need to be 1; it can be any number.

- **Playback Start Time.** Indicates the start time of a playback sequence.

- **Range Slider.** Shows the playback range of an animation within the total number of frames.

- **Current Time.** Indicates the current frame of animation.

- **Playback Controls.** Used to view animations or navigate through an animation. These controls are similar to the controls on a DVD player.

- **Playback End Time.** Indicates the last frame of the playback range.

- **End Time.** Indicates the last frame of the animation.

- **Current Character.** Shows what the current character is.

- **Auto Keyframe.** Indicates whether the Automatic Keyframe feature is turned on or off.

Now that you know a little about the controls, take a look at how they work. You will start with a simple ball animation. In the top-left corner of the Maya display is a small drop-down box that contains the word Modeling. Click on the down arrow and scroll to the word Animation.

This will bring up the animation menu set.

1. Create a polygon sphere, as shown in Figure 11.2.

2. You will animate the ball from the Side view. Go to the Side view, as shown in Figure 11.3.

3. Move the sphere up and to the left in the view window.

4. Set a keyframe by choosing Set Key from the Animate menu, as shown in Figure 11.4.

5. Move the current frame to 7 on the Timeline.

6. Move the sphere to the position shown in Figure 11.5.

7. For the next keyframe, move the current frame to 8 and the sphere to the position shown in Figure 11.6.

8. The next keyframe is 9 and the position of the sphere is up and to the right, as shown in Figure 11.7.

9. Set the next keyframe at 14 with the sphere up and to the right in the view screen, as shown in Figure 11.8.

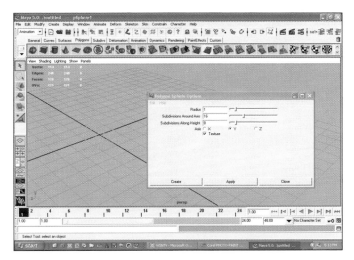

Figure 11.2 Create a polygon sphere.

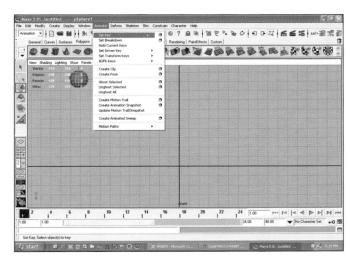

Figure 11.4 Set a keyframe.

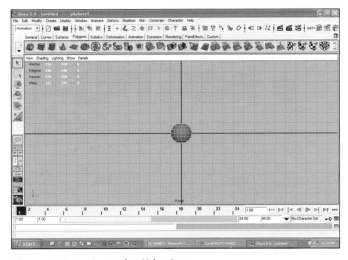

Figure 11.3 Go to the Side view.

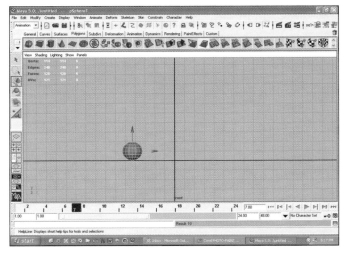

Figure 11.5 Move the sphere down and to the right.

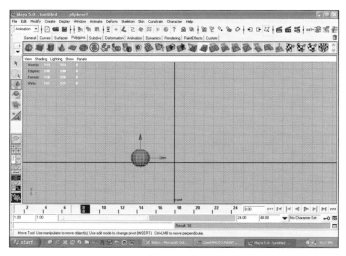

Figure 11.6 Move the sphere to the next keyframe of the animation.

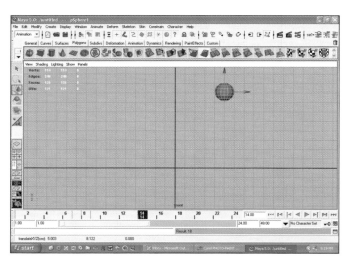

Figure 11.8 Move the sphere to the next keyframe of the bounce.

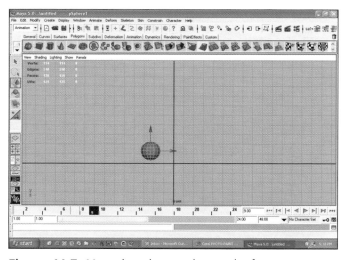

Figure 11.7 Move the sphere to the next keyframe.

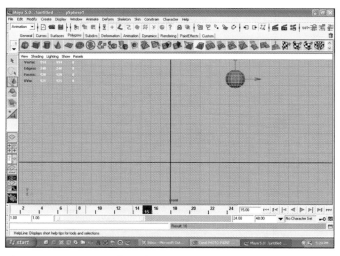

Figure 11.9 Move the sphere to the top of the bounce for the next keyframe.

10. Now move the sphere up and to the right a little, as shown in Figure 11.9, and set another keyframe.

11. The next keyframe is down and to the right, as shown in Figure 11.10.

12. Set the last keyframe of the animation down and to the right, as shown in Figure 11.11.

13. Press the Play button to see how the sphere moves from frame to frame. Notice that Maya automatically computes the position of the sphere between keyframes.

14. The sphere is moving but the animation still needs work. Use the Rotate and Scale tools to change the shape of the sphere, as shown in Figure 11.12. Reset keyframe 1.

15. Adjust keyframe 7 to the same shape as keyframe 1 and reset the keyframe.

16. Now flatten the sphere at frame 8, as shown in Figure 11.13. Reset the keyframe.

17. Change the shape of the sphere in frame 9, as shown in Figure 11.14, and reset the keyframe.

18. Play the animation.

Notice how much more dynamic the animation is with the sphere changing shape. It now looks like the sphere is hitting the ground and bouncing off it. You can go ahead and adjust the shape of the sphere for the rest of the animation.

So far you have seen how to move an object. You also have seen how an

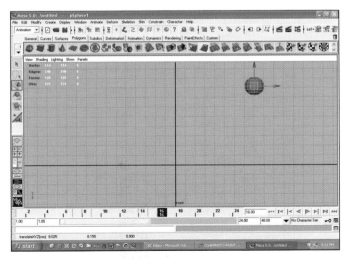

Figure 11.10 Move the sphere to the next keyframe as it begins to descend once more.

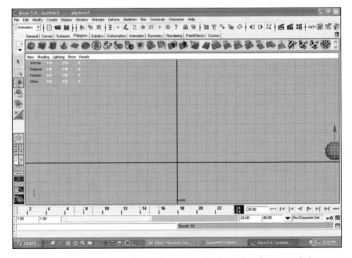

Figure 11.11 Move the sphere to the last keyframe of the animation.

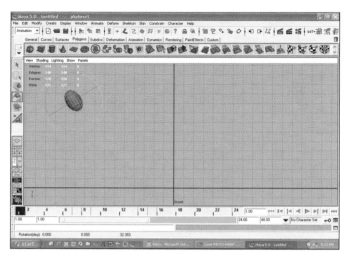

Figure 11.12 Adjust the shape of the sphere.

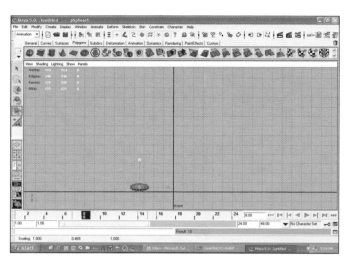

Figure 11.14 Change the shape of the sphere in frame 9.

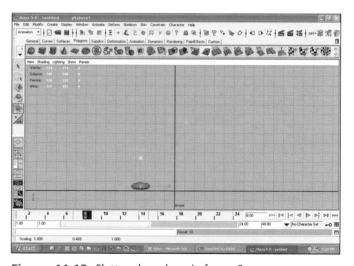

Figure 11.13 Flatten the sphere in frame 8.

object's shape can change in an animation. In the last example, you learned how to set keyframes and how to reset them after adjustments to an animation. Practice animating simple shapes until you become comfortable with the animation controls.

Character Animation

Character animation is one of the most complex things you will come across when preparing art for games. The complexities can be overwhelming. In this chapter I have attempted to simplify the process so it will be easier to understand. I will be touching only the surface of all the controls and options for animating characters. Wherever possible, I will indicate where additional features are used, but it would be impossible to explain everything about 3D character animation in one chapter.

I want to start with your character that you built in the last two chapters, so go ahead and load Polyman. Characters are many times more complex than spheres. Simple shape changes are not good enough to get characters to move correctly. To solve this problem, Maya and most other good animation programs have developed a system of joints and bones. These joints and bones work the same way that the bones and joints in your body work. In fact, studying your own skeletal structure is a good way to learn how to set up joints and bones in your characters.

Before you start, you will need to change the joint display size to fit your model. Maya has four default sizes and a custom size. For this project, change the joint size to 25 percent by selecting Joint Size, 25% from the Display menu, as shown in Figure 11.15.

1. Go to the Side view and select the Joint tool in the Skeleton menu.

2. Using the tool, click inside the hip area, as shown in Figure 11.16. Notice that a green sphere indicates the joint. The

joint tool works best in an Orthographic view.

3. Now place joints in the knee, ankle, and toes of the character, as shown in Figure 11.17. Notice that a cone is created between each joint. The cone and the joint make up a bone.

4. Now go to the Front view and center the joints in the leg, as shown in Figure 11.18. Because the joints are created in a hierarchy, moving the first joint will cause all of the subsequent joints to move with it. Moving

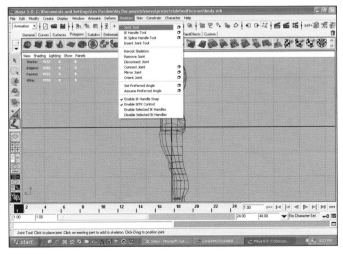

Figure 11.15 Select the Joint tool.

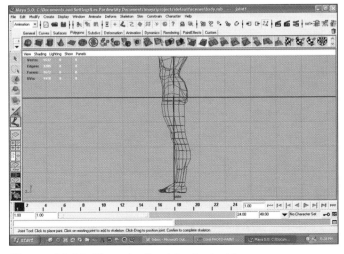

Figure 11.16 Place the first joint in the hip.

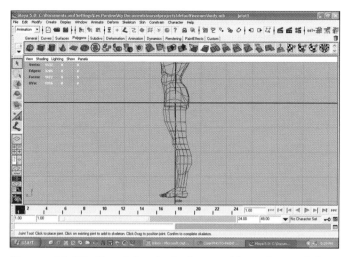

Figure 11.17 Place joints in the knee, ankle, and toes of the character.

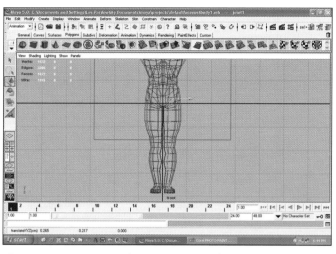

Figure 11.18 Center the joints in the left leg.

one of the later joints will only move the lower joints; this action leaves those joints above the moved joint in place.

5. Now go to the Front view and create another joint that will be centered in the pelvis area to connect to the hip joints from either side, as shown in Figure 11.19.

6. The pelvis joint needs to be connected to a bone in the hip joint. Notice that the bones are shaped like cones, with the larger ends pointing toward one joint and the smaller ends pointing toward the other. The larger end indicates which joint is the control joint over the bone. The control joint is called the *parent*. You will want the pelvis joint to be the parent joint and the hip joint to be the child joint. First select the hip joint, and then the pelvis joint, as shown in Figure 11.20.

7. Press the P key on the keyboard to parent the pelvis joint to the hip joint.

8. The joints for one leg are complete. Now you need to create joints for the right leg. You could do this by creating joints using the Joint tool, just as you did for the left leg, but there is a much easier way to create these joints. Select the hip joint.

9. From the Skeleton menu, select Mirror Joints to bring up the Mirror Joint Options dialog box.

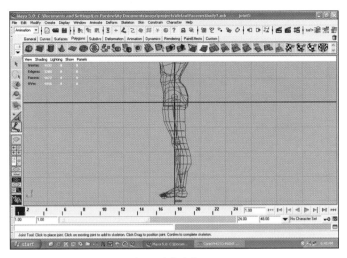

Figure 11.19 Create the pelvis joint.

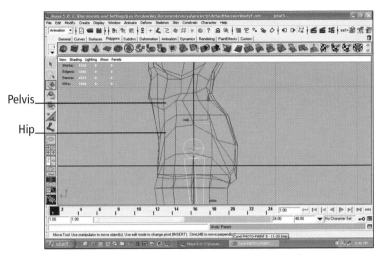

Figure 11.20 Select the hip joint and then the pelvis joint.

10. Set the options to those shown in Figure 11.21 and mirror the left joints and bones to the right leg as shown. Notice how this automatically parents the new leg to the pelvis.

11. Now you need to name each joint. This will be very important when you attach the model to the skeleton. Open Hypergraph and move the graph to where the new joints are located.

12. Rename each joint by right-clicking on the block and

selecting Rename from the menu. Rename the joints as shown in Figure 11.22.

13. In many game engines the game needs to have a root joint that is separate from the other joints in the model. This joint needs to be exactly at the origin point of the scene. Create a root joint and place it at the origin. *Root joints* are used for base locations of the character in some engines. The engine keeps track of the location of the root joint to set up character movement in the game.

14. Parent the pelvis joint to the root joint so the resulting skeleton looks similar to Figure 11.23.

15. Rename the root joint *root* in Hypergraph.

16. Now you need to make a series of joints for the back, neck, and head of your character. Use the Joint tool to create joints similar to the ones in Figure 11.24.

17. Parent the new joints to the pelvis joint, as shown in Figure 11.25.

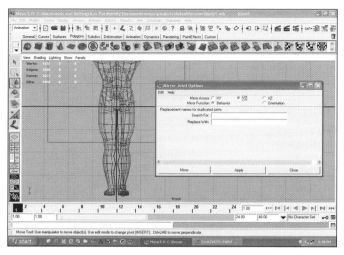

Figure 11.21 Mirror the joints of the left leg to the right.

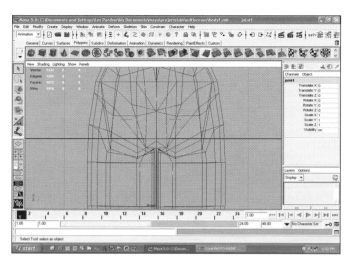

Figure 11.23 Create a root joint.

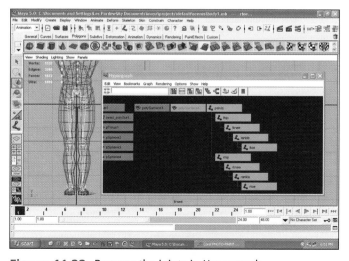

Figure 11.22 Rename the joints in Hypergraph.

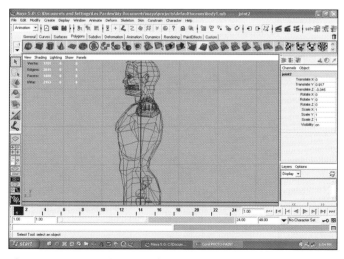

Figure 11.24 Make joints for the spine, neck, and head of the character.

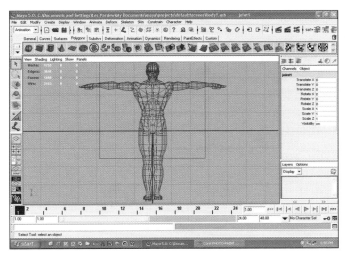

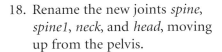

Figure 11.25 Parent the new joints to the pelvis joint.

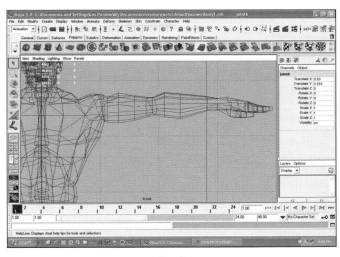

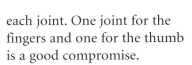

Figure 11.26 Create joints for the arm.

18. Rename the new joints *spine*, *spine1*, *neck*, and *head*, moving up from the pelvis.

19. In the Front view, create joints for the left arm, as shown in Figure 11.26.

20. In the Top view, create a thumb joint and parent it to the wrist joint, as shown in Figure 11.27. You could make separate joints for each knuckle of the hand, but that many joints will cause the engine to slow because of all the calculations needed for each joint. One joint for the fingers and one for the thumb is a good compromise.

21. Now you need to adjust the thumb joint in the Front view because by default the joint will be placed on the origin line. Use Figure 11.28 for a guide.

22. Name the joints of the arm *lshoulder*, *lelbow*, and *lwrist*.

23. Parent the shoulder joint to the neck joint, as shown in Figure 11.29.

24. Mirror the arm joints from the left arm to the right, as shown in Figure 11.30.

25. Rename the arm joints to indicate that they are on the right side of the character by changing the *l* to *r*, as shown in Figure 11.31.

26. Now you have a completed skeleton for your character. You need to create some animation controls to help you animate the character. Select the left knee joint and rotate it in the z-axis, as shown in Figure 11.32.

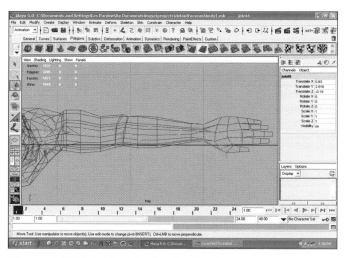

Figure 11.27 Add a joint for the thumb.

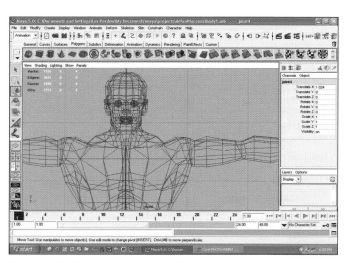

Figure 11.29 Parent the shoulder joint to the neck joint.

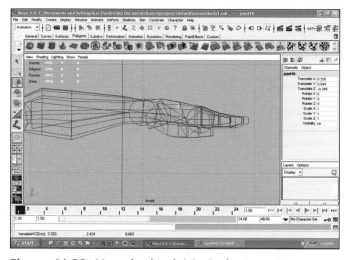

Figure 11.28 Move the thumb joint in the Front view.

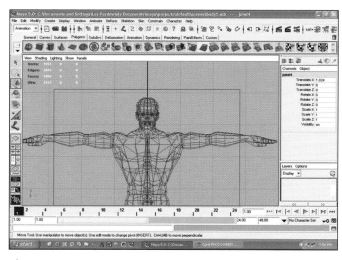

Figure 11.30 Mirror the joints of the arm.

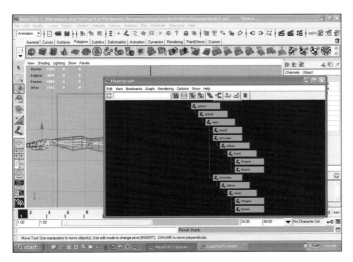

Figure 11.31 Rename the arm joints.

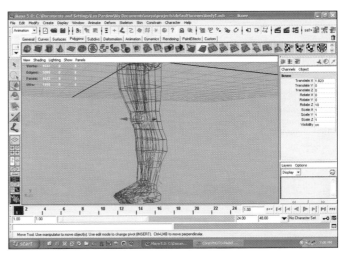

Figure 11.32 Rotate the left knee joint.

27. Select the left hip and set the preferred angle, as shown in Figure 11.33. Setting the preferred angle gives the animation controller you will create next a direction for moving the leg.

28. Next you will create an animation controller called an *IK chain*. IK stands for *Inverse Kinematics*, which is a way to create control over joints in reverse order from the hierarchy. An IK chain will allow you to move the foot and have the

leg follow in a natural movement. This makes it much easier to control the movement of the legs and arms of your characters. Go to the Skeleton menu and select the IK Handle tool.

29. Click on the hip joint and then on the ankle joint to create the IK chain, as shown in Figure 11.34.

30. The IK chain has its handle near the ankle joint. Look for the lines radiating out from it and select one of them. It will

turn green. Now use the Move tool to move the handle so you can get used to how it controls the leg. Notice that moving the handle will cause the joints to move in a natural way, as shown in Figure 11.35.

31. Position the ankle joint back in its proper spot, as shown in Figure 11.36.

32. Create an IK chain for the right leg the same way you did for the left leg.

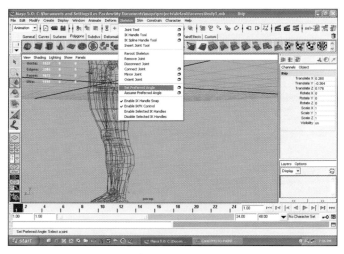

Figure 11.33 Set a preferred angle for the leg.

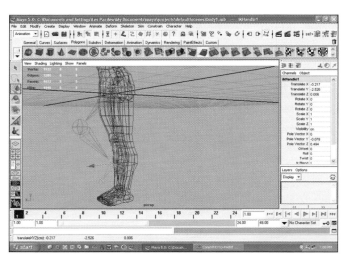

Figure 11.35 Move the IK chain handle.

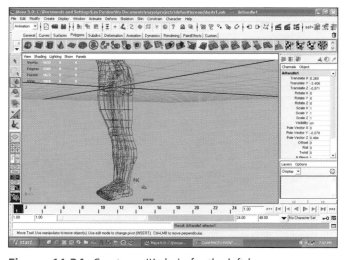

Figure 11.34 Create an IK chain for the left leg.

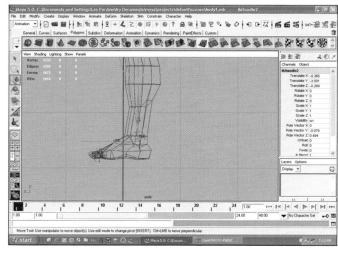

Figure 11.36 Put the ankle joint back in its proper position.

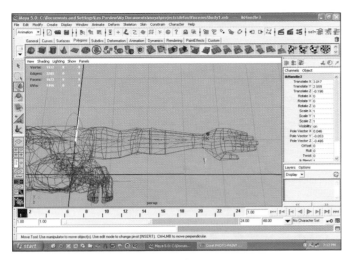

Figure 11.37 Create IK chains for the arms.

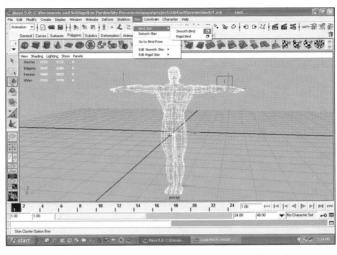

Figure 11.38 Choose Bind Skin, Smooth Bind from the Skin menu.

33. Go to the arm joints and rotate the elbow joint to set the pre-ferred angle as you did for the leg.

34. Create an IK chain for the arm from the shoulder joint to the wrist joint, as shown in Figure 11.37.

The skeleton is now ready to attach to the model. The process of attaching a skeleton to a model is called *skinning*. There are two types of bindings used to skin characters in games—smooth and hard. Hard binding attaches one vertex to one joint; smooth binding attaches one vertex to multiple joints. The advantage of smooth binding is that the vertices move in a more natural way than they do in hard binding. The problem with smooth binding is that it takes more calculations and is therefore more processor expensive than hard binding. Smooth binding is becoming more common in games, so for this example you will use it to skin your character.

1. Select the model and then the root joint of the skeleton.

2. In the Skin menu, select Bind Skin, Smooth Bind to access the Smooth Bind Options dialog box (see Figure 11.38).

3. Set the skin attributes to those shown in Figure 11.39 and click on Apply. The model will change color to indicate that it is now bound to the skeleton.

4. Test the binding by moving one of the legs, as shown in Figure 11.40.

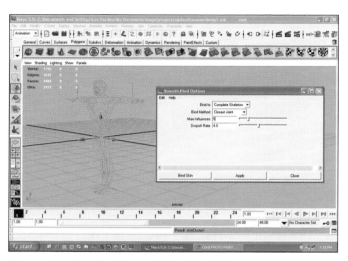

Figure 11.39 Bind the model to the skeleton.

Figure 11.40 Test the binding.

5. Smooth binding works pretty well for most of the vertices on the model, but not for all of them. Some will need to be adjusted by hand. Pull the arm down and look at the shoulder area. Some of the vertices around the chest collapse with the arm, as shown in Figure 11.41.

6. The problem with the chest is that the vertices are influenced too much by the shoulder joint and not enough by the spine. The influence each joint has over a vertex is called *skin weighting.* You can adjust skin weighting in Maya. I will go over a couple methods for adjusting the skin weight. Select the model (not the skeleton) and open the Paint Skin Weights tool, as shown in Figure 11.42.

7. Painting skin weights on a model is a little like painting a 3D object; the model turns black with the influence of the joint in white. If a joint has 100% influence over an area, the area will be white. If the joint has no influence over an area, the area will be black. See Figure 11.43 for reference.

8. You will work on the chest first. Select spine1 from the joint list.

9. Adjust the settings of the tool as shown in Figure 11.44 and paint the area of the model's rib cage until it is mostly white.

10. Painting skin weights is an intuitive way to adjust the weights. Do some painting and then check the weighting by moving the arm. Remember to press Ctrl+Z after you move the arm to have it return to the original position.

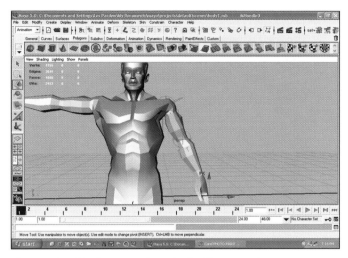

Figure 11.41 Some vertices don't skin correctly.

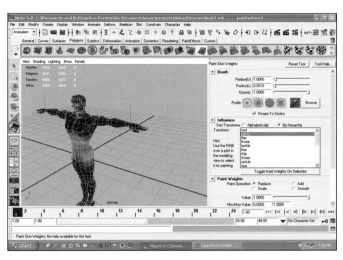

Figure 11.43 The Paint Skin Weights tool

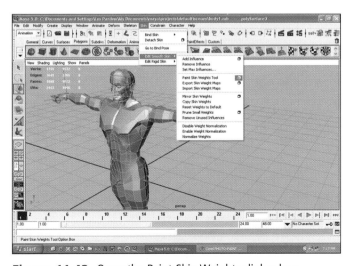

Figure 11.42 Open the Paint Skin Weights dialog box.

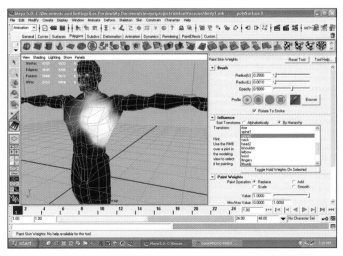

Figure 11.44 Paint the rib cage area with weighting from spine1.

11. You also need to adjust the weighting of the shoulder joint to get it to work correctly, as shown in Figure 11.45.

12. Now you will take a look at another way to change the skin weights. Go to Component mode and select all the vertices of the head, including the eyes and mouth. If you were going to do facial animations you would weight the vertices of this area differently, but for your purposes in this chapter, you can tie all the weights of the face to the head joint.

13. Now bring up the Component Editor, as shown in Figure 11.46.

14. The Component Editor is a very useful tool for isolating elements of a model. Click on the Smooth Skins tab at the top of the tool.

15. Select the column heading that is labeled head. The column will change to black.

16. Use the slider on the bottom of the tool to adjust all the weights in the column to 1.0, which is 100% weighting. You want the selected vertices of the head to all be tied to the head joint. Refer to Figure 11.47.

17. Test the skin weights in the head by using the Rotate tool to move the head, as shown in Figure 11.48. You might need to paint skin weights in some of the neck areas to get the neck to look just right.

18. You should check and adjust every joint in the model to get the weighting as close to the natural movement of the body as possible. This is a

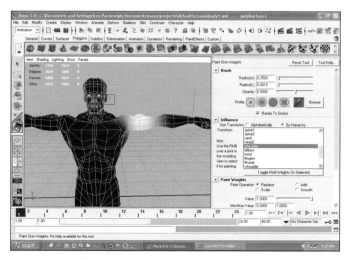

Figure 11.45 Adjust the weighting of the shoulder joint.

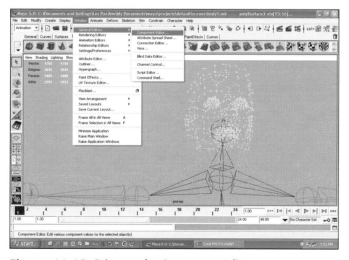

Figure 11.46 Bring up the Component Editor.

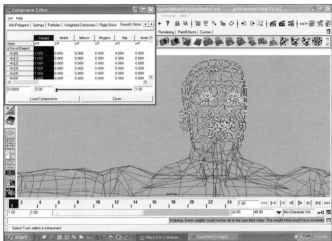

Figure 11.47 Adjust the weights of the vertices to 1.0.

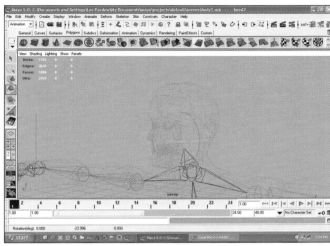

Figure 11.48 Test the skin weighting of the head.

time-consuming task, but it is necessary if you want the model to look right when you animate it. Figure 11.49 shows the weighting of the pelvis joint.

19. Continue to adjust the weighting of the body. Figure 11.50 shows the adjusted weighting of the hip joint.

20. Figure 11.51 shows the adjusted skin weighting of the left knee.

21. After you have finished weighting all the joints, you can move on to animating your character.

First, however, you will need to make a few adjustments in Hypergraph to get the animation to work correctly. Select the handle nodes of the IK chains and parent them to the root joint, as shown in Figure 11.52.

22. Create a polygon plane to act as your ground, as shown in Figure 11.53.

23. Now you need to create a couple of keyframes. In Hypergraph, select all of the joints and controls in the skeleton.

24. Set a keyframe at frame 1.

25. Set a keyframe at frame 24, as shown in Figure 11.54. Also, turn on the Auto Keyframe button.

26. Start by creating a crouch at frame 6. Go to frame 6.

27. Pull the arms down and bend them slightly, as if the character is about to jump.

28. Rotate the chest forward by rotating the spine and spine1 joints.

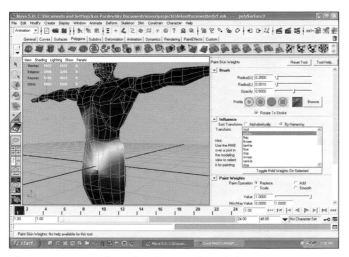

Figure 11.49 Adjust the skin weights of the pelvis joint.

Figure 11.51 Adjust the skin weights of the knee joint.

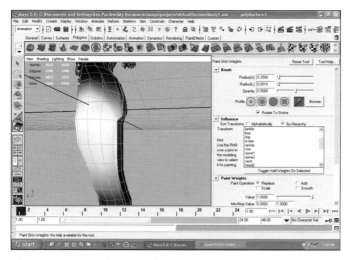

Figure 11.50 Adjust the skin weights of the hip joint.

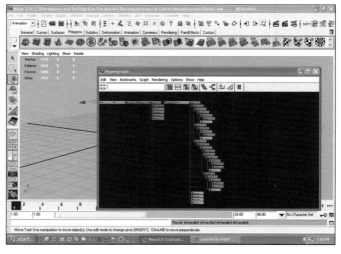

Figure 11.52 Parent the IK chain handles to the root joint.

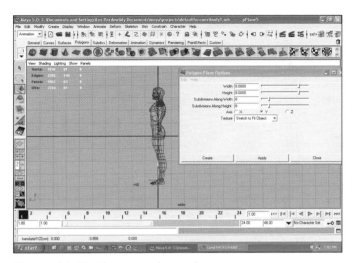

Figure 11.53 Create a polygon plane.

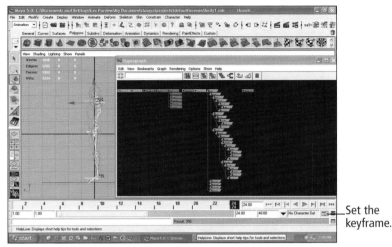

Set the keyframe.

Figure 11.54 Set the beginning and ending keyframe of the animation.

29. Rotate the head and neck joints so the character is looking straight ahead.

30. Now bring up the legs so the character is in a crouch.

31. You will notice that as you bring up the legs, the knees are too close together. Not a very manly pose, is it? Select the Show Manipulator tool to bring up the Pole Vector component of the IK chain.

32. Rotate the knees out, as shown in Figure 11.55.

33. Once you have the crouch just right, select the root joint and pull the character down so his feet are planted on the ground. You will need to rotate the ankle joint to get the feet to line up with the ground.

34. Now go to frame 10. Notice that a keyframe was automatically created at frame 6. This is because you turned on the Auto Keyframe button.

35. Adjust the model in frame 10 to look similar to Figure 11.56.

This will be what the character looks like at the height of his jump.

36. At frame 16, have the character land, as shown in Figure 11.57.

37. Play the animation.

Congratulations! You have just created your first character animation. That wasn't so bad, was it? Actually, I left out a lot of controls, but now you know the basics of character animation. Save this file and try animating some other motions. As you learn to

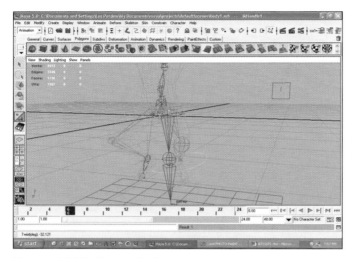

Figure 11.55 Rotate the knees out.

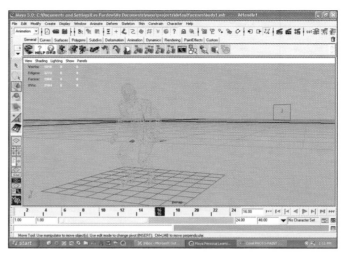

Figure 11.57 Set the character's landing at frame 16.

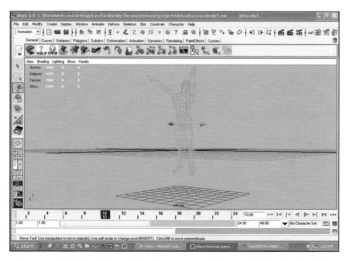

Figure 11.56 Adjust the character at frame 10 for the height of his jump.

animate, read up on some of the more advanced animation controls in Maya.

Summary

This was a somewhat complex chapter, but I tried to keep it as basic as I could. Maya is a very deep software program with a rich animation system; I only scratched the surface of its power. I showed you how to control animation in Maya, and I covered creating skeletons and skinning characters. You created some basic animation controls in the IK chains. You are now armed and ready to start experimenting with the animation system. Try setting up your own character model. Create some animations of your model. The more you practice with the animation system, the better you will get. Study the way people move in real life as an example for your animations.

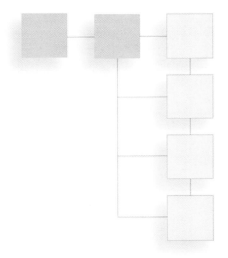

CHAPTER 12

SPECIALIZED GEOMETRY AND SPECIAL EFFECTS

So far in this book you have covered a lot of territory. If you have followed the examples and experimented on your own, you have gained the beginning of what you will need to know to be a game artist. In this last chapter, you need to learn about two more important areas of game art—the creation of specialized geometry and the basics of developing special effects for games.

Creating Specialized Geometry

Many game engines require the creation of polygon models that are never seen in the game. These models are used for setting up boundaries, triggering special events, creating spawning points, and any number of other functions. These models are usually exported separately from the other models and are used primarily by programmers to store information for the engine to use when the game is running. The most common type of specialized geometry for games is a collision map.

Collision Maps

Collision maps derive their name from the early days of game development, when all games were created in 2D. In those days a collision map was a two-color invisible picture in which one color represented where a character could walk and the other color represented where he couldn't. As games have advanced, so have collision maps. Now collision maps not only define the boundaries of character movement, they also can have other information, such as surface qualities or physics.

In theory, game engines could use the model geometry from the game models for collision maps. The problem with the game models is that they often use significantly more polygons than necessary for a collision map.

When you use a collision map with fewer polygons, you are left with a greater number of polygons available for the models you actually see in the game.

Let's build a collision map so you can see how it is done. Bring up Maya and load the room you created in Chapter 5. You will build a collision map for this model.

1. The first thing you must do is turn the room model into a template. Select all the objects in the scene and then choose Object Display, Template from the Display menu, as shown in Figure 12.1.

2. The room will no longer be in Shaded mode; it will be in Wire-Frame mode. Click beside the model and notice that the wire-frame turns gray.

3. Try selecting the model. You cannot select a template in Maya in the view screen. This comes in very handy when you are building collision maps because it makes it easier to build new geometry without interference from the older geometry.

4. Create a polygon cylinder, as shown in Figure 12.2. Notice that you are using fewer polygons than the original model.

5. Scale the cylinder so it is just inside the wall of the dome model, as shown in Figure 12.3.

6. From the Front view, move up the cylinder so the bottom is about the same level as the floor.

7. Adjust the top of the cylinder so it is about level with the bottom of the balcony, as shown in Figure 12.4.

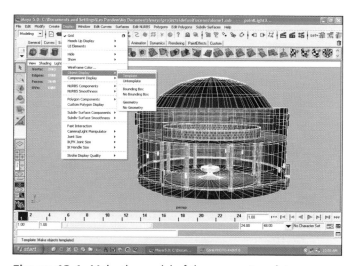

Figure 12.1 Make the model of the room a template.

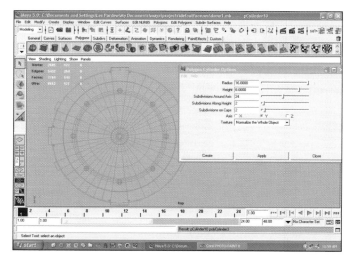

Figure 12.2 Create a polygon cylinder.

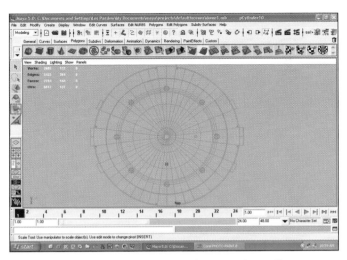

Figure 12.3 Scale the cylinder to fit inside the wall.

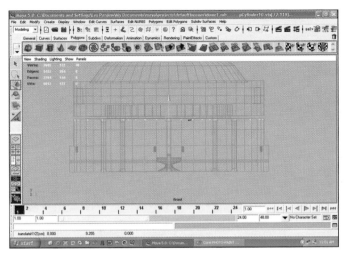

Figure 12.4 Fit the cylinder into the bottom of the room.

8. Select the inside ring of vertices on the bottom of the cylinder and scale them to match the platform on the floor of the room, as shown in Figure 12.5.

9. Extrude the faces on the inside ring of polygons to form the platform, as shown in Figure 12.6.

10. Now select the faces on the inside of the top of the cylinder and scale them to fit just inside the balcony, as shown from the Top view in Figure 12.7.

11. Extrude the faces to follow the rail of the balcony, as shown in Figure 12.8.

12. Extrude the faces again and scale them to fit over the top of the rail.

13. Extrude the faces again to fit down the other side of the rail.

14. Extrude the faces again to follow the floor, as shown in Figure 12.9.

15. Extrude the faces again to follow the wall. Only go as high as the doors.

16. Extrude the faces again to follow the walls to the top.

17. Continue extruding faces following the shape of the ceiling, as shown in Figure 12.10.

18. Now for the doorways. The collision map needs to be rotated so that it lines up with the doors. Rotate the collision map 7.5 on the y-axis.

19. Extrude the face in the doorway to fit the doorway, as shown in Figure 12.11.

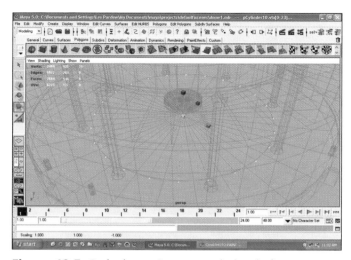

Figure 12.5 Scale the vertices to match the platform.

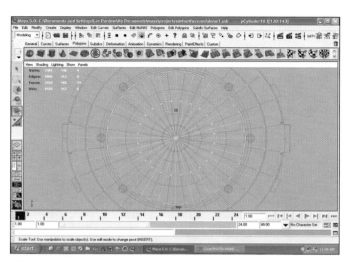

Figure 12.7 Scale the faces of the top to fit inside the balcony.

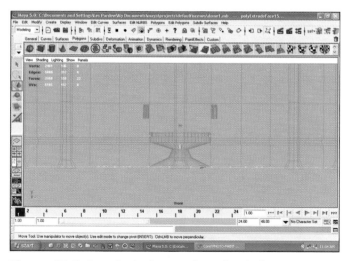

Figure 12.6 Extrude the faces to form the platform.

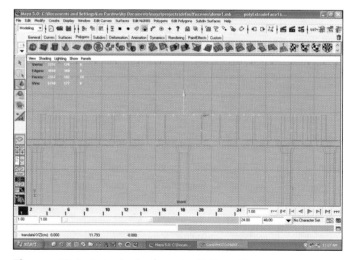

Figure 12.8 Extrude the faces to fit the rail.

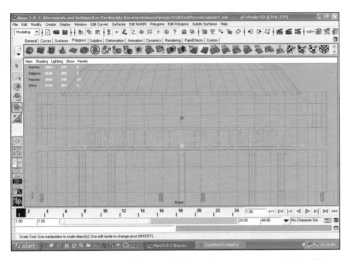

Figure 12.9 Extrude faces to follow the geometry of the floor.

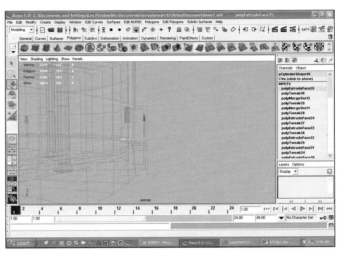

Figure 12.11 Flatten the polygons to match up with the door.

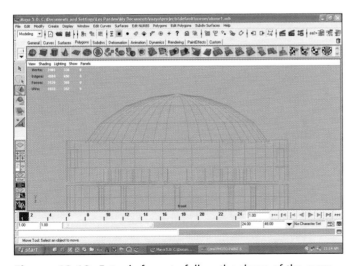

Figure 12.10 Extrude faces to follow the shape of the room.

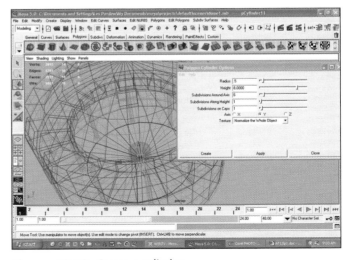

Figure 12.12 Create a cylinder.

20. Repeat Steps 18 and 19 for the other three doors on the bottom floor and the two doors on the balcony level.

21. Create a cylinder, as shown in Figure 12.12.

22. Move and scale the cylinder to fit just outside one of the columns, as shown in Figure 12.13.

23. You don't need the faces on the top and bottom of the cylinder because they will be above the ceiling or below the floor.

Therefore, you can select and delete the faces on the top and bottom of the cylinder, as shown in Figure 12.14.

24. Move the new cylinder in the Front view so it fits over the column, as shown in Figure 12.15. You might need to scale the column to reach from the floor to the ceiling.

25. Group the column to center the pivot point.

26. Duplicate the column and rotate it to fit over the next column.

27. Repeat the steps until all the columns are covered, as shown in Figure 12.16.

28. Create a new cylinder, as shown in Figure 12.17.

29. Adjust the new cylinder to fit around the chalice pool, as shown in Figure 12.18.

30. Delete the faces on the bottom of the pool cylinder.

31. Delete the faces on the top and bottom of the cylinders covering the columns.

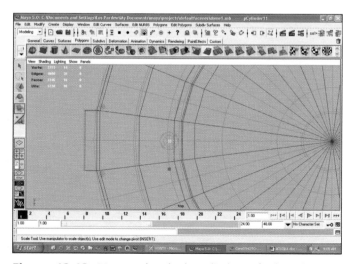

Figure 12.13 Move and scale the cylinder to fit the column.

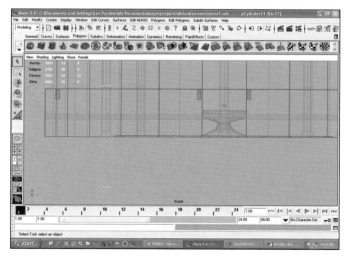

Figure 12.14 Delete the faces on the top and bottom of the cylinder.

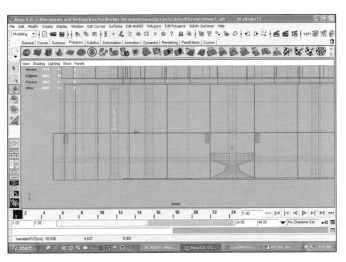

Figure 12.15 Move and scale the column from the Front view.

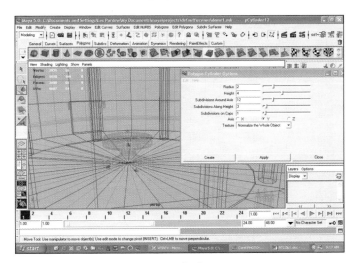

Figure 12.17 Create a new cylinder.

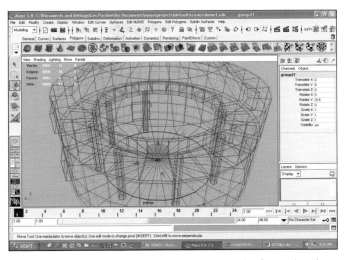

Figure 12.16 Place a duplicate of the cylinder for each column.

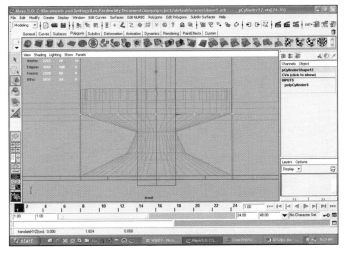

Figure 12.18 Shape the cylinder to fit the pool.

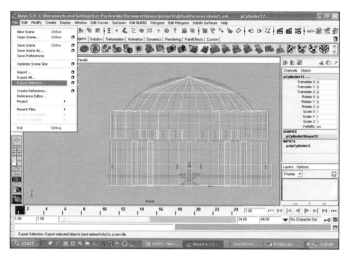

Figure 12.19 Export the collision map.

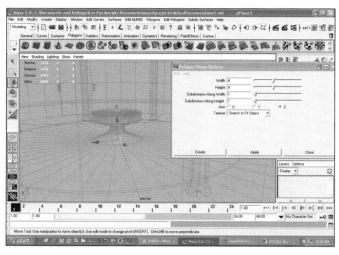

Figure 12.20 Create a single polygon plane.

32. The collision mask is now finished and ready to export. Select all the objects in the collision map.

33. Select Export Selection from the File menu, as shown in Figure 12.19, to export the collision map.

The collision map is now finished. Notice that it has far fewer polygons than the original model. The collision map does not contain any textures, so it should run very fast in the engine.

Triggers and Other Invisible Objects

Many engines use polygonal objects to store game information. These objects are set up so they can be used to trigger events in the game. They also are used to place objects in the game, such as characters, vehicles, traps, pick-ups, breakable items, doors, spawning points, and so on. The list is endless, limited only by the engine and the imagination of the development team.

In some game engines, these invisible objects are placed in the game world using a world editor, which is a program that is part of the engine. In other game engines, the artist uses the 3D modeling software to place the objects in the world. In either case the process is similar; I will show you how to do it in Maya.

1. If you don't have it open already, load the dome room and set the model to a template.

2. Create a single polygon plane, as shown in Figure 12.20.

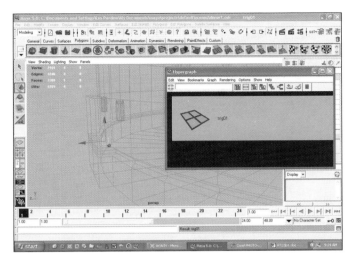

Figure 12.21 Rename the polygon.

3. Select Polygon Components, Normals from the Display menu to show the direction of the face of the polygon.

4. Move the polygon over to one of the doorways and scale it to cover the doorway area.

5. In Hypergraph, rename the polygon *trig01*, as shown in Figure 12.21.

That's about it; it's not too hard. You just created a trigger object. When your character enters the room and walks through that doorway, he will pass through the trigger object. When that occurs, it will cause something in the game to happen. The face is pointing toward the door, so the trigger will only go off if the character is entering the room.

The name of the trigger could be anything; in this case, you called it trig01. In the game engine, all objects with the trigXX name will cause the same action to happen. The name is used to tell the programmers what action to tie to the geometry.

Game levels are filled with places where actions or events must occur. A typical level might have anywhere from a few to a few hundred invisible objects in it. Placing these objects is a time-consuming task, but getting them just right can make all the difference in how the game plays. It is an important job for the game artist.

Some game companies hire artists to do nothing else but set up great levels. These artists are called *level editors*, and they perform a very important function in game development.

Creating Special Effects

Games today are filled with special effects. The term *special effect* comes from the movie industry. In motion pictures, special effects are elements added after filming to enhance the movie. In games, special effects include lighting effects, particle effects, or other elements that simulate the type of effects seen in movies. Over the years, special effects in movies and games have grown to include almost any fantastic or unique visual elements. Next, you will learn about some of the basic special effects used in games.

Particle Effects

Particle effects are the most common type of special effect used in games. Particles are small single polygons. Many of these polygons grouped and moving together can simulate effects such as smoke, fire, or rain. Particle effects have some common elements, which include:

- Emitters
- Paths
- Turbulence
- Dissipation

An *emitter* is the origin point or area of a particle effect. In a game the artist will designate a place for an emitter. For example, your game might have a torch in a sconce by the door to a castle. You can place a directional emitter near the top of a torch, pointing up. Then you specify the type of particle

the emitter will release—in this case, a flame particle.

The *path* is the line of movement of the particle. In the case of the torch, the line of movement is upward and away from the top of the torch.

Turbulence is the variation in the path of each individual particle. If all the particles of the torch moved in exactly the same direction, the flame effect would not be very believable. By adding variability to the paths of each particle, you can achieve a more believable flame effect.

Dissipation is the gradual transition of each particle from solid to transparent. The *dissipation rate* is the time it takes for a particle to go from solid to transparent; the *dissipation range* is the range in which a set of particles will go from solid to transparent.

To understand how particle systems work in games, you can create one in Maya.

1. Create a cylinder, as shown in Figure 12.22.
2. Create two materials and load the bark.bmp and end.bmp

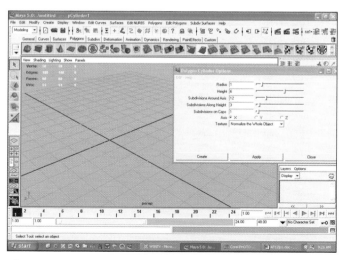

Figure 12.22 Create a polygon cylinder for a log.

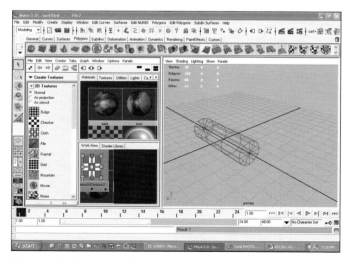

Figure 12.23 Load the textures.

textures on the CD in the directory for Chapter 12, as shown in Figure 12.23.

3. Use the Cylindrical Mapping tool to apply the bark to the cylinder, as shown in Figure 12.24.

4. Use the Planar Mapping tool to apply the end material to the cylinder, as shown in Figure 12.25. You now have a nice-looking log.

5. Now you need to go to the Dynamics menu set. Select it from the drop-down menu on the top-right portion of the screen, as shown in Figure 12.26.

6. In Hypergraph, change the cylinder's name to Log, as shown in Figure 12.27.

7. Now you need to bring up an effects dialog box. Select Fire from the Effects menu to bring up the Create Fire Effect Options dialog box.

8. Adjust the settings to match those shown in Figure 12.28 and apply them to the log object.

9. The small ball that appears inside the log is the particle emitter. The other settings in the dialog box are for adjusting the fire. Change the frame to 24, as shown in Figure 12.29. The green circles represent the particles.

10. To see the particles, you will need to add a light. Create a light, as shown in Figure 12.30.

11. Position the light, as shown in Figure 12.31.

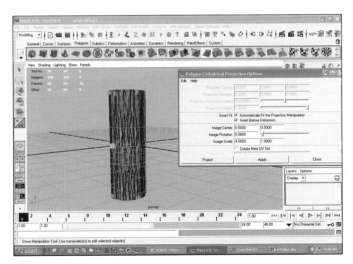

Figure 12.24 Apply the bark material to the cylinder.

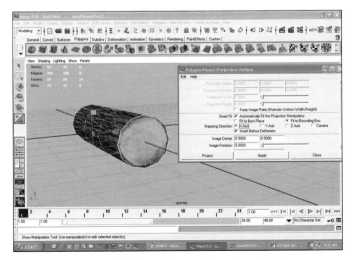

Figure 12.25 Apply the end material to the cylinder.

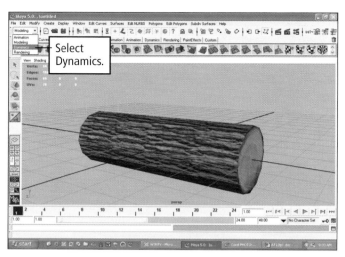

Figure 12.26 Change the menu set to Dynamics.

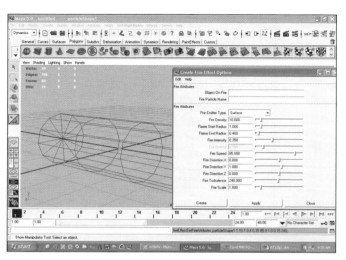

Figure 12.28 Apply a particle emitter to the log object.

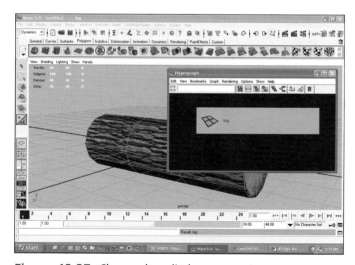

Figure 12.27 Change the cylinder name to Log.

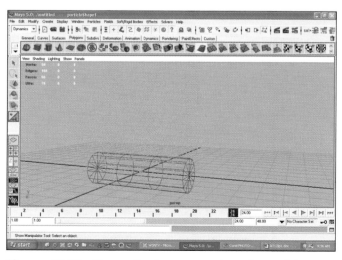

Figure 12.29 Change the frame to see how the particles work.

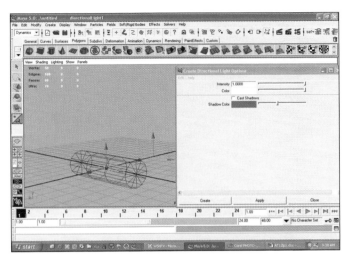

Figure 12.30 Create a directional light.

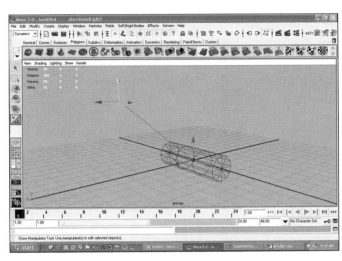

Figure 12.31 Position the light.

12. Change the menu set to Rendering, as shown in Figure 12.32.

13. Select Render Current Frame from the Render menu. A small Render View window will appear, as shown in Figure 12.33.

14. You can render a couple more frames of the animation by setting the current frame to another number and then selecting Render Current Frame again.

15. Now you can set some rendering attributes and render the whole animation so you can take a good look at how the particles work. In the Render view, select Render Globals from the Options menu, as shown in Figure 12.34.

16. Set your options to match the options shown on the Common tab in Figure 12.35.

17. Now switch to the Maya Software tab and set those options, as shown in Figure 12.36.

18. Now you can batch render the animation. Select Batch Render from the Render menu, as shown in Figure 12.37.

19. When the Batch Render Animation dialog box appears, you will notice that the options are in gray. This is because the Personal Learning Edition of Maya does not support rendering on multiple machines. You should be fine rendering this project on one machine. Click on the Batch Render button to start the render.

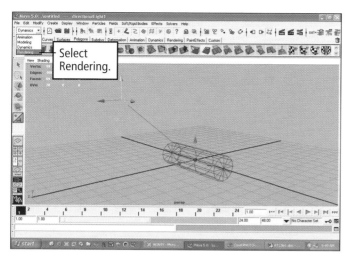

Figure 12.32 Change to the Rendering menu set.

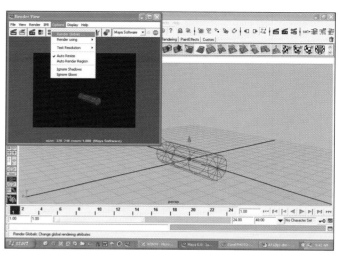

Figure 12.34 Select Render Globals from the menu.

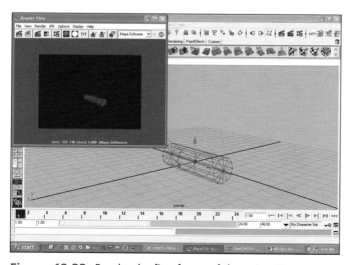

Figure 12.33 Render the first frame of the animation.

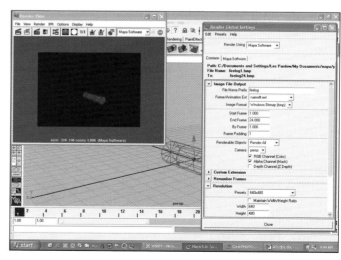

Figure 12.35 Set the options of the Render Globals dialog box on the Common tab.

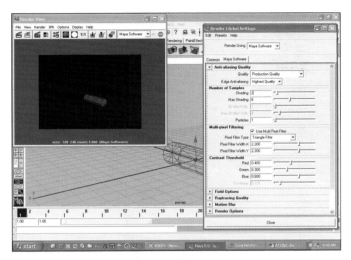

Figure 12.36 Set the Maya Software options.

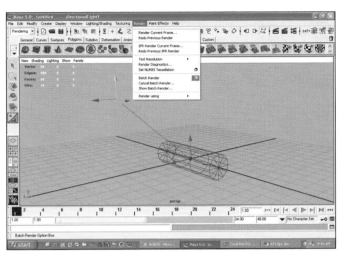

Figure 12.37 Select the Batch Render option.

20. If you want to see the progress of the rendering, click on the Script Editor in the lower-right corner of your display to expand that window, as shown in Figure 12.38. The Script Editor will show you the progress of each frame and the location to which the frame is saved.

Once the rendering is finished, you can look at the results of your flame particles. Figures 12.39 and 12.40 are examples of how the particles should look.

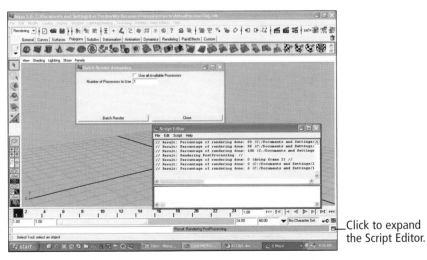

Click to expand the Script Editor.

Figure 12.38 The Script Editor shows the progress of each frame.

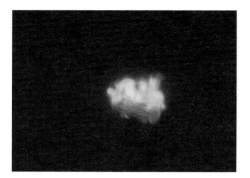

Figure 12.39 A rendered frame from the firelog animation

Figure 12.40 Another rendered frame from the firelog animation

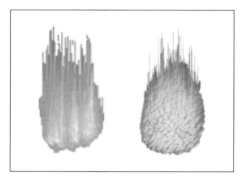

Figure 12.41 Particle textures used in a game

Take some time and experiment with the settings of the flame effect. Change the turbulence and see how it affects the flame. Try adjusting some of the other attributes to see what happens. You will quickly see that even small adjustments can sometimes have dramatic effects. Try creating some other effects from the Effects menu options.

Creating Particles

In Maya you can have as many particles as you want because you are not rendering them in real time. In games, on the other hand, you are rendering in real time so the number of particles is limited. Most particles in games are small polygons with textures applied. The way you create the textures for your game will depend on how your game engine treats transparency. Most game engines support an alpha channel; however, some use a mask. Particles almost always have some element of transparency.

Figure 12.41 shows two particles; one is a flaming rock and the other is a shard of ice. These two particles were created for a fantasy game in which the main character could call fire or ice from the sky. By combining these textures with some semi-transparent cloudlike particles, I was able to get a nice-looking effect.

Animated Billboards

A *billboard* is a single polygon that is programmed to always face the camera. Billboards are often used to simulate effects that might require more particles than the game machine can run successfully. With a billboard effect, the texture of the billboard is animated through a series of animations. Figure 12.42 shows an example of a billboard animation. Here I used a color map and a mask for the transparent area to create an explosion. The explosion was created in Maya using more than a thousand polygons. The billboard animation only required one polygon.

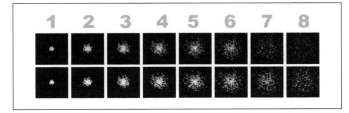

Figure 12.42 A billboard animation sequence

You can use billboard animation for other things than simply special effects. I have seen them used successfully for animated crowds, individual characters, signs, and lights.

Summary

In this chapter I covered some elements of game art that aren't seen by the player, as well as some that are. The specialized geometry for games might not be seen, but it is a critical part of game development. The special effects are definitely seen by the player. Both are extremely important for making a good game.

This is a beginning book about the fascinating world of game art development. If you have gone through everything in this book, you have only just begun your journey to becoming a real game artist. There is still a lot to learn. I suggest you practice the skills you have learned thus far and see what you can create. If you are interested in a career in game art development, I suggest that you learn as much as you can about art. The better artist you are, the better game artist you will become. Good luck! This is a fascinating and exciting field.

INDEX

License Agreement/Notice of Limited Warranty